Sentencing
in a Rational Society

Nigel Walker

Allen Lane The Penguin Press

Allen Lane The Penguin Press
Vigo Street, London W1

SBN 7139 0107 1

Printed in Great Britain by
Western Printing Services Ltd, Bristol

To my wife

Contents

Preface

This book is written for a particular sort of society: one which is peaceful, affluent and ignorant, but aspires to rationality. Peaceful enough, at any rate, to keep order without the help of troops. Affluent enough to devote quite a lot of money and highly trained manpower to the handling of offenders. Ignorant enough to be forced to rely on superstition rather than science in using these resources; but sufficiently rational, or in love with rationality, to feel the need of more scientific knowledge to replace the superstition. Rational enough, also, to want to know how to approach the problem of sentencing in the interim, until more scientific knowledge is available; in other words, thinking it reasonable to ask 'What is it rational to do until we know more?'

The subject of the book is a penal *system*. It is not about techniques of penal treatment, or even about alternatives to penal treatment. Someone who wants to know how to supervise a probationer, manage a prison or socialize psychopaths will not find the answer here. Nor does the book discuss explanations of criminal behaviour. I am not depreciating books on these subjects, although I believe that important advances, conceptual as well as technical, are needed before they can be of much practical value. But what this book tries to deal with is the *systematic* aspects of our approach to the problem of crime: that is, its aims and assumptions, the decisions which it calls for, the people who have the task of making them, and the considerations which they should have in mind.

Another thing which this is not is a textbook. That is not merely an excuse for my failure to deal exhaustively with every topic, or for my assumption that the reader already knows a little about courts and sentences (although if he does not he can look up unfamiliar terms in Appendix B). It also means that I have made no attempt to achieve the dignified impartiality which is the ideal of textbooks. Sometimes this impartiality is due to genuine, scientific doubt in the face of inconclusive evidence. Sometimes it is nothing more than a dodging of issues for tactical reasons: if you don't like climbing down, you can sit on a fence. Many of the issues which I shall raise – especially in the first two chapters – can be dodged, and usually are. But penology is more interesting if they are not.

N.D.W.

Nuffield College,
Oxford
December 1968

Acknowledgements

I owe a debt of gratitude to a number of people, without whose help this book would have been even more imperfect. Professor Johannes Andenaes of Oslo University provided me with statistics about the Norwegian system of appeal against sentence, as well as with the text of Appendix C. Dr Britt-Mari Persson Blegvad, of the University of Aarhus, provided me with information about Swedish Child Welfare Boards. Mr Vernon Bogdanor of Brasenose College was kind enough to criticize Chapter 2. Mr John Conrad, formerly Director of Research at the California Department of Corrections, gave me great help in tracing information in the U.S.A. about penal systems. M. Paul Cornil, formerly head of the Belgian Ministry of Justice, gave me information about the institution called '*semi-détention*'. Edinburgh University Press allowed me to reproduce illustrations from my book *Crime and Punishment in Britain*, and virtually the whole of my James Seth Memorial Lecture on 'The Aims of a Penal System'. Professor Thomas Ferguson, formerly of Glasgow University, allowed me to reproduce the table in Chapter 3 from his book *The Young Delinquent in his Social Setting*. Dr Werner Geisler, of Kiel University, provided me with information about West Germany's ordinances regarding unlocked vehicles. The Home Office's Statistical Branch provided me with the figures on which Table 3 is based. Mr H. D. Willcock of the Government Social Survey allowed me to see an advance copy of his report on deterrents for teenage males. Mr Michael Willmer of Nuffield College and Mr Roy Carr-Hill, also of Nuffield College, collaborated with me in writing Appendix A. Mr John Wilson and Mr Barry Sugarman of the Farmington Trust Research Unit helped me in my rather fruitless search for assessments of moral education in schools. Finally, many of the ideas throughout the book occurred to me as a result of seminars with Professor Rupert Cross and Professor Herbert Hart, although they would not necessarily agree with all of them.

Miss Jenny Parsons of Nuffield College typed the whole book with great speed and accuracy; and Mrs Patricia Simmons of St Hilda's College helped me with notes and bibliography.

N.D.W.

Chapter 1

The Aims of a Penal System

This first chapter is an exercise in penal philosophy. Philosophizing is distrusted by most of the professions that are concerned with the penal system. It is suspect for lawyers because they are conscious that if the criminal law as a whole is the Cinderella of jurisprudence, then the law of sentencing is Cinderella's illegitimate baby. It is poison to administrators because there is nothing which splits legislators – whether they are ministers, or members of either House – so much as discussion of the aims of punishment; and it is hard enough to secure parliamentary time for penal legislation without having to cope with divided back-benches as well. It is disturbing for penal agents – by which I mean the staffs of prisons, probation departments, and so forth – who have to act upon the sentence of the court, because they are already torn between their own instinctive reaction to the offender or his offence, their belief as to the intention of the court, and the barrage of criticism to which they are subjected by penal reformers. As for penal reformers, many are afraid that philosophizing might complicate the simplicity of their humanitarianism. Finally, it is also distrusted by penologists, who seem to regard discussion of penal aims rather as doctors regard discussion of the ethics of euthanasia or abortion – something that they ought not to think about while on duty. As for the ordinary person who is interested in penal questions, the very word 'philosophy' has a discouragingly academic aura, and the word 'academic' in its turn means 'difficult and pointless'.

Many of these misgivings are based upon a mistaken assumption: the assumption that penal philosophy is just a sector of moral philosophy – the philosophy of punishment – under a more fashionable name. I think that this is an important mistake. Some issues are common to both, but more often what seems to be the same issue arises in a different form.

For example, it will soon become obvious that I do not believe that retribution is a proper aim for a secular penal system. This declaration will give rise at once to several misunderstandings, so that I must quickly make the following points:

(a) I am not necessarily advocating a more *lenient* penal system than would a retributivist;

(b) on the other hand, I am not attributing *inhumanity* to retributivists (that is the sort of oversimplification which brings discussion to a dead end);

(c) most important of all, I am not going to argue that there is no place for retribution outside the penal system.

The last point needs more explanation than the rest. I see no harm or illogicality in holding both that the penal system should be as free as possible from retributionism and, at the same time, that it is natural (and perhaps also morally permissible) for me – as a private individual – to hope that an offender, or class of offenders, will atone by suffering. If I felt like this, I could even argue that, as a private individual with these views, I would not be inconsistent if I reported an offender to the police in the hope that the penal consequences for the offender would be unpleasant (whatever their official objective might be). What I cannot consistently do is to urge that the penal system should be officially designed with a view to imposing unpleasant consequences on the offender simply because he deserves them.

Whether these private feelings are morally permissible or even desirable is a question to which the answer is both independent and outside the scope of this book. No doubt the answer will vary with one's ethical and religious views, and also with the exact nature of one's private feelings. At one end of the scale the desire for revenge for an injury personally suffered tends to incur moral disapproval in our society. At the other end of the scale a disinterested belief that a moral or divine law calls for the expiation of a wrong done to someone else tends to be regarded as morally sound. All that I wish to emphasize is that what follows has no implications of this kind.

Nor does the order in which I propose to discuss the possible aims of a penal system beg any questions. I intend to take notice in turn of all the aims which seem to be put forward nowadays, and have chosen an order which seems to me the best one in which to proceed from simple to more complex issues.

I. MONTERO'S AIM

An aim which is easy to define and dispose of is

Aim 1: *to protect offenders and suspected offenders against unofficial retaliation.*

If it needs a name, it could be called 'Montero's aim', after the Spanish jurist (1916) who emphasized it. Since it is hard to imagine circumstances in which this aim could be achieved only at the expense of others, and since it seems to command unanimous support in any discussions of penal objectives, I need not spend much time on it.

It is perhaps worth pointing out, however, that if we wholeheartedly subscribed to Montero's aim we should pay more attention to certain aspects of the penal system. For example, since stigma is an unofficial penalty, which can often impose suffering that is excessive by any criterion, we should seriously consider whether it is not possible to exercise more control over it. In case this sounds impossible, it should be noted that this is what we already do in the case of juvenile offenders when we prohibit the publication of their names and other identifying particulars unless the court permits. A similar provision for adult offenders would allow courts to decide for or against public identification in each case.

If asked to justify Montero's aim, most people would argue either

(a) that unofficial retaliation leads to further disorder: this justification appeals to Aim 2 (below); or

(b) that unofficial retaliation often imposes excessive suffering on the offender or suspected offender. This justification may be an appeal either to the humanitarian or to the retributive principle, which will be discussed in that order.

2. REDUCTIVISM

This brings us to

Aim 2: *to reduce the frequency of the types of behaviour prohibited by the criminal law.*

There seems to be no recognized name for those who emphasize this objective. To call it 'utilitarianism' or 'Benthamism' implies more than is intended, and I am therefore forced to give it the rather ugly title of 'reductivism'.

Reductivism sounds unexceptionable commonsense; nor does it seem to beg any questions. The question 'What types of behaviour should the criminal law prohibit?' can be answered independently, preferably after agreement has been reached on the aims and techniques of a penal system; and I shall deal with it in Chapter 2.

The *pure* reductivist is prepared to use any measure that is likely to be effective in reducing the incidence of any conduct which his society decides to bring within the scope of the penal system. He will approve measures of *social hygiene*,[1] such as slum-clearance, if they can be shown to reduce crime. He will encourage *measures to reduce opportunities*[1] for crime (such as the payment of wages by cheque). He will accept *general deterrents*[2] which seem to discourage potential criminals. He will consider with an open mind any *corrective*[3] which is *prima facie* likely to reduce a known offender's criminal tendencies, whether it acts as an *individual deterrent*, or as a *reformative influence*. If he is asked to choose between such policies (although for the most part they are complementary and not inconsistent), he would simply ask 'Which is the most effective in the case of the type of conduct which you have in mind?' But obviously he must in practice take into account other considerations.

For example, he must accept economic limitations on the policies which he is prepared to advocate. No society can afford a policeman at everyone's elbow. The number of people willing or suitable to be psychiatrists, probation officers, or custodial staff, under present or foreseeable conditions of service, is already insufficient for our *present* penal system. Situations are conceivable, however, where there is a genuine choice between policies neither of which is too expensive in resources to be contemplated. If he were limited by no other considerations, the 'economic reductivist' would simply ask which was likely to yield the biggest reduction for the money (or the manpower).

3. HUMANITARIANISM

But there are other possible considerations. Penal humanitarians assert what is not so much an aim as a principle:

Aim 3: *that the penal system should be such as to cause the minimum of suffering (whether to offenders or to others) by its attempts to achieve its aims.*

I shall call it the 'humanitarian' principle, although Bentham, who was the first to emphasize it, referred to it as the 'frugality' of punishment (1789). It is a principle which seeks to impose

---

1. Discussed in Chapter 3.   2. Discussed in Chapter 4.
3. Discussed in Chapters 5 and 6.

limitations on the pure or economic reductivist. In its strongest form it is in conflict with reductivism, since it asserts that there are some penal measures so inhuman that they ought not to be inflicted even if they represent the minimum of suffering needed to reduce the incidence of a given type of offence (thus, for example, some opponents of capital punishment argue that even if it *were* the only effective deterrent for some potential murderers, it is too cruel to be inflicted). In its milder form the humanitarian principle permits whatever the reductivist can show to be an effective deterrent or corrective: but it insists that their severity should be kept to the necessary minimum.

4. RETRIBUTIVISM

In either form the principle is genuinely humanitarian so long as it does not appeal for support to other justifications. It is some-times confused, however, with a rather sophisticated variety of retributivism. In its unsophisticated form penal retributivism asserts

Aim 4: *that the penal system should be designed to ensure that offenders atone by suffering for their offences.*

This must be clearly distinguished from Montero's aim, as well as from reductivism and humanitarianism. The genuinely retri-butive penologist believes that the enforcement of atonement is a proper aim of penal systems whether or not this enforcement reduces the incidence of the offences in question, and whether or not it protects the offender against unofficial retaliation. Indeed, if he is both consistent and courageous the pure retributivist must be prepared to argue that the penal system should enforce atone-ment even if by doing so it *increases* the frequency of the offence in question (as imprisoning some homosexuals is said to do), or even if it renders the offender *more* exposed to unofficial retalia-tion (as the pillory did).

The relationship between penal retribution and humani-tarianism is not easy to analyse logically. It would be unfair to point to the fact that in other centuries or other countries retri-butivists have supported punishments which here and now would be labelled 'inhuman' or even 'sadistic'. A civilized retributivist would probably accept that certain punishments are too inhuman to be regarded as just atonement, no matter what the crime. If so, he would of course have to give up the idea that every offender must suffer as much as his victim.

Most penal retributivists seem prepared to compromise with

the first three aims or principles which I have discussed, by claiming only

> Aim 4a: *that the penal system should be designed to exact atonement for offences in so far as this would not impose excessive unofficial retaliation, or inhumane suffering on the offender, and in so far as it would not increase the incidence of offences.*

I shall call this 'compromising retributivism'.

It is a curious fact that people who lay a great deal of stress on atonement as an aim of secular penal measures are usually people whose religion promises that atonement for wrong-doing will be arranged by a supernatural authority. The two beliefs are not necessarily inconsistent. For example, one may think that God uses human beings as agents for enforcing atonement, although if this is the case he must be assumed to tolerate something less than perfect justice or efficiency in his agents. Or one may believe that the secular penal system enforces atonement for some sorts of behaviour, God for others: but this view is plausible only if one holds the implausible view that no crime is a sin and vice versa. Or one may simply see nothing objectionable in the possibility that many sinners will atone twice – once under a fallible secular system and once under an infallible supernatural justice.

Atheists, agnostics, and people whose religion is not preoccupied with morals can be penal retributivists with less difficulty. If *no* supernatural authority enforces atonement, and if atonement *ought* to be enforced, it is natural to assume that the obligation rests on human shoulders. In fact, most atheists and agnostics would probably disown the retributive aim. But even so, they are likely to accept several essentially retributive assumptions about the way in which the penal system ought to operate.

Consistency. The best example is the assumption that similar acts must be dealt with by similar measures. Although Parliament, judges, and other sentencers have accepted the notion that the measures which are applied to this or that offender should be 'individualized'[4] (so as to fit assessments either of his culpability or of his prospects of reform, according to one's interpretation of 'individualization'), in practice great efforts are made to achieve consistency. The lengths to which they can be carried are illustrated by the case of *R.* v. *Reeves* (1963). Reeves and another man had been convicted of receiving twenty stolen pitch-fibre

4. A notion which is discussed in Chapter 8.

pipes. The other man, who had been tried summarily, had been fined £25; but Reeves, who had elected to be tried by a higher court, was sentenced to nine months' imprisonment. When he appealed, the Court of Criminal Appeal did not consider this sentence excessive; on the contrary, they criticized the other man's fine as too lenient. But such was their respect for consistency that they felt obliged to reduce Reeves's sentence by an amount which ensured his immediate release. In other words, although it was within their power to ensure that at least one of the pair received what they considered the right[5] sentence, they considered it more important to ensure that both received the same sentence, and therefore reduced Reeves's sentence to one which they considered inadequate.

Legal Naturalism. This veneration of consistency sometimes combines with another phenomenon to produce a particularly unfortunate result. There is a tendency (which is very hard to resist unless one is constantly on guard) to regard acts which have the same legal name as being to some extent equally culpable. It is the persuasive effect of a legal name which makes some people so reluctant to accept the idea that some 'murderers' need not be imprisoned. Such is the power of what might be called 'legal naturalism' that one way of weakening their objections is to reclassify some forms of murder as 'manslaughter', 'culpable homicide', 'child destruction', or 'infanticide'. Again, people who use the word 'murder' to support prohibitions on abortion are exploiting our legal naturalism.

Irrevocability. Another retributive aspect of sentences is their theoretical irrevocability. It is true that this can be explained historically (hanging, mutilation, branding, and whipping could not be undone); and that – as we shall see in Chapter 9 – the principle of irrevocability has been modified to a considerable extent by expedients such as the appeal against sentence, the use of the prerogative of mercy, and remission of prison sentences and release on licence. But expedients such as these serve to emphasize the difficulty which we have in ridding ourselves of the assumption that the sentence of the court is not to be interfered with later. One can try to justify this on the grounds that the possibility of later modification would weaken the deterrent effect of sentences (although, if so, it is inconsistent of us to allow

5. It is not clear whether they had in mind retributive or reductive rightness.

courts to remove disqualifications from driving). But the real justification is certainly the assumption that the sentence is retributively appropriate, and that what is retributively appropriate today cannot cease to be so at a later date.

Harm. Another assumption which is built upon a retributive foundation is that the severity of the sentence should be related to the amount of harm done by the offence. This assumption is embodied in statutes which provide lesser maximum penalties for unsuccessful attempts than for successful attempts. Even offences which are committed unintentionally are sometimes distinguished in this way: the maximum penalty for dangerous driving is two years' imprisonment, but for causing death by dangerous driving it is five years. Statutes apart, sentencers are often moved to leniency by the argument that the offender has undone, or partially undone, the harm resulting from his offence. The petty embezzler who is able to say that he has paid back most of the money often earns a favourable comment and a lighter sentence from the court.

It is true that some retributivists would repudiate these naïve distinctions, and would argue that the amount of blame and therefore the severity of the penalty should be governed by the offender's intentions and not by the actual result. The view that the severity of punishment should depend upon the harm done is thus only a natural and not a necessary inference from the retributive view of penal measures.

But the greater the emphasis which the retributivist places on the offender's state of mind the harder it is to be sure that penal measures are achieving the aim of enforcing atonement. For if the atonement must be appropriate not to the harm done, but to the state of mind in which the offender did it, the task of ensuring that the severity of the punishment shall be fairly adjusted becomes very difficult indeed. So obvious is this difficulty that at least one religion assumes (or used to assume) the existence of a full-time angel for the purpose, endowed with complete insight into the minds and hearts of men, and known as 'The Recording Angel'.

It is true that the impossibility of complete accuracy is not a conclusive objection. Rough justice is usually considered better than no justice. But even a penal system whose *sole* objective was the enforcement of appropriate atonement would be very rough indeed; and if other objectives are accepted as proper it is very doubtful whether it can be regarded as achieving even the roughest sort of retributive justice. For Aim 2, the reduction of the frequency of certain types of behaviour may necessitate prolonged detention of the very offenders who are least able to control their behaviour, and therefore, on retributive principles, the least culpable.

Doli Capax. Another example of this paradox is the legal maxim which until recently used to guide English courts, at least in theory, in deciding whether a child between his tenth and fourteenth birthdays should be 'found guilty' of an offence. Scottish courts seem to have abandoned the principle some time in the nineteenth century; but in England, even if it was clear that the child performed an act prohibited by the criminal law, it was presumed that he did not know that he was doing 'wrong'[6] unless evidence was given which made it probable that he did know; and if no such evidence was given he should be acquitted. If this principle were conscientiously applied, the result would be that the young thief who did not know that stealing is wrong would be exempt from interference by the penal system, while the young thief who did could be dealt with. Yet if anything the one who did not know that stealing is wrong or illegal was in greater need of intervention, since a boy of ten or eleven who does not know this must either be very abnormal or have had a very abnormal upbringing.

But perhaps the hardest question which the retributivist has to answer is 'How should we decide the form or degree of suffering which is appropriate to the offence?': a question which must be answered whether the offence consists of the harm done or the harm attempted. This question is least difficult to answer if one takes the unsophisticated view that the punishment which is retributively most appropriate is that which most closely resembles the offence. It is on this view that capital punishment is the right way to enforce atonement for murder, although in civilized societies it is not carried to the logical extreme at which the murderer's choice of weapons is imitated. Imitation is recognized to be either too inhumane or too impracticable, depending on the circumstances; but once it is abandoned retributivists find it difficult to suggest any *objective* measure of appropriateness.

6. It was not entirely clear whether 'wrong' meant 'morally wrong' or 'against the criminal law', although the same ambiguity had long since been cleared up so far as the M'Naghten Rules were concerned.

Some seem to appeal to a kind of intuition, which seems to be stronger in the case of those with strong moral or religious convictions. Others seem to appeal to a consensus of opinion: if they are judges they consult their colleagues; so do criminals. Legislators consult a wider variety of people and organizations, short of actually holding plebiscites. In any case, one logical consequence of the appeal to consensus is that a sentence which was retributively right in 1969 could become excessive or inadequate as opinions change – a position which retributivists as well as others would find uncomfortable.

On the other hand, the reductivist who wants to eliminate retribution as a penal aim has to overcome at least one practical difficulty. This is the impossibility of exercising complete control over the considerations which influence the agents in the penal system. No doubt it would be possible to declare explicitly in a statute what the aims of a sentencer may or may not be, as, for example, the Yugoslav Code of 1951 appears to do.[7] It would be possible to enact that in sentencing any offender the court should have regard *only* to his correction and the protection of society, so that it would at least be possible for the offender to appeal against a court whose decision was explicitly or demonstrably influenced by retributive reasoning; but since a fine or a sentence of imprisonment can be imposed either for reductive or for retributive reasons it would be impossible to infer the intentions behind most sentences. I shall return to this problem in Chapter 11.

It would be equally out of the question to ensure that the penal system was *invoked* only for reductivist purposes. Most of the victims who report an offence which has affected them personally do so in order to retaliate against the offender. Consequently even if it were possible to devise a penal system in which the aims of all the official agents were non-retributive it would be impossible to prevent the public from using it for retributive purposes.

7.   'Purpose of Punishment'
                          Article 3
'The purpose of punishment is:
  to prevent activity perilous to society;
  to prevent the offender from committing criminal offences and to reform
    him;
  to exercise educational influence on other people in order to deter them
    from committing criminal offences;
  to influence development of social morals and social discipline among
    citizens.'

These practical limitations, however, are not arguments in favour of an official retributive aim. At most the retributivist can argue that, since penal systems require human agents and since human agents are vindictive or at best moralistic, it is inevitable that a penal system should often be invoked or manipulated for retributive reasons. To which the reductivist can reply that it is at least possible to design a system so that its penalties, even if invoked for retributive reasons, are justifiable by reductivist aims and are used in accordance with a reductivist policy.

If the retributivist tries to go further and argue that the penalties of a penal system should be designed with his aim in view, neither he nor his reductivist opponent can produce conclusive arguments. What the reductivist can argue is that attempts to achieve the retributive aim as well as other aims lead to difficulties, and that even if no attempt is made to achieve other aims it is impossible to tell how accurately one is achieving the retributive aim.

At this stage in the argument the retributivist might retort that the reductivist is no better able to tell when *he* is succeeding in *his* aim of reducing the frequency of the behaviour of which the penal system takes notice. It is true that the difficulties of measuring the success of reductivist measures are all too great. But this is a debating point rather than a genuine *tu quoque*. In the first place, the difficulties of assessing reductive efficacy are practical rather than theoretical, and are therefore not impossible to overcome, as some recent research has shown; whereas the difficulties of assessing retributive accuracy are theoretical, fundamental, and insuperable. Secondly, even if this difference did not exist, the reductivist is aiming only at efficacy, whereas the retributivist is aiming at accuracy. In other words, reductivists' mistakes at worst make them less effective than they would like to be, but retributivists' mistakes have consequences which, on their own assumptions, are moral 'injustices', and therefore more serious.

I must now repeat a point which I made at the outset. Since I have been discussing *penal* retributivism – that is, the view that retributive justice in some form should be an aim or principle of penal systems – I am not saying anything about retributivism in its other aspects. For example, I am not condemning either the morality or the logic of the view that there are acts which, as 'sins', call for atonement. It seems to me inevitable that at our present early stage in our cultural evolution most people should feel vindictive towards someone who has harmed them or their friends or kin; inevitable, too, that some people should feel a slightly more disinterested vindictiveness when someone whom they do not know is harmed; and inevitable that this feeling should be promoted to the status of a moral precept – divinely approved or otherwise – by the notion of retribution. Private feelings of this sort are not to be abolished by rational argument. Moreover, the same person can quite consistently feel vindictive or retributive towards people who have infringed the criminal code, and yet believe that his private feelings are irrelevant to the question 'What should be the aims of the penal system?'

But these observations allow the penal retributivist to fire two more shots. Private feelings of this sort, he can argue, may be *consistent* with a pure reductivism in the penal system, but will they tolerate it? Must not the penal policy-maker ensure that his system satisfies the retributive demands of the man in the street, especially if the latter no longer has sufficient confidence in the existence of a retributively efficient deity? And since modern penal policy-makers cannot share Bentham's hope that the public can be deceived by making penal measures *appear* to be retributive when they are not, penal measures must be at least partly retributive in aim. Otherwise, the retributivist might add, Montero's aim, the protection of the offender against unofficial retaliation, might be frustrated.

This argument, which asserts in effect that even if retributive aims are undesirable in a penal system it must embody them in order to avoid being destroyed, would be more formidable if penal policy-makers were faced with a genuine choice between pleasant and unpleasant measures. In concrete terms, a system which *prescribed* a free holiday on the Costa Brava for bank-robbers (instead of merely failing to prevent it now and then) would certainly be so unpopular that it could hardly survive. But, since virtually all penal measures which we seriously contemplate for mentally normal adults are unpleasant (although in varying degrees), it is possible for the man in the street (or on the bench) who thinks that penal measures should be retributive to reassure himself that they are, and indeed to accept an imperceptibly decreasing degree of unpleasantness. What is more, when it is a question of measures for the very young, he is prepared even to accept the notion that unpleasantness is not always essential; and it is a fact of penal history that principles which one generation applies to the immature are sooner or later applied to the mature. Probation is an example.

The last shot left in the retributivist's locker is the argument that retribution is after all not an end in itself but one of the means by which we improve offenders. I am not sure that many retributivists would take this line, but I have heard some do so. If they believe that it improves secular conduct, then retribution becomes merely another corrective technique in the repertoire of the reductivist. But is this really retributivism? After all, those who argue in this way have to concede that if it is to have this beneficial effect the punishment must be seen and accepted as just retribution by the offender himself. This could have paradoxical consequences. Is the severity of the penalty to be regulated by the offender's conscience? If so, is the man with the tenderer conscience to suffer a more severe penalty than the man who does not admit that he deserves his punishment?

If, on the other hand, the retributivist is arguing that punishment is justified by spiritual improvement, he is asking that the penal system should do the work of the Church. He is certainly entitled to ask that it should not make the work of the Church impossible (for example by placing obstacles in the way of contact between offender and priest). But if he asks that it should adjust the nature of the penalty to assist in the work of the Church he is raising awkward questions. For example, would this justify longer (or shorter) prison sentences for Christians than for atheists? But I do not think that genuine retributivists regard retribution as a means in this way. For them it is an end in itself.

What must be conceded, even by the purest of reductivists, is that offenders' notions of what is retributively appropriate – in colloquial language 'fair' – must sometimes and at some point in the system be taken into account. If the offender is merely to be eliminated – for instance by deportation or by death – or incapacitated – for instance by secure custody – his acceptance of the fairness of the penal measure cannot make much difference to its success. If the aim, however, is to reform him, his acceptance may well be a necessary condition of success. How much attention must sentencers pay to the criminal's sense of justice? Must the reductivist, having shown the retributivist the door, let him in again by the window? Not necessarily. If he is very bold he could argue that the task of reconciling the criminal to his sentence is not for the sentencer but for the penal agent – the probation officer or the prison staff. Penal agents sometimes say that they are able to achieve this; but as a general solution to the problem it is rather visionary, and when we ask 'Who is to reconcile the motorist to his fine?' its absurdity becomes obvious.

The solution is to be more precise about the sort of things that strike offenders as unfair. One of these is inconsistency: so far as this is concerned Reeves's views almost certainly coincided with those of the Court of Criminal Appeal. Another is severity, when this appears to exceed the norm. Not surprisingly, offenders do not complain about lenient departures from the norm. In short, offenders do not seem to be demanding a system in which sentences are retributively appropriate; merely one in which they are consistent and not on occasion unpredictably severe. What they find it difficult to accept is 'individualization' and 'exemplary sentencing'; and I hope to show that even from the reductivist's point of view the value of both these ideas is doubtful.[8]

The Limiting Retributivist. There are, however, more sophisticated forms of penal retributivism which must be discussed. It can be maintained that, while penal measures should not be designed or applied with atonement in view, their severity should be *limited* by retributive considerations (Longford, 1961). On this view, what is done to offenders can be planned with a view to reducing the frequency of repetitions of their offences so long as the principle is observed that

> 4b: *the unpleasantness of a penal measure must not exceed the limit that is appropriate to the culpability of the offence.*

In concrete terms, the length of imprisonment imposed on a burglar should be such as to maximize his prospects of reform (or protect society against him for a substantial time if his prospects of reform are small), *so long as it is not too heavy a price to pay for burglary*. A principle of this sort can be used to justify a system which – as in England – fixes the maximum penalties for offences but leaves the court free to impose less than the maximum.

Retribution as a limiting principle must be clearly distinguished from the strong form of humanitarianism, which asserts that there are some forms or degrees of suffering that should not be imposed, however effective they may be from the point of view of prevention. For example, assuming that detention until the age of sixty is the only effective means of preventing a violent

8. See Chapters 4 and 9.

recidivist aged thirty from committing further injuries to other people, a retributivist would ask whether the injuries he had so far committed were so bad as to justify thirty years of custody, whereas a humanitarian would ask whether so long a sentence should be permissible in *any* circumstances.

This sort of retributivist – who might be called a 'limiting retributivist' – is less likely to find himself in conflict with reductivists. True, the lower the limits which he sets the more likely the reductivist is to object that he is not being allowed to achieve *his* aim. And when faced with an offender who is very likely to do serious and irremediable harm for the rest of his active life the limiting retributivist (whose principle allows him to have regard only to the harm which the offender has already done or attempted) is almost bound to want to release the offender before reductivists would. In any case, he must still try to answer the very awkward question 'How do you tell what is a retributively appropriate maximum?' and his answers are no less lame than those of the ordinary retributivist.

Retribution in Distribution. The third and most refined sort of retributivist surrenders not only the idea that penal measures should be designed with an eye to atonement, but also the idea that there should be a retributively appropriate limit to their severity (although he can consistently accept the humanitarian principle that some forms of penalty are too severe to be applied to anyone). This retributivist points out that so long as we confine penal measures to people who have committed a criminal offence and do not allow penal measures to be applied to someone who has not, we are honouring a retributive principle – the principle that

4c: *society has no right to apply an unpleasant measure to someone against his will unless he has intentionally done something prohibited.*
Kant was probably the first moral philosopher to enunciate it, but Professor Hart (1959) was the first to discuss it fully, and he has called it the principle of 'retribution in distribution'.

The distributive retributivist is in a much stronger position than his less sophisticated brethren, the ordinary, compromising or limiting retributivists. He does not have to answer the question 'How do you know what penalty – or maximum penalty – is appropriate to this offence or that?' He is not in conflict with reductivists over offenders who seem to need very long periods of detention. For he leaves both the nature and the duration (or severity) of the penal measures entirely to the reductivist (with or without a humanitarian at his elbow); and he concerns himself entirely with the question 'Who is to be liable to whatever measures the reductivist thinks necessary (and the humanitarian considers permissible)?' To which his answer is 'Only those people who have intentionally committed acts prohibited by the penal system'.

Two forms of distributive retributivism have to be distinguished. One asserts that this is the only principle on which a workable penal system *can* be founded. This could be called the 'practical' form, to distinguish it from the 'moral' form which asserts that this is a principle which *ought* to be honoured by any penal system, even if it were practicable to do without it.

The moral version is on the whole harder to maintain than the practical version. Imagine a situation in which it is as certain as it can be that a man will commit serious and irreparable harm – such as murder or mutilation – to another person (he may, for instance, be a jealous and violent husband whose wife has eloped with another man). The only method of ensuring that the harm is not done may well be to put him in custody for a while. Strictly speaking, the moral kind of distributive retributivist is bound to object to this, on the grounds that the man has not yet done something to justify his detention. Or suppose that the man is paranoid, that his murderous intentions are uncontrollable and based on delusion. Here again, if Hart is thinking in moral terms, we have no right to impose detention on him. Yet in both cases we feel, somehow, that it would be wrong to do nothing to prevent murder being done. It is in such cases that the conflict between the philosophy of retributivism and the philosophy of social defence or reductivism seems irreconcilable.

At the moment we side-step this conflict by double-think of one sort or another. If the man is mentally abnormal we expect a psychiatrist to arrange for his compulsory admission to a mental hospital, and we keep our retributive consciences quiet by pointing out that the mental hospitals are not part of the penal system. If he is too sane for this expedient, we expect the police to keep an eye on him until he does something which can be regarded as a 'breach of the peace' – for example, prowling around the house where his wife and her paramour are living. He can then be brought before a court and 'bound over to keep the peace', although he has really committed no breach of the criminal law. As a manual written by a police officer for policemen says, 'this charge is useful where the breach of the peace does not amount to any other [*sic*] offence . . .' (Devlin, 1961). Another expedient is to select an easily definable and testable circumstance which is often associated with the future commission of an offence and to enact that this shall in itself be a crime. An example is the carrying of an offensive weapon.

All these represent efforts to avoid the admission that we are officially intervening in a manner objectionable to the person concerned merely on the strength of a probability that he will commit an offence. Our reason for wanting to avoid this is that it would be an admission that Hart's principle of retribution in distribution is sometimes contrary to commonsense. To admit this directly seems a dangerous step on to a slippery slope.

Neither of these forms of double-think, however, will salve our consciences in a much more frequent type of situation. Many modern statutes penalize behaviour which is not intentionally harmful, but merely negligent, and do so even if the negligence has caused no actual harm. An everyday example is the offence of driving without due care and attention. Indeed we sometimes go further, and apply the criminal law to situations in which it can hardly be argued that negligence is involved. A shop-keeper who sells adulterated food may be convicted of an offence under the Food and Drug Acts even if he had no means of knowing whether it was adulterated, for example because it was tinned. Such cases worry not only Hart but practising lawyers as well, and they try to salve their consciences in several ways. If negligence is an element of the offence, they insist that it should be greater than is necessary in a civil action, so that it can be called 'gross' or 'criminal' negligence, or in extreme cases 'recklessness'. What they are trying to do is to reassure themselves that, even if the accused did not intend harm, he is to some extent morally culpable. They ask 'Did he know that he was likely to cause it, but without caring?' or (accepting a lesser degree of culpability) '*Ought* he' (presumably in a moral sense) 'to have given the matter sufficient thought to realize what might happen?' (Many academic lawyers, of course, are unhappy about these subterfuges and their objective.) If not even negligence is required to satisfy the statute, so that what is often called 'strict liability' is involved, courts are willing to entertain unusual defences – for instance, that the driver of a car who ignored traffic lights was not 'driving' because he had had a blackout. Or they may convict the offender but discharge him if he does not appear to have acted intentionally or with a culpable degree of negligence.

Our laws for preserving public order, for dealing with the dangerously insane, and for discouraging certain kinds of inadvertence demonstrate that, however much Hart's principle appeals to our moral sense, we are prepared to modify it in the interests of expediency, if three conditions are satisfied:

(1) that the danger thus avoided is a *serious* one;

(2) that there is some fairly objective and not too crude way of *defining* circumstances in which the probability that the danger will materialize is much greater than usual;

(3) that the preventive measures which are permitted are not *drastic.*

Thus while no one would accept a system which imposed death on people who were suspected of hanging around Woolworth's in order to shoplift, it is not intolerable to contemplate the prevention of serious violence and sexual molestation of unwilling victims by measures which involve tactful and unobtrusive supervision of persons who can be shown to be likely to behave in this way.

Another kind of conflict between the reductivist and the distributive retributivist arises when the former considers it essential to deal with an offender in a way which imposes hardship or distress on his family (as a heavy fine or a prison sentence may do). The man who upholds the principle that it is morally wrong for penal measures to fall on the innocent is bound to worry about this. We salve our consciences in several ways. The state provides material assistance to families rendered destitute by the imprisonment of the wage-earner. Judges sometimes mitigate their sentence because of its probable effect on dependants, especially if the convicted person is a mother. The man in the street simply tells himself that the offender should have thought of his family before risking their happiness.

On the whole, however, it is easier to reconcile vicarious punishment with distributive retributivism when the latter is regarded not as a *morally binding* principle, but simply as a *practically desirable* one. If one adopts this practical justification one is prepared to tolerate exceptions in cases of expediency so long as the principle governs *most* of the operations of the penal system. Otherwise a man could not order his life rationally, and would go about in fear and trembling lest he be locked up because his wife has run away with his best friend. Certainly a penal system which operated in this way with great frequency would arouse so much opposition that it would not be tolerated. *But it is important to realize that the strongest case for this sophisticated form of retributivism is not that to breach it occasionally is unthinkable or morally insupportable, but that to abandon it completely is politically out of the question.*

5. DENUNCIATION

One more possible aim of penal measures must be considered:
Aim 5: *to show society's abhorrence of crime.*
Since the word 'denounce' is commonly used in formulating this aim, I shall call it the 'denunciatory aim'. At various times and in various words it has been put forward by Beccaria (1764), Fitzjames Stephen (1883), Émile Durkheim (1895), Lord Denning (1950), and at least one Home Secretary, Gwilym Lloyd George (1956). Most of them had in mind the crime of murder, and it was argued that a justification for the death penalty was that so drastic a penalty denounced the crime as peculiarly abhorrent to society.

Historically this argument did not come to the fore until the death penalty had been virtually restricted to murder and treason, and did not become fashionable until other justifications for the death penalty (that is, elimination, deterrence, and retributive appropriateness) had been to some extent discredited. But a suspicious history does not disqualify it from serious consideration. Moreover, there are signs that it is taking the place of penal retributivism as a justification for drastic sentences for crimes other than murder.

A pure, or non-retributive, denunciator would not worry overmuch whether the condemned man was innocent or guilty, and would no doubt be satisfied if, as Bentham proposed (1830), the public could be deceived into thinking that criminals suffered terrible punishments, even if this did not in fact happen. He might believe, of course, that this is impracticable, and that the criminal must therefore actually suffer the punishment. The point is not quite so academic as it seems at first sight, because it could be argued that the suspended sentence achieves the denunciatory aim without actually imposing the suffering. But I fancy that most denunciators would argue that unless the criminal is known to suffer the penalty society's abhorrence is not adequately demonstrated.

What has to be asked, however, is *why* it is being demonstrated, and *to whom*. If the demonstration is intended to discourage potential offenders, the denunciation is a technique of reductivism, and if one is a practical reductivist one then asks whether the gain is enough to justify the cost and hardship. One can also ask how the denunciation works. Does it simply deter those who fear society's condemnation, or does it set up some subtler psychological process which leads to conformity? In either case, is the effect one which would not be achieved by the mere fact of public conviction? Certainly those who simply fear society's condemnation should be deterred by the mere stigma of public conviction.

Professor G. D. Morton (1962) has suggested that the drama of trial and conviction emphasizes society's disapproval in a particularly forceful way, and it is conceivable that we are even more impressed if the last act in the drama is a hanging or a long sentence of imprisonment. But this raises the question 'Who is supposed to be impressed?' If the aim is mere reduction of offences, there is no point in providing a frisson for the law-abiding. As for potential law-breakers, how impressed are they by the drama? Since I know of no scientific research into this aspect of the penal system I can only say that my regular informal discussions with groups of prisoners, extending over many months with the same men, do not suggest that they *are* impressed.

But I do not think that this is what the denunciators really have in mind. If I read correctly between the lines, they mean that the denunciation is not a means to an end but just as much of an end in itself as the retributive aim which it seems to be replacing. There are analogies: people get real satisfaction from listening to public condemnations of conduct of which they already disapprove (sermons are a good example of this). An even more dignified analogy is a commemorative act (not necessarily religious) like the two minutes' silence on Armistice Day. If this is a fair comparison we might call this aim 'ritual denunciation'. The question is whether those who believe in it are satisfied by a ritual which does not actually involve the imposition of hardship on the victim. Anthropologists describe rituals which have evolved from human sacrifice to animal sacrifice and finally to token sacrifice. If the only point of imposing a drastic penalty is the completion of a ritual, I wonder whether modern denunciators would accept token sacrifices.

It is difficult to escape the feeling, however, that the denunciatory theory is nothing more than a sophistical version of old-fashioned retributivism. My suspicions are aroused by the sort of people who preach it, by the fact it tends to be used in support of drastic penal measures such as hanging, and by the opportune way in which it became popular at a time when more obvious justifications for hanging – deterrence, elimination, and retributive suitability – were becoming discredited. How closely denunciation can be linked with retribution was demonstrated by the Archbishop of York (1965) in the House of Lords' debate on the suspension of capital punishment:

> Society must say, through its officers of law, that it repudiates certain acts as utterly incompatible with civilized conduct and that it will exact retribution from those who violate its ordered code. . . .

The test question which should disclose a denunciator's underlying philosophy would ask whether the criminal must actually suffer, or whether it is sufficient merely to indicate society's abhorrence of his crime – for example by a suspended sentence. If he says that the criminal must suffer, he must answer the question 'Why?' If he says 'To reduce crime' he is really just a desperate reductivist. If he says 'To satisfy our feelings' he is asking us to treat the criminal sacrificially, as a mere instrument in a ritual. But if he says, as he probably will, 'Because he ought to suffer', he is just a retributivist in fancy dress.

Let me summarize what I have been arguing. The reduction of prohibited conduct must be the main aim of any penal system, but must be tempered by both economic considerations and humanity if the system is to be practicable and tolerable. The aims which raise serious difficulties are ordinary retribution and denunciation. Retribution as a limiting principle raises more difficulties than humanity as a limiting principle, and there is little point in adopting both. Retribution as a distributive principle has a strong appeal, but cannot be universally applied unless we give up several very desirable forms of preventive interference, or indulge in double-think by regarding them as outside the penal system.

A penal system designed by an economic reductivist, observing limits dictated not by retributive justice but by humanity, would differ in some important respects from our present one. It would be less ambiguous and illogical. It would distinguish less sharply between actual and likely harm, and between intention and inadvertence. It would lay far less emphasis on consistency in sentencing. On the other hand, it would not be either intolerably severe or unrealistically lenient. In short, it is not unthinkable. The rest of this book is an attempt to show roughly what it would be like.

Chapter 2

The Scope of the Criminal Law

Let us imagine, then, a reductivist and a humanitarian, both purged by some psychotherapeutic process of all retributive aims and assumptions, conscious or unconscious, sitting down to plan an effective system for lowering the frequency of crime. In this joint planning operation the role of the reductivist would be to suggest measures that seemed likely to be effective, while the humanitarian had the right of vetoing or at least suggesting limits to those which might impose suffering.

One of the questions which they would have to discuss at an early stage would be 'At what sort of behaviour should our plans be aimed; that is, what should "crimes" include?' This is the sort of question which has hitherto been answered by accident and implication rather than by a direct and reasoned statement. In the nine hundred years since the Conquest a criminal code which once took notice only of treason and a handful of felonies such as murder, robbery, arson, rape and serious thefts has widened until nobody knows how many separate offences are distinguished by common law, statute and subordinate legislation. New offences have been added to it under pressure from the Church, from revenue-collectors, from social reformers, from government departments and from the agencies of law enforcement themselves. In this century alone the new additions to the English statute-book range from incest (1908) to litter-dropping (1957). The objectives of all these additions have been so varied that it is impossible to describe in a single sentence the function which the criminal law nowadays performs. In one way or another it tries to achieve at least thirteen sorts of purpose which not only can but must be distinguished from each other:

(1) the protection of the human person (and to some extent animals also) against intentional violence, cruelty or unwelcome sexual approaches;

(2) the protection of people against some forms of unintended harm (for example, from traffic, poisons or infections);

(3) the protection of easily persuadable classes of people (that is, the young or the weak-minded) against the abuse of their persons or property (for example, by sexual intercourse);

(4) the prevention of acts which, even if the participants are adult and willing, are regarded as 'unnatural' (for example, incest, sodomy or bestiality);

(5) the prevention of acts which, though not included under any of the previous headings, are performed so publicly as to shock other people (for example, nakedness, obscene language, or heterosexual copulation between consenting adults which takes place in public);

(6) the discouragement of behaviour which might provoke disorder (such as insulting words at a public meeting);

(7) the protection of property against theft, fraud, or damage;

(8) the prevention of inconvenience (for example, the obstruction of roads by vehicles);

(9) the collection of revenue (for example, keeping a motor-car or television set without a licence);

(10) the defence of the state (for example, espionage);

(11) the enforcement of compulsory benevolence (for example, the offence of failing to send one's child to school);

(12) the protection of social institutions such as marriage or Christian worship (for example, by prohibiting bigamy or blasphemy);

(13) the enforcement of the processes regarded as essential to these other purposes (for example, offences connected with arrest, assisting offenders to escape conviction, and testimony at trials).

The objectives in this list are so varied that it is extremely difficult to formulate a general principle which will help to decide whether a given sort of behaviour should or should not be treated as a crime. For example, we are several centuries past the era in which the criminal law was thought of simply as the secular institution for the punishment of moral wrong-doing, and we now recognize that many sorts of conduct which we condemn morally are outside its scope, while other sorts within its scope are from the moralist's point of view trivial, neutral or even defensible.

Does this mean, however, that it is impossible to formulate any rules or principles to which we can appeal if we are asked to decide whether a new crime should be created or an old one abolished? Is the issue to be decided simply by the strength of feeling that can be aroused in Parliament at an opportune moment? Certainly this is how many such decisions have been taken in this century over the last hundred years. The crime of 'gross indecency between males' was created in 1885 by Henry Labouchère, a back-bench member of Parliament who – for some reason which has never been satisfactorily explained – successfully moved this amendment to a bill which was designed to protect immature girls from sexual exploitation. The crime of incest was created in 1908 in response to pressure from the Church of England, which had only recently begun to discover how many slum-dwellers were unaware of the prohibitions of Leviticus, Chapter 18. The Litter Act of 1957 was the result of a private member's bill, supported by the Association for the Preservation of Rural England. But perhaps the oddest story of all is that of the Hypnotism Act of 1952.

In December 1948, a Miss Rains-Bath, then aged nineteen, attended a stage exhibition of hypnotism given in the Brighton Hippodrome by the well-known stage hypnotist, Mr Ralph Slater. She was one of the members of the audience who were induced to become his subjects. A week after the performance she began to have fits of depression, weeping or apathy, which recurred constantly until fourteen months later she was relieved of them by a medically qualified hypnotist. Early in 1950 she brought a successful action against Mr Slater for negligence and assault, and was awarded £1,132.

The news of her action was, of course, reported in *The Times*. Meanwhile, rural England had also roused itself: the *Gloucestershire Echo* of 8 March 1950 reported that the year before a girl who had been hypnotized in a public performance had taken twelve days to emerge from the trance. It was only a matter of months before the Midlands realized their peril, and the *Sheffield Telegraph* of 12 July reported the case of a man who had been told to fall asleep when the band played a certain tune, and continued to do so in his engineering office when his colleagues whistled this tune. Medically qualified psychiatrists wrote to *The Times* about the dangers of hypnotism in the hands of practitioners who lacked a medical qualification. Questions began to be asked in Parliament. . . .

In the general election which occurred soon afterwards, none of the parties seem to have regarded stage hypnotism as a menace worth mentioning in their election programmes. But in the new Parliament a private member introduced a bill to ban stage hypnotism altogether. More or less by accident, this was given a second reading one Friday morning against the Government's advice. But by this time the theatrical interests and the local authorities had realized what was happening, and the private member was persuaded to accept amendments which allowed stage hypnotism if the local authority gave permission for it, but made it illegal for people under twenty-one to be used as subjects. In practice, few local authorities refuse permission, and all the stage hypnotist does is to ask each of his volunteer subjects whether they are under twenty-one. That is how one of the rarest types of casualty in medical literature found its way into the criminal law.

It is easy by examples such as these to discredit our present method of drawing and redrawing the boundaries of criminal law. Is it possible to improve on it?

LIMITING PRINCIPLES

Now and again there have been attempts to formulate what might be called 'limiting principles', which declare that the criminal law should not be used for certain purposes, or in certain circumstances.

If the conclusions of the preceding chapter are accepted, at least one limiting principle follows from them:

(A) *Prohibitions should not be included in the criminal law for the sole purpose of ensuring that breaches of them are visited with retributive punishment.*

It is probably not too far-fetched to ascribe this principle to Beccaria, whose *Of Crimes and Punishments* (1764) was the first treatise on penal theory to deal with the subject on utilitarian premisses. His assertion that 'It is better to prevent crimes than to punish them. This is the ultimate end of all good legislation...' is the assumption upon which the approach of all later utilitarians, such as Bentham, Mill and Baroness Wootton, is based.

A few years later, Bentham's *Introduction to the Principles of Morals and Legislation* (1789) stated three more limiting principles. The first was

(B) *The criminal law should not be used to penalize behaviour which does no harm.*

In his phraseology, punishment was groundless when, on the whole, there was no evil in the act. It is a principle to which everyone would give general assent, and would agree that it was the reason why we do not use the law to discourage bad manners or bad art. Nevertheless there would be many disagreements over other sorts of conduct. The idea of prohibiting bad art by law sounds ridiculous, but one of the things which town and country planning legislation tries to control is bad architecture, and a man who flouts it can suffer heavy penalties. How offensive must something be, and to how many people, before it is counted as harmful?

Another of Bentham's principles was

(C) *The criminal law should not be used to achieve a purpose which can be achieved as effectively at less cost in suffering.*

For instance, suggested Bentham, if the objection could be achieved 'by instruction . . . as well as by terror', terror should not be used. The trouble about this principle is that Bentham talks as if deterrence and instruction were interchangeable so far as everyone in a given class is concerned. He may simply have meant, of course, to exempt from punishment very young offenders who needed only to be warned that what they had done was a crime. But if he meant, as he probably did, to exclude whole classes of harmful conduct from the criminal law, he overlooked the possibility that some of the people who indulge in such conduct might respond to deterrence but not instruction. A better formulation of the principle would be

(CC) *The criminal law should not be used where measures involving less suffering are as effective or almost as effective in reducing the frequency of the conduct in question.*

Bentham's third principle was

(D) *The criminal law should not be used if the harm done by the penalty is greater than the harm done by the offence.*

For in such cases punishment would be 'unprofitable' when the felicific balance-sheet was added up. The difficulty about this principle is that it requires us to weigh, let us say, the unhappiness caused by bad architecture against the unhappiness caused by a large fine. Since the two sorts of unhappiness are inflicted on different people we cannot simply leave it to individual choice, as we do when we ask someone whether he would rather be fined or imprisoned. The difficulty of choosing between incommensurables is one of the weaknesses of Benthamism which have been exploited by its opponents.

A variant of this principle, however, seems to underlie a modern argument that has been used against the wholesale prohibition of abortion or homosexual acts. It has been pointed out that such sweeping laws give rise to practices which, on any point of view, are more undesirable than those against which they are aimed. If legal abortions were not so difficult to arrange, there would not be a black market in illegal ones, with its high mortality. The outlawing of private homosexual behaviour between consenting men provided excellent opportunities for blackmail (although the fear of stigma or of a broken marriage provides some opportunity for blackmail even when the fear of the law does not). The undiscriminating prosecution of bigamists must have endangered many unions between men and women which, though unhallowed, were stable and happy. The prosecution of narcotic addicts is said by sociologists such as Dr Schur (1963) to turn them into criminals. If Bentham had written today his comment would probably have been that

(DD) *The criminal law should not include prohibitions whose by-products are more harmful than the conduct which they are intended to discourage.*

Unfortunately this involves the same difficulty as principle D, although to a lesser degree. For principle DD is of help only when the prohibited conduct is so clearly less harmful than the by-products of the prohibition that there can be little disagreement on the subject. It is not surprising, therefore, to find that principle DD is invoked only when the conduct under discussion is of a kind which makes it possible to maintain either that the harm which it does is illusory or negligible, or that it harms only the person who indulges in it. It has been argued, for example, that marijuana-smoking is not in itself harmful to the body or mind, and that what does harm is the black market, created by the prohibition, which leads marijuana-smokers to associate with criminals, and especially with sellers of 'hard' drugs.

Others would argue that even if drug use is harmful – and there can be little doubt that *some* drugs are destructive – they harm only the user, who has freely chosen to use them (often, it is added, as an escape from some other kind of misery). Bentham himself recognized the existence of what he called 'self-regarding offences', which harmed only the offender, and which he thought it 'inexpedient' to punish. It was J. S. Mill, however, who in 1859 developed this into a full-blown principle in his essay *On Liberty*:

The object of this Essay [wrote Mill] is to assert one very simple principle, as entitled to govern absolutely the dealings of society with the individual in the way of compulsion and control, whether the means used be physical force in the form of legal penalties, or the moral coercion of public opinion. That principle is, that the sole end for which mankind are warranted, individually or collectively, in interfering with the liberty of action of any of their number, is self-protection. That the only purpose for which power can be rightfully exercised over any member of a civilised community, against his will, is to prevent harm to others. His own good, either physical or moral, is not a sufficient warrant.

Leaving aside for the moment the fact that Mill was talking about other forms of coercion as well as the law, a modern statement of his assertion might be this:

(E) *The criminal law should not be used for the purpose of compelling people to act in their own best interests.*

Mill himself recognized that there should be exceptions to this rule. 'Despotism', he thought, 'is a legitimate mode of government in dealing with barbarians provided that the end be their improvement'; and he took much the same view of the upbringing of children. So far as children were concerned, therefore, he would not have said that his principle ruled out compulsory benevolence such as enforced attendance at school, although he might well have objected to obligatory social insurance.

What he himself had in mind were 'infringements of liberty' such as legal restrictions on the sale of poisons, on drunkenness unaccompanied by violence, on gambling and on Sunday amusements. He was not concerned with the question whether these were morally wrong or not; he was arguing that even if they were wrong nobody should attempt to use the law – or indeed the pressure of public opinion – to discourage others from such behaviour, since it did no harm to anyone except possibly the drug-addict, the drinker or the gambler himself. Other would-be reformers of the law have of course gone further, and argued that some of the acts which the law prohibits on the assumption that they are morally wrong are not wrong at all, or wrong only in special circumstances. Suicide, euthanasia, gambling, drinking, drug-taking, abortion and private homosexual behaviour have all been defended in this way. If their defenders had used Bentham's language they would have said that in such cases punishment is 'groundless'. For Mill, however, this was not the point. Whether such behaviour was wrong or not, the law should not be used against it.

Mill's principle has gained wide support in this country over the last century, probably because of its emotional appeal to a freedom-loving intelligentsia rather than the strength of the reasoning on which it was based. He himself thought that the strongest argument for it was that although an 'over-ruling majority' was likely to be right more often than not about conduct that affected the interests of other people, when it came to 'self-regarding conduct' it was quite as likely to be wrong as right: and he cited a number of obviously ridiculous discrepancies between the moral beliefs of different religions and cultures. The argument seems to imply that if a majority was in fact in the right it would be *justified* in interfering with self-regarding conduct. A stronger argument would have been that the object of such interference is usually to force people to behave morally, but that – as Professor Hart has pointed out – there is no virtue in morality if it is imposed from without.

Mill also had to meet the counter-argument that many of the types of behaviour which he wished to protect against interference were not, in the long run, self-regarding after all. As our subsequent experience has emphasized, the drinker, the drug-user, the gambler are likely to cause suffering to their dependants, relatives and friends and to become eventually a burden which society has to carry. Mill's answer was rather forced and moralistic:

> I cannot consent to argue the point as if society had no means of bringing its weaker members up to its ordinary standard of rational conduct, except waiting till they do something irrational and then punishing them, legally or morally, for it. Society has had absolute power over them during all the early portion of their existence: it had the whole period of childhood and nonage in which to try whether it could make them capable of rational conduct in life.

If (he is saying) society has failed to take its opportunity of ensuring that their upbringing protects them against the temptations of drink, drugs and gambling, it should not try to remedy its failure by punishing them when they are adults.

The argument is at once utopian, perfectionist and penologically out-of-date. Utopian because it assumes that society can control the upbringing of children and teenagers to this extent. Perfectionist because it asserts that if one has failed to achieve something desirable in the best way one should not be allowed to try the next best (an odd principle). Penologically out-of-date because it overlooks the possibility that the law might be a means – perhaps the only means – of compelling the alcoholic, the drug-addict or the gambler to undergo therapeutic treatment (Mill himself was of course writing in an era of deterrent penal measures, and could hardly be expected to envisage this).

The pragmatic approach. The principles which Beccaria, Bentham and Mill formulated were moral prescriptions, which said that the penal system *ought not* to attempt this or that task. Other writers, however, were pursuing a more pragmatic line of thought and asking what the law could reasonably be expected to achieve. This is how Montesquieu approached the subject in Book XIX of *The Spirit of the Laws*. He recognized that prohibition by law can be carried further in some societies than in others, but thought that in any kind of society there were areas of conduct (which he called '*les mœurs et les manières*') in which it was most unwise to use the law in the hope of effecting changes.

Even Mill's most violent opponent, the Victorian judge Fitzjames Stephen, accepted pragmatic limits of this sort to the interference of the criminal law. In *Liberty, Equality, Fraternity* (1874), which was a bitter attack on Mill's essay, he admitted that 'you cannot punish anything which public opinion, as expressed in the common practice of society, does not strenuously and unequivocally condemn. To try to do so is to provoke gross hypocrisy and furious reaction'.

In the less emotional language of the twentieth century this principle might read

(F) *The criminal law should not include prohibitions which do not have strong public support.*

The principle has its own weaknesses – such as the difficulty of measuring public opinion in a morally pluralistic society. Like Mill's principle its justification is not self-evident, and it raises the question 'Why not?' Stephen's own reason seems to have been 'because of the gross hypocrisy and furious reaction which would result if one failed to observe this principle'.

Whether Stephen could have supported his argument with convincing examples is doubtful: certainly subsequent experience suggests that he overstated it. Our attempts to improve people's driving of motor-cars by means of the criminal law have certainly been made without the 'strenuous and unequivocal condemnation' of public opinion. It is true that each successive attempt to strengthen penalties or improve means of enforcing the law has met with organized opposition from the motorists' associations, some of which might have been regarded by Stephen as 'gross hypocrisy'. Yet this can scarcely amount to the 'furious reaction' that he predicted.

The importance of Stephen's principle, however, lies in the recognition that there are practical limits to the scope of the criminal law. Bentham and Mill wrote as if there were no difficulty in detecting and punishing any sort of offence, even self-regarding ones; and their principles were moral prescriptions. Punishment *ought* not to be inflicted if it is groundless, needless, unprofitable or inefficacious, said Bentham; self-regarding offences *ought* not to be discouraged by law or any other form of coercion, thought Mill. Stephen, who was a lawyer and a judge, lifted the problem out of the armchair of moral philosophy and into the fresh air of practical politics. The fact that he was arguing in favour of punishing many offences which Mill would have exempted from the criminal law makes him, by modern standards, reactionary; but it does not mean that *all* his utterances should be disregarded.

On the contrary it is worth asking in the light of modern experience what are the practical, as distinct from the moral, considerations that suggest limits to the scope of criminal law.

An obvious practical consideration is the economics of enforcement. The chief agencies of enforcement are police forces, whose size is restricted by the amount of public money which the society in question is willing to spend on them. Even if this were not a limiting factor, it would be found that the number of suitable men and women willing to be recruited to the police was not large enough to make an enormous expansion possible. Allocating policemen's time to the best advantage will always be a major problem, but the extent to which it regulates the rigour of law enforcement is not fully appreciated. In at least one large city of the U.S.A., if a theft involving property of less than a certain amount is reported to the police the report is not even passed to the detective branch for fear of wasting their time; and there are many British police forces which follow much the same policy. In 1963 the Chief Constable of an English city caused some controversy when he announced that he would not 'waste public money' on prosecutions for shoplifting where the value of the stolen goods was small and the offender unlikely to repeat the offence.

Another important consideration is the law-enforcement agencies' need for the assistance of the private citizen. Apart from a selection of driving and parking offences, of revenue offences and breaches of health or safety regulations which can be detected and brought home to the offenders entirely by the observation and evidence of police, inspectors and other officials, very few offences would come to official knowledge if they were not reported by private citizens, and very few of these would be traced to their perpetrators if it were not for the information which the police are able to obtain from the same source.

There are some offences, indeed, which could seldom be prosecuted without the evidence of one of the participators. One of the reasons why women who have resorted to criminal abortionists are so seldom prosecuted in England is that their evidence is usually needed to secure the conviction of the abortionists. Most police forces are so determined to convict blackmailers that they will refrain from prosecuting the victims who give evidence against them.

One of the dangers inherent in the extension of the criminal law to a multitude of peccadilloes is that by making a larger percentage of the population into targets for law-enforcement agencies it may forfeit the co-operation of this percentage in the enforcement of the more important prohibitions. An obvious example of this possibility is traffic offences, which now account for two thirds of all convictions in higher and lower courts. It is impossible to assess the amount of co-operation which the police forfeit by such prosecutions, but it must be considerable.

Even when police forces could initiate prosecutions without too much trouble they often refrain from doing so in cases where they believe that strict enforcement would alienate the public. In England, youths who can be proved to have had sexual intercourse with girls not far below the statutory age of consent (sixteen) are often not prosecuted, largely because the police feel that public opinion would not support them. Another rather unpopular indictment is bigamy, which is not prosecuted nowadays unless there is evidence that the guilty party went through the form of marriage in order to deceive the other party into having sexual intercourse or into parting with property. In countries where private homosexual behaviour between consenting adult men is still criminal, prosecutions for this are often restricted to cases in which there is evidence or suspicion of proselytizing, commercial exploitation, blackmail or 'orgies'.

An assumption which seems to underlie some arguments against certain prohibitions is that

(G) *A prohibition should not be included in the criminal law if it is unenforceable.*

The word 'unenforceable', however, is used very loosely in such arguments. Does it mean 'such that *some* breaches of it would not be detected'? Hardly, for in this sense every prohibition is unenforceable. Does it mean 'such that *all* breaches of it would be undetected'? Again, hardly; for it is no easier to think of any prohibition that would be unenforceable by this criterion. (Perhaps the nearest thing to a genuinely unenforceable prohibition in the history of English law was the form of treason which consisted of 'imagining' the death of the king, the queen or the heir apparent, before it became established by case-law that an overtly treasonable act must be proved.) What the principle must mean is that

(GG) *A prohibition should not be included in the criminal code if only a small percentage of breaches of it could be proved against the perpetrators.*

In this form the principle at once raises the question 'How small must the percentage be?', which is impossible to answer precisely, and not at all easy to answer even roughly until some reply has been given to the more fundamental question 'Why is relative unenforceability an argument against the inclusion of the prohibition?' The stock answer to this is that it 'brings the law into disrepute'.

Like so many stock answers this needs a very close examination. It can hardly mean that a complete absence of attempts to enforce a particular law discredits the whole criminal code, or law-enforcement agencies in general; for the history of every criminal code has plenty of instances in which prohibitions have been allowed to fall into desuetude, without any evidence that this weakened respect for the operative parts of the code. Does it mean that the agencies of law enforcement make themselves ridiculous by unsuccessful attempts to secure convictions? If so, this could be remedied very easily by taking action only when the prospects of succeeding are very good, as the police do with speeding offences.

A more plausible form of the argument might be that if those who are prosecuted for a given offence are regarded by their fellow-citizens as a small and unlucky selection from those who have actually committed it, the public may come to feel that their prosecution is 'unfair'. That such a feeling might well be irrational – especially if the offenders knew that they were risking prosecution – would not prevent it from being widespread. Certainly offenders who are unlucky enough to be prosecuted for a commonly undetected offence – such as exceeding speed limits – seem to feel it.

At most, however, this would be an argument for extreme caution in actually prosecuting detected breaches of the prohibition, and not an argument against including the prohibition in the criminal code. For quite a strong argument can be put forward for retaining, or indeed inserting, even unenforceable prohibitions.

The argument is that the law influences conduct, not merely because people are deterred by the possible consequences of infringing it, but also because it is taken as a declaration of what the society in question condemns. This theory – which I have elsewhere called 'the declaratory theory' – resembles the denunciatory justification of penalties which was discussed in the previous chapter, but is distinguishable because it asserts that even if no one were ever penalized for a breach of a prohibition (indeed even if no one knew what the penalty was) it would still help to maintain standards of conduct.

Certainly the clearest examples of the use of this argument have been connected with prohibitions whose enforceability was doubtful at the very least. It was put forward to the Wolfenden Committee on Homosexual Offences and Prostitution by witnesses who were against the relaxation of the law on homosexual acts between men; and the sole member of the Committee who dissented from this relaxation expressed the objection by saying

Many citizens . . . regard the prohibitions expressly imposed by law as the utmost limits set to their activities . . . and the removal of the present prohibition from the criminal code will be regarded as condoning or licensing licentiousness. . . .[1]

More recently, at least one Home Secretary has used the argument to defend legislation which was avowedly designed to influence opinion rather than penalize conduct. During the second reading of the Race Relations Bill of 1968 Mr Callaghan said

I attach great importance to the declaratory nature of the first part of the Bill. I believe that . . . the very process of giving the law brings an instinctive response from the great majority of our citizens. [Hansard, Commons, 23 April 1968.]

1. See Mr Adair's Minority Report appended to the main report.

Whatever one's views on these particular laws may be, the argument is not implausible. We know that in other areas of opinion, such as politics, people are apt to alter their judgements to correspond with what they believe to be the view of the majority. Experiments in which I have collaborated with Mr Argyle and Professor Berkowitz confirm that university students' views on the morality of certain actions can be strongly influenced by telling them the results of fictitious opinion-surveys of their peers. Might not the criminal law function as a powerful means of inducing people to believe that a given type of conduct is strongly condemned by their peers?

The same experiments, however, showed that in the case of most students it was not possible to influence their moral judgements by inducing them to believe that a given action was or was not prohibited by the criminal law. Two reservations must be made at this point. One is that in both experiments there was a minority of students whose moral judgements probably were influenced in this way. In the first experiment these were identified as students who believed that if a law was passed, for example against heavy smoking, it became morally wrong to disobey that law. In the experiment designed by Professor Berkowitz the minority was identified as students who were 'deeply involved in their society, traditional and conventional and socially responsible'. (In all probability the two experiments on different samples pointed to much the same sort of minority: the student who thought that legislation could *ipso facto* render an act morally wrong was probably a student who was also traditional, conventional and socially responsible.) An equally important reservation is that these experiments measured only short-term effects on a rather special sub-group of the population. They do not prove – and it is difficult to see what sort of experiment could prove – that alterations of the law do not have long-term effects on moral attitudes.

POSITIVE JUSTIFICATIONS

What is noticeable about practically all the arguments which I have been summarizing is that they have been concerned with what may be called 'limiting principles', which offer rules to tell us where the expanding boundaries of the criminal code should stop. There have been few attempts to approach the problem from the other aspect, and formulate positive principles to tell us what tasks the criminal law should attempt. As a result the defenders of individual liberty – Mill, Morley, the Wolfenden Committee, and Professor Hart – have been manoeuvred into a defensive position. Because the criminal code is so old an institution, and has been enlarged so gradually, the onus of proof is assumed to lie on those who wish to see the process halted or reversed.

This assumption is encouraged by the obvious difficulties of shifting the burden. The very diversity of functions to which I have already drawn attention makes any attempt to approach the problem in this way sound naïve. Nevertheless, if an institution is as costly – whether in terms of economic resources or of human happiness – as the penal system undoubtedly is, it seems more realistic to ask for positive justifications whenever it is to be used against a given sort of conduct.

If possible, these justifications should not appeal to moral sentiments of the sort that condemn certain kinds of behaviour. They should not assert that the criminal code should prohibit this or that because it is wicked. To assert this is to invite argument as to what is or is not wicked, and in any society – let alone one which contains such a diversity of moral views as Britain – areas of disagreement will quickly be found.

Something like a non-moralistic justification was offered by Sir Patrick (now Lord) Devlin, in his well-known lecture on *The Enforcement of Morals* (1959), where he said

> The State must justify in some other way [than by reference to the moral law] the punishments which it imposes on wrongdoers and a function for the criminal law independent of morals must be found. This is not difficult to do. The smooth functioning of society and the preservation of order require that a number of activities should be regulated. . . .

It was unfortunate that the main purpose of his lecture was to repudiate the Wolfenden Committee's recommendation that homosexual acts in private between consenting adults should not be criminal. For it led him to argue, in effect, that private homosexual acts between men arouse such 'general abhorrence' that they did in fact threaten our society with disintegration. This was so obviously unrelated to the social and political facts that – together with other weaknesses in his argument – it laid him open to telling attacks from Professor Hart, Dr Wollheim and other spiritual descendants of Mill.

Nevertheless, the misapplication of a principle does not necessarily invalidate it; and, with all his intolerance, Lord Devlin was in fact stating one of the main axioms of a philosophy which seems to underlie a good deal of modern penal legislation.

The need to ensure 'the smooth functioning of society' must, after all, be the main justification for the parts of the criminal code which are concerned with the collection of revenue, the protection of health and the defence of the realm – functions 9, 2 and 10 on pages 23–4. Most, though probably not all, of the other prohibitions can be regarded as necessary for 'the preservation of order', to the extent at least that, if they were not enforced on some occasions, there would be disorder. Not all theft or damage would provoke public disturbances; some victims, for example, would be afraid to retaliate. But some would not, and their methods of protecting themselves or avenging their losses would lead to breaches of the peace. The same is true of intentional violence against the person or unwelcome sexual advances. The prohibition of these can be justified because they are classes of actions of which by no means all, but a substantial number, would provoke disorder.

Nevertheless there are some prohibitions which it is not very plausible to justify in this way. The obvious examples are in my group 4, which consists largely of sexual behaviour that has come to be regarded as 'unnatural', and is prohibited by many criminal codes even if it takes place in private, and between participants who are adult, sane and under no coercion or inducement other than their own desires. (It is interesting to note how difficult it is to think of any form of non-sexual behaviour that is regarded as so 'unnatural' as to call for the intervention of the criminal law. Coprophagy, for instance, strikes an enormous majority of people as unnatural, but is not prohibited in any criminal code of which I know.) So long as incest[2] or homosexual acts are genuinely private, and do not involve advertisement, coercion, deceit or the persuasion of the young or mentally disordered, they are most unlikely to provoke disorder. What arouses resentment, and on occasion violence, is importuning by homosexuals.

The difficulty of arguing, however, that such prohibitions are in the interests of public order or the smooth functioning of

2. Virtually all the *prosecuted* cases of incest involve fathers who have had intercourse with daughters who are under the age of consent, and could thus be prosecuted as unlawful sexual intercourse. It is incest between consenting adults which is hardly ever prosecuted and which could without loss be excluded from the criminal code.

society is not an argument for seeking some other kind of justification. For it is just this sort of prohibition about which modern legislatures are uneasy. In the minority of civilized societies in which the criminal code still prohibits homosexual behaviour between consenting adult males, the prohibition seems to be enforced with less and less enthusiasm or efficiency, and its justification is questioned with increasing frequency.

At first sight there is another category of penal legislation which is not easy to justify on Lord Devlin's principle: what I have called 'compulsory benevolence'. It is implausible to argue that the evasion of universal education or national schemes of social insurance is likely to lead to breaches of the peace. It is not so unrealistic, however, to suggest that children who are allowed to grow up illiterate or more than usually ignorant in a technological society, or people who make no provision for sickness or old age, become economic burdens on their society, and perhaps nuisances of other kinds. This being so, compulsory benevolence can fairly be said to be in the interests of the 'smooth functioning' of society.

Without discussing all the frontiers of the criminal code in detail, I have tried to show that it is not out of the question to formulate both limiting principles and positive justifications which are considerably less dependent on moralistic assumptions and values than, for example, Mill's principles. It is true that they are no more precise. There is just as much room for argument as to what is necessary for the smooth functioning of society or the preservation of order as there is over the question of what is or is not a purely self-regarding offence. But whereas arguments over self-regarding offences are apt to end in deadlock between two or more moral viewpoints, disputes as to what is or is not detrimental to smooth functioning or order do allow for some sort of appeal to observable fact and experience.

It must also be admitted that instead of attempting, like Mill, to draw an eternal boundary between what may and what may not properly be regulated by official sanctions, Lord Devlin offers only a shifting frontier. What may provoke disorder in one generation or one society may not so do in a more tolerant one. In a society which is thrown into a panic by rumours of witchcraft it may be desirable to prohibit witchcraft, as colonial administrators found in Africa. This does not mean, of course, that the prohibitions should be enforced by medieval penalties. What it does mean is that those who see no harm in witchcraft must make some progress in communicating their enlightened viewpoint to the society in question before demanding the abolition of the law that prohibits it.

It cannot be maintained, of course, that a justification based on the smooth functioning of society and the preservation of order is completely value-free. The desirability of these objectives is no more than an assumption, although one that few would question. Perhaps the most convincing way, however, of demonstrating the extent to which it is independent of ordinary moral judgements is to apply it to an imaginary situation. Let us suppose that in a given country there begin to occur sporadic cases of a new type of behaviour which I shall call Xing, in order to avoid arousing irrelevant emotions in the reader. Some of the inhabitants of the country are so shocked by Xing that they mob the homes of those suspected of it, and occasionally there is bloodshed between the Xers and the anti-Xers. Fortunately both are in a minority, and the people who are emotionally neutral about Xing are sufficiently numerous to be free to decide what to do in order to prevent further outbreaks of violence. What they must decide is whether to rely on the prosecution of anti-Xers for assault or to legislate in order to make Xing a crime.

As far as can be ascertained by some rather hasty research, Xing is not an uncontrollable form of behaviour, merely very enjoyable: Xers can refrain from it if necessary. It does not seem to incapacitate them for work or the responsibilities of marriage and parenthood, although one or two marriages have broken up because one spouse could not tolerate the other's Xing. Admittedly, Xers seem to be rather boring as companions, because it takes up most of their spare time, and they talk about little else. If prevented from Xing they become apathetic, saying that most of the enjoyment has gone from their lives, but do not seem to suffer severely. Physically they do not seem to suffer from it, although there are statistics which suggest that male Xers are slightly more likely to have coronary thromboses in their sixties than comparable non-Xers. Apart from the annoyance it causes to anti-Xers, it seems to do no harm to others; but since it is rather noisy it is almost always obvious when it is taking place.

Some research has also been carried out on the subject of anti-Xism. This seems to be an involuntary reaction which affects both sexes and is independent of social class, intelligence, religious belief and type of education. Anti-Xers seem to be disturbed not merely by Xing in their presence but by the belief that Xing is taking place in their vicinity. Many of them are of the opinion that it is a habit acquired through the persuasion and example of other Xers, that it is rapidly increasing in prevalence, and that it is physically and morally harmful (if asked to be more specific about its moral harm they point out that it is so enjoyable that Xers spend all their spare time in this way). Ninety-nine per cent of anti-Xers consider that it should be made an offence punishable with imprisonment.

The neutral but peace-loving majority might reason on several lines. Moralistically, they might argue that since Xing does no demonstrable harm apart from the annoyance which it causes to the anti-Xist minority, the latter ought not to resort to violence and should simply be penalized for doing so. Equally moralistically they might argue that since Xers cause such intense annoyance to anti-Xers, and since they can apparently refrain from it at will without real suffering, they should not do it, and if necessary should be penalized for it. On the whole there seems to be little to choose between either argument. On the other hand, if the majority really wished to arrive at a decision by non-moralistic reasoning, they would ask themselves – and people experienced in law enforcement – whether prosecuting people for Xing or prosecuting those who attacked Xers would prevent disturbances at the less cost; and in this context costs would be reckoned in terms of people penalized as well as man-hours of work by law-enforcement agencies. This might or might not be an easy question. It is just possible that the aim of minimizing the number of people penalized and the aim of minimizing the man-hours worked by police, courts and other agencies might lead to different answers, although this seems unlikely.

The idea of requesting information from the police rather than advice from the moralists will startle quite a number of people, who will protest that law-enforcement agencies should be the servants and not the advisers of the legislature. This is an assertion of a prejudice rather than an argument, and is in any case slightly unrealistic, since it ignores at least two facts of nature. One is that consultation between administrators and their law-enforcement agencies on the practicability of enforcing prohibitions is inevitable in a competent bureaucracy. The other is that, as I have pointed out, prosecutors and police just as inevitably develop their own rules for enforcing controversial prohibitions. This is not to suggest that police (whose prejudices can be very moralistic) should dictate criminal codes. What should be sought – and very carefully sifted to disentangle prejudice from experience – is their estimate of the cost of a prohibition in terms of manpower and other scarce resources.

In any case, the neutral peace-lovers should not overlook the possibility that the frequency of Xing (or of opposition to it) can be effectively reduced by means other than law-enforcement. If this seems to be so, they should ask whether these alternatives cause less distress and resentment; and if this seems to be so, whether this advantage is outweighed by undesirable side-effects. (For example, if a drug can be put on sale which gives Xers more pleasure than their controversial activity, has it detrimental consequences for them or their families?) If the answer is still favourable to the alternatives, are they costlier than law enforcement in terms of money or manpower, and, if so, by how much? For the peace-lovers might well be prepared to choose alternatives which were costlier by a small, or even not so small, margin.

Since Mill's arguments were more than slightly moralistic, the sort of reasoning which I am outlining can hardly be labelled 'utilitarian' if it is to be distinguished from them. Perhaps 'administrative' or 'pragmatic' are the best terms. They make it sound less inspiring than Mill's battle-cry of 'Liberty', and the fact-finding which it entails demands harder work than the exchange of ethical arguments from armchairs. In the long run, however, it provides more solid ground than the bogs of moral assertions, and it is much more likely to lead to a workable and humane list of penal prohibitions.

In practice, although I have used Lord Devlin's formulation of the administrative principle, it would usually lead to conclusions more acceptable to Mill than to him. For example, it would support the exclusion from the criminal code of private homosexual, incestuous or sodomitic acts between consenting adults; of abortions performed with the consent of the woman by a suitably qualified medical practitioner; of bigamy committed without any intention of defrauding, deceiving or seducing a man or woman.

Chapter 3

The Techniques of Crime-reduction

Anyone who is trying to reason administratively about the inclusion of this or that sort of behaviour in the criminal code will soon find it necessary to ask 'What techniques are likely to be most effective in reducing its frequency?' or, a more sophisticated question, 'What techniques are likely to yield the biggest reduction in relation to their cost?'

Although we are a long way from being able to answer questions of this sort with the precision that would satisfy an economist, it may be possible to make a few helpful generalizations. The first step is to distinguish the kinds of techniques which modern societies employ in the hope of reducing breaches of their criminal codes. The most useful distinction is based on the extent to which a technique can be regarded as 'focused' – that is, the confidence with which it can be assumed that all the people to whom it is applied are, or would otherwise be, offenders. Thus for example the sentences which courts impose on convicted thieves are focused, whereas propaganda intended to encourage people to take precautions against thieves is 'unfocused'.

UNFOCUSED TECHNIQUES

Most, though not all, of what are called 'preventive measures' are unfocused, or only partially focused. They consist chiefly of:

General deterrents, that is, measures intended to discourage potential offenders by their unpleasantness. Examples are the death penalty, corporal punishment, financial penalties, deprivation of liberty. General deterrence is one of the traditional aims of the official measures which are put at the disposal of courts; but it is also believed that the unofficial consequences of being identified as a thief, a sex-offender or a man of violence – the consequences which are loosely summed up by the word 'stigma' – act as deterrents, at least to people who have not yet been stigmatized.

The efficacy of penalties and stigma as unfocused preventive measures is a subject which requires a fuller discussion than it can receive at this stage; and the next chapter is devoted to it. Meanwhile, other unfocused techniques must be briefly mentioned.

The reduction of opportunities includes any expedient intended to make the successful commission of crimes less easy. Examples are control over the sale of firearms, explosives, poisons; control over the holding and conduct of public meetings; propaganda about the protection of buildings against illegal entry, or about the carrying of wage-packets and other large sums of money; and improvements in the lighting of public places.

Some offences provide very little scope for precautions. In many cases the only effective precaution would be the abolition of the social institution which provides the occasion or opportunity for them. Fights at football matches or in public houses are examples. Even when it is possible, however, to take precautions it is seldom possible to answer the question 'To what extent are they reducing the total frequency of the behaviour against which they are directed, and to what extent simply protecting specific places or people against offenders who find their opportunities elsewhere?' The answer – if it could be given at all – would certainly vary greatly for different offences. Many petty thefts are committed impulsively by men who suddenly see the opportunity, but who would not otherwise have stolen at that time. At the other end of the scale are bank-robberies and wage-snatches by men who specialize in this sort of crime and have been on the look-out for situations which can be turned into opportunities. Increasing precautions against them may simply drive them either to find opportunities elsewhere or to use greater violence in overcoming the precautions. They are not mere opportunity-takers but opportunity-seekers or even opportunity-makers. Similarly, some sexual offenders are mere opportunity-takers, while others – the more compulsive ones – actively seek situations in which they can find victims.

Education and propaganda. Efforts are sometimes made to persuade the public to become more intolerant of some undesirable form of conduct, especially if it is so prevalent that enforcement of the law against it is difficult. A recent example was the campaign in Britain against drunken driving, which featured posters with the message 'Don't ask a man to drink and drive'. Another was the campaign to 'Keep Britain Tidy'. Neither were spectacularly successful, and both drunken driving and litter-dropping have been the subject of criminal legislation in recent years.

As we saw in the previous chapter, it is sometimes argued – usually by lawyers – that the very existence of a law prohibiting this or that type of conduct is to some extent an unfocused form of prevention, since it declares to the public at large that the conduct in question is not tolerated by the society to which they belong. Here again, as we saw in Chapter 2, such evidence as we have is negative, though not conclusive.

On the other hand, we have hardly begun to explore systematically the possibilities of ethical training in schools. Part of the reason is the discredit which has now fallen on the values and methods of schools which did pay attention to this aspect of education, and especially those run by religious orders, or modelled on the English public school. Certainly both their techniques of moral education and the values they taught were unsubtle enough. A contributory cause, too, has been the Freudian emphasis on the importance of the parents' treatment of the child in the pre-school years, which has distracted attention from the extent to which moral values learned at home are modified by later influences.

There can be no doubt that one of the most important of these later influences is the educational system. The code of conduct inculcated by the English public school has been the subject of both admiration and ridicule, but never disbelief. Scientific research, however, into the efficacy of deliberate attempts to alter schoolchildren's attitudes to such things as personal violence, sexual promiscuity, stealing or dangerous driving does not so far seem to have been reported.[1]

There is some evidence, on the other hand, of the *negative* effects which schools can have on conformity with the law. The graph in Figure 1 seems to point to a close association between compulsory attendance at school and the peak age for being found guilty[2] of indictable offences (which, so far as schoolchildren are concerned, usually means shoplifting and other petty

1. Some idea of the difficulties of any such research, and of the conceptual groundwork that must precede it, can be got from the publications of the Farmington Trust Research Unit, and in particular J. Wilson, N. Williams and B. Sugarman (1967).

2. The shape of the graph is only slightly altered if police 'warnings' for indictable offences are included.

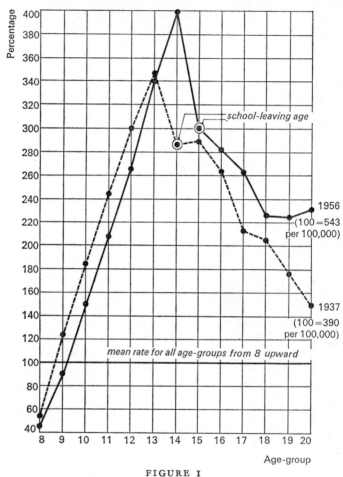

FIGURE I
SCHOOL-LEAVING AGES
AND THE PROBABILITY OF
BEING FOUND GUILTY OF THEFT
OR OTHER INDICTABLE OFFENCES

thefts). When the school-leaving age was fourteen the peak occurred just before it; when it was raised by a year the peak also moved up by one year. Better evidence still is provided by the Social Medicine Research Unit's study of delinquency rates in secondary schools in Tower Hamlets (Power, 1967). Even when the schools were divided into those whose boys lived in high-delinquency districts and those whose boys lived in low-delinquency districts, there were schools in both groups with consistently low rates and schools with consistently high rates over a period of seven years: and the school which a boy attended seemed to make more difference than the location of his home to his chances of appearing in the juvenile court. On the whole it is more plausible to attribute these effects to the influence of peer-groups than to teachers. A child's chances of being detected in delinquency seem to increase with each year of exposure to school whereas if the teachers were effectively active they should decrease. This lends some support to the public-school technique of using boys' own leaders to influence school morality, in preference to more direct tactics of precept and example.

When we turn to the other important factor, mass media of entertainment, we find that although there is a considerable corpus of reported research there is still a good deal of uncertainty about the ways and conditions in which the morality of the young is affected. One or two traditional assumptions have certainly been discredited, among them Aristotle's comforting belief in vicarious catharsis. A potentiality for violence or sexual satisfaction does not seem to be lessened by tales or scenes of love or war. Nor, on the other hand, is imitation necessarily stimulated by this sort of spectacle: before this is likely to happen a number of complex conditions must be fulfilled. Research into the exact nature of these conditions is still in its infancy (see, for example, Halloran, 1964 and 1967). Meanwhile the onus of proof still lies on those who wish, for whatever reason, to argue that mass media which report or depict violence and other undesirable behaviour do not contribute to increases in its frequency.

PARTIALLY FOCUSED TECHNIQUES
Some measures are aimed not at the population as a whole but at age-groups, areas or other sub-groups which are believed to have a higher-than-average rate of crime or other anti-social conduct. Some of these measures – such as the establishment of clubs for teenagers in crime-prone parts of cities – have the reduction of crime as their main aim. Others – such as slum-clearance or case-work with problem families – are measures of social hygiene with wider aims; but one of the hopes which inspire them is that they will reduce delinquency.

The assessment of efficacy is no easier in the case of partially focused techniques than in the case of unfocused ones. One or two examples will show the difficulties involved.

The effect of slum-clearance on the delinquency of teenage Glasgow boys was investigated by Professor Ferguson shortly after the 1939–45 war. He analysed the convictions for theft and other crimes of 1,349 schoolboys who had left school about the age of fourteen in January 1947. Of these, 960 lived in privately owned properties, ranging from 'residential' and 'good working-class' to slums, while 389 lived in local authority housing schemes built for the most part between the wars. Since Glasgow's policy had been to rehouse families from slums in special housing schemes, and 85 per cent of the boys rehoused from slums had been in these special housing schemes since the age of eight, many of them all their lives, Professor Ferguson was able to draw up the following table:

TABLE I

INCIDENCE OF DELINQUENCY (AS PERCENTAGE OF BOYS 'AT RISK') IN RELATION TO TYPE OF HOUSING DISTRICT

| Type of district | No. of boys 'at risk' | Boys convicted | | Boys convicted at least once between ages of 8 and 18* | Boys with more than one conviction |
		During school years	After leaving school		
		%	%	%	%
Residential and good working-class	188	4·8	2·6	6·9	2·6
Fair working-class	381	5·8	4·7	9·1	4·9
Bad working-class	252	5·2	9·5	14·2	6·3
Slum	139	7·9	15·8	22·3	8·6
Local authority housing	389	4·6	8·7	12·3	3·3
'Rehousing' (slum-clearance)	142	10·6	13·3	21·8	7·7
Other L.A. housing	247	1·3	6·0	6·8	0·8
All boys in study		5·4	7·6	12·2	4·8

* The figure shown in this column may be rather less than the total of the two preceding columns because of the inclusion in each of these of a few boys convicted both during and after school years.

The table shows the differences which one would expect between the conviction rates of boys from 'good working-class districts' and from slums; but hardly any difference between those still in the slums and those rehoused from slums.

It can be argued with justice that the primary aim of Glasgow's slum-clearance schemes was not the reduction of delinquency; that the special housing schemes were very badly planned, with no attention to recreation or other amenities; and that to move slum families *en bloc* to the same neighbourhood did nothing to break up the delinquent sub-culture of the slums. It is also possible that we have not yet come to the end of the story, and that the next generation in the new housing schemes will be better behaved.

Arguments of this kind, however, cannot be used to explain away the negative results of another investigation, this time of efforts to improve the behaviour of delinquent gangs by means of what is called the 'detached worker' technique.

The Midcity Project was carried out in a lower-class district of Boston from 1954 to 1957, a major objective being to reduce illegal activity by resident adolescents. The 'community-program' was aimed at developing and strengthening local citizens' groups which could take direct action against delinquency, and at co-ordinating the work of professional agencies in the area. But the main efforts of the project were directed at 'problem families' and at adolescent gangs, the former through psychiatric case-work, the latter through 'detached workers'. These workers consisted of five men and two women who established and maintained contact with twenty-one gangs for periods varying from ten to thirty-four months, making efforts to modify their behaviour by organizing legitimate activities, acting as a liaison with adult institutions, and using 'techniques of direct influence'.

The impact of the Project on the gangs was measured in three ways. The court appearances of the members of four Project gangs throughout their adolescent period (up to the age of twenty-three) were compared with the records of members of five control gangs, who were matched for age, ethnic classi-fication and social status. The comparison showed negligible differences. The possibility that nevertheless there had been a reduction in illegal behaviour, whether detected or not, during the 'contact period' was investigated. The results, based partly on official records, partly on the detached workers' own reports, suggested that there had been no such reduction. The possibility that nevertheless there had been a reduction in 'disapproved behaviour' (i.e. conduct which, whether illegal or not, is contrary to ethical norms) was also investigated, again relying on workers' reports and official records. Once more the results were negative (Miller, 1962).

Not all the evidence is quite so discouraging. When the juvenile-delinquency rates for 1951 in twenty-two English towns were compared, it was found that those which spent more on their services for teenagers had lower delinquency rates, even when allowances were made for occupational and other differences between the towns (Bagley, 1965). It is possible, of course, that high expenditure of this kind simply reflected a greater general concern over juvenile delinquency, and that this, rather than the services provided, was the true explanation of the lower rates.[3] This is an example, however, of the sort of investigation in which negative results, which would have been much more conclusive and disquieting, were fortunately absent. It leaves room for hope that an experimental test of the effectiveness of different sorts of 'youth service' will yield positive results. What must be recognized and faced is the fact that these positive results are so far lacking.

FOCUSED TECHNIQUES

Finally, there are techniques which are focused on individuals. Sometimes these are preventive. Individuals who are identified as likely to become delinquents are subjected to special attention in the hope of preventing this. An example of this approach in which a careful attempt was made to assess its effectiveness was the expensive Cambridge-Somerville Youth Study which was carried out in Massachusetts in the 1940s (Powers and Witmer, 1951, and McCord and Zola, 1959).

Nearly 2,000 names of boys regarded as troublesome or not troublesome were obtained from schools, police, probation officers and other social agencies. Data were collected on each boy from their homes, schools and other agencies. Boys who had passed their twelfth birthday, or moved out of town, or could not be traced were eliminated. A selection committee of experts (not on the project's staff) rated each boy's likelihood of becoming delinquent on an eleven-point scale (from plus to minus five). The boys were then paired: a likely delinquent with an unlikely delinquent of the same age. The result was 650 pairs, of which half (325) were distributed between ten 'counsellors', each

---

3. Or even that the police in these towns were readier to deal with young delinquents in ways that did not lead to appearances in court.

'counsellor' getting roughly equal numbers of likely and unlikely delinquents. The case-loads of thirty-four or thirty-five proved too heavy, which led to the discarding of some boys later. In assigning them, the counsellor's own preferences – e.g. for ethnic groups – were consulted. All treatment ceased in 1945, having gone on for an average of nearly five years, but for periods ranging from two and a half to eight years. The remaining 325 pairs received no special treatment or attention. The results were compared up to November 1948, three years after the end of the project. The conclusion was that 'the special work of the counselors was no more effective than the usual forces in the community in preventing boys from committing delinquent acts'. It must be admitted that the 'counsellors' were not, by modern standards, trained for their task; but the almost completely negative results are discouraging.

Most focused techniques, however, are applied to identified offenders, and are intended either to correct or to incapacitate.

Corrective techniques are intended to remove or reduce a known offender's disposition to repeat his offence (or, if they are more ambitious, to remove or reduce his disposition to break the law in any way). They include

> *reformative techniques*, which are intended to achieve this by removing or reducing his motives for offending, or by strengthening his self-control (for example, probation); and *individual deterrents*, which are intended to discourage him by their unpleasantness from offending again, even if he still has the motives for doing so (for example, fines).

It is so difficult to be sure whether a technique is functioning as an individual deterrent or whether it is reforming the offender's character that it is best to use the designation of 'corrective', which does not beg the question. For example, it is usually assumed that if probation is effective it is because it reforms: but in a survey by Mr Willcock (to be described in the next chapter) some young males seemed to regard the prospect of being put on probation as more of a deterrent than a fine. Admittedly few of them had been on probation, so that we can infer with safety only that probation can function as a *general* deterrent; but offenders who have been on probation sometimes refer to the irksomeness of weekly reporting to the probation department, and it is not implausible to conclude that supervision of this kind can be tiresome enough to function as an individual deterrent.

Incapacitating expedients. The other important group of focused techniques consists of expedients for incapacitating the offender from repeating his offence. Traditional expedients of this kind include hanging, branding, the amputation of a limb and transportation (of which a modern echo is the deportation order which can be imposed on certain offenders). The most widely used modern expedient, however, is the prison sentence. Another common example is disqualification from driving a motor vehicle, although its effectiveness in actually preventing people from driving is often questioned. A much less frequent example is the castration of men who have committed several harmful sexual offences, which – until recently at least – was offered to some sexual offenders in Denmark as an alternative to the continuation of a long and indefinite prison sentence. Incapacitating expedients are not usually adopted until the offender has demonstrated, by repeating his offence, that he is unlikely to respond to correctives.

The efficacy of imprisonment as a corrective and incapacitating expedient will be discussed in later chapters. Meanwhile a few points should be made about the respective attractions of focused, partially focused and unfocused measures.

Because they are applied to whole populations, or to groups of which not all members have been identified as law-breakers, unfocused and partially focused measures are less drastic in their operation, and are therefore regarded as more humane. So far as partially focused measures are concerned, however, it is difficult to point to evidence that any of them are markedly effective; and since virtually all of them are expensive, in terms both of money and of trained manpower, this raises in its most acute form the question whether it is rational to expend money and manpower on them.

It is even possible that some social improvements actually contribute to crime. As we have seen, there is some evidence for a causal connexion between compulsory schooling and juvenile thieving. When the school-leaving age is raised by another year, will the peak move with it, and become higher still?

Nobody in their senses would argue that even conclusive evidence of such a causal connexion would justify, for example, the lowering of the permissible school-leaving age. Although the reduction of crime was one of the original aims of compulsory education, it is no longer an important consideration in the minds of educationists. There are very few measures of social hygiene for which the main justification is the hope that they will counteract delinquency (the best examples are probably the penetration of teenage gangs by young social workers – a measure developed in the U.S.A. – and the more widespread technique of establishing clubs for teenagers in areas with high delinquency rates). Even when this hope is the main justification, it would be short-sighted to argue from lack of statistical evidence for its success to the conclusion that the effort should be abandoned. Only positive evidence that the technique was actually contributing to delinquency, or that the resources – and in particular the skilled workers – could be more effectively employed, would be good reasons for discontinuing projects of this kind.

As for unfocused measures, general deterrents are cheap, especially since the more effective they are the less often they are actually applied. This is a highly theoretical generalization, however: we have still to examine the extent to which they can be said to *be* effective. Prohibition by law is relatively cheap, since even paid legislators do not spend much of their time over *penal* legislation; but its efficacy is at best doubtful. The same is true of education and propaganda, although we have not yet developed the technique of ethical training in schools beyond a rather crude stage.

The economics of opportunity-reduction are a complex subject which has hardly been considered as yet. Every shop-keeper, for example, has to make some sort of decision about his precautions against shoplifting (not to mention shop-breaking). Stringent precautions are expensive, and may discourage custo-mers; but without them he will have steady losses through theft. If his goods consist of relatively inexpensive items, so that the theft of one or two does not mean a heavy loss, he will settle for fairly simple precautions, such as a detective or two. If they consist of high-priced, portable items, such as gems or watches, he will put them under toughened glass and make sure that there is always an assistant at the customer's elbow. The prudent car-owner weighs the cost of special locks against the troublesome alternative of taking his valuables with him every time he parks.

An interesting and important question, however, is whether such decisions should be left entirely to the shop-keeper or the car-owner. Should shops which take only perfunctory steps to prevent shoplifting be able to rely on a publicly financed police force to protect them? Should a car-owner who leaves his car unlocked be allowed to waste the time of the police when he finds his car or its contents gone? Is propaganda enough to discourage carelessness of this sort? I have already mentioned the Chief Constable who declared that he would not waste the time of his hard-worked police force in dealing with petty non-professional shoplifters. Many other police forces, less frank but no less realistic, do not waste more time over petty thefts than is necessary to record the particulars politely.

West Germany has gone further in this direction, and has made it an offence to leave one's car parked in the open without securing it against theft. The reductivist and the retributivist – even a distributive one like Professor Hart – will take very different views of this policy. The retributivist will point out how grossly unjust it is to impose a penalty on a victim, actual or potential, and may argue that if someone wishes to risk his property in this way it is his own affair. The reductivist will retort that it is not entirely his own affair. Quite apart from the fact that goods stolen from many commercial vehicles are not the property of the person in charge of the vehicle, and quite apart also from the fact that many thefts from vehicles lead to claims on insurance companies and complaints which take up the time of overworked police forces, the potential victim's carelessness may increase the risk for others, since every opportunity of which a pilferer takes successful advantage increases his readiness to pilfer again: *l'appétit vient en mangeant*. A fine for drivers who leave vehicles unlocked in public places might well offend a naïve sense of justice, but might yield a more substantial reduction in such thefts, and at less cost, than any other form of police action.

If I do not devote more space to the reduction of opportunity and other preventive measures it is not because I am belittling their importance. On the contrary, I believe that there are several sorts of frequent offences against which opportunity-reduction is the best weapon we have, either because other policies are ineffective or because they are uneconomic. This is an area, however, which is almost entirely outside the scope of penology. What it requires is new ideas in engineering and administration, coupled with intensive education of the public.

As for social hygiene, this is an area into which social scientists are only beginning to make their first tentative expeditions; systematic surveying has not yet begun. Few if any measures of social hygiene have the reduction of crime as their sole or even their main objective; their aims are less easy to define, though none the less worth while.

There is little point, however, in scratching the surface of so enormous a subject in a book which is concerned with the penal system. The only unfocused measures which are an integral part of this social institution are general deterrents, and it is with these that the next chapter will be concerned.

Chapter 4

General Deterrence

Deterrence has become a dirty word in penological discussion, partly because it has so often been the battle-cry of those who support capital or corporal punishment, partly because of a fashionable assumption that it is more enlightened and scientific to talk about social hygiene and reformation. Even penologists who think more logically than this are apt to succumb to a pseudo-scientific assumption. Because the statistical evidence for the effectiveness of deterrents is scarce and of limited applicability they regard it as irrational to act on the expectation that *any* deterrent will be effective.

It is true that the very nature of the process of deterrence makes its operation very hard to study objectively. While a deterrent is in operation it is very difficult, if not altogether impracticable, to devise a satisfactory way of finding out the number of occasions on which it has been the decisive consideration in the mind of a person who rejected an opportunity for law-breaking.

Moreover, we are seldom, if ever, in a position to measure what can be called the 'absolute efficacy' of a deterrent: that is, to compare a situation in which there is *no* deterrent with a situation in which there is *only that* deterrent. This is sometimes forgotten in discussions of the effect of abolishing or reimposing a type of penalty, such as capital or corporal punishment; and the fact that 'abolition' really means 'replacement with long sentences of imprisonment' is overlooked. For this reason, the most that we can usually hope to measure is 'comparative efficacy': that is, the extent to which a given deterrent is more effective than the alternatives to it.

Even when we are fortunate enough to find a situation in which some type of conduct has recently been made criminal, and punishable with a more or less specific penalty, such as a fine, we are seldom in a position to answer the question 'How frequent was it before it became punishable?' since it is not until conduct becomes a crime that police begin to keep statistical records of it.

Only in rather special conditions is it possible to make even cautious inferences from official statistics. The necessary conditions are

(a) that statistics of the frequency with which a given type of offence is reported are kept in a uniform way over a period;

(b) that during this period the penalties for the offence are changed, whether by statute or by an alteration in sentencing policy. The sharper the change the better from the scientist's point of view;

(c) that this change is publicized;

(d) that it does not coincide with any other development that is likely to affect the frequency of the offence in question (such as an increase or decrease in opportunities, or in police activity);

(e) that the probability of incurring the usual penalty for the commission of the offence is fairly high.

The relevance of most of these conditions seems obvious, but they are easily overlooked. For example, a recent report to the Californian legislature[1] cites a study of the bad cheque problem in Nebraska and other states (Beutel, 1957) in support of the statement that regional variations in the severity of penalties have no effect on crime rates. The study had certainly demonstrated that in Colorado – and other states – where penalties for bad cheques were more lenient prosecutions for this type of offence were relatively *less* common. It had also disclosed, however, how few bad cheques were ever brought to the notice of the law: the percentage in the Nebraska sample was about 2 per cent! If the chance of actually incurring the penalty was as low as this[2], it is hardly surprising that the difference between a short and a medium term of imprisonment seemed to have no effect in reducing the frequency of the offence.

The importance of ensuring that publicity is given to any changes in the penalty is illustrated by a Finnish experiment (Tornudd, 1968). This is one of the very few instances in which social scientists have been able to persuade agencies of law

1. By the Assembly Office of Research (1968).

2. In fact it was even less, because a substantial percentage of cases reported to law-enforcement officers were settled unofficially by payment of the debt.

enforcement to alter their policy as a deliberate test of a penological hypothesis. The ethical reactions to proposals of this
kind are usually so adverse that it is only when the offence in
question is not regarded as serious and the penalties are not
considered drastic that this sort of experiment seems practicable.

This one was concerned with the offence of public drunkenness. Drunks are notoriously apt to reappear in court again and
again for this offence, a fact which casts doubt on the effectiveness of fining and imprisonment as deterrents in their case. In
Finland, where police not only make the arrests but also decide
in the first place whether the drunk should be fined[3] (subject to
confirmation by the court), the police forces in three medium-
sized towns were persuaded to reduce the percentages which
were fined in the three years 1962–4. In one of the towns the
percentage of arrests for drunkenness which led to fines was
reduced from more than 50 to less than 20 per cent, and the
reductions in the other two, though less spectacular, were very
marked. Three similar towns were used as controls, and in them
the fining percentages remained fairly stable, between 50 and
60 per cent.

In the first year of the experiment the rate of arrests for
drunkenness remained much the same as they had been in the
experimental towns. In the second year there was a sharp rise
in one of the towns, almost certainly the result of a new highway
project which brought many migrant workers – always heavy
drinkers – to the area; the rates in the other two towns did not
increase, and were if anything a little below average. Two of the
control towns showed slight increases, one showed a marked
decrease!

In short, there were no changes in the rates – in an upward or
downward direction – which could be attributed to the experimental reduction in the percentage of arrests leading to fines.
Unfortunately, it had been deliberately decided[4] not to publicize
the reduction, and investigators who mixed with the chronic
drunks in the experimental towns found that in fact they had
not guessed that there had been a change of policy; those who
were released by the police without a fine simply explained their
good luck by saying 'I suppose I wasn't so drunk after all'. All

3. As in England, failure to pay the fine – which is frequent – almost always
led to imprisonment for a short period.

4. Perhaps because the police were afraid of the public's reaction; but the
reason for the decision is not explained.

that the experiment demonstrated, therefore, was that even a marked change in sentencing policy, lasting for at least three years, did not seem to have been noticed by the offenders directly affected. The difficulty of altering people's estimates of the probability of incurring a penalty is a point to which I shall return later in this chapter.

The nearest approach to a sound and successful experiment in testing a deterrent is probably that achieved by Professor Richard Schwartz and Miss Sonya Orleans, with the help of the United States Internal Revenue Service. Nearly 400 taxpayers were divided into four matched groups. Members of the 'sanction' group were interviewed, and asked questions designed to remind them indirectly of the penalties which they might suffer if they tried to evade taxes. Members of the 'conscience' group were interviewed with questions designed to arouse their civic sense and feelings of duty. The third, or 'placebo' group were asked only neutral questions, which avoided both sorts of stimulus. The fourth group were not interviewed at all, in order to test the possibility that even a 'placebo' interview produced some effect (which on the whole it did not seem to do). The interviews took place in the month before the taxpayers were due to file their returns for 1962. Without disclosing information about individuals, the Internal Revenue Service compared the returns of the four groups for the year before the experiment and the year 1962. The reported gross incomes of both the 'sanction' and the 'conscience' groups showed an increase, compared with small *decreases* in the 'placebo' and uninterviewed groups. In other words, the attempts to stimulate both fear of penalties and civic conscience seemed to have had effect.[5]

For an example of negative evidence, let us turn to the well-known controversy over the efficacy of capital punishment as a deterrent for potential murderers, which has led to several statistical studies of murder rates. Those worth considering have either compared contemporary rates in areas which do and areas which do not make use of the death penalty, but which have roughly similar definitions of murder; or compared rates for the same country during periods when the death penalty was and

5. See Schwartz and Orleans (1967). They drew a slightly bolder conclusion: that appeals to conscience were *more* effective than threat of sanctions; but this inference assumes that the appeal and the threat were of equal potency, whereas it is conceivable that unintentionally they had made their 'conscience' interview a more powerful stimulus.

was not used. The best example of the first sort of study is Professor Sellin's comparison of abolitionist and retentionist states of the U.S.A., to be found in the appendices to the Report of the British Royal Commission on Capital Punishment, 1949–53. For a study of the other sort, look at this graph (Figure 2) of New Zealand's murder rate from 1924 to 1962, a period

KEY

●   moving five-year averages per million inhabitants
     of murders known to the police
⚥   number of executions carried out in the year

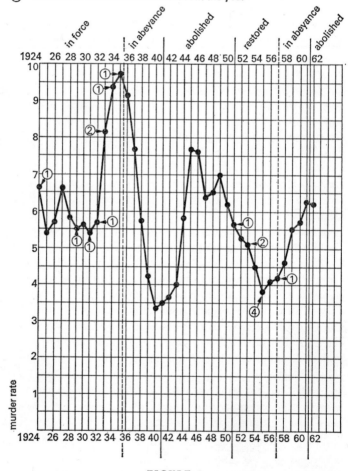

FIGURE 2

MURDER RATES AND THE DEATH PENALTY IN
NEW ZEALAND

during which capital punishment was at first in force, then in abeyance, then abolished, then restored, then in abeyance and then abolished again. Although New Zealand was not deliberately experimenting, the result of its changes of policy is as close as we are likely to come to an experimental use of the death penalty. The changes were well publicized throughout this small country (as were the cases in which the death penalty was actually carried out); and murder is a crime which is solved more often than any other.

Neither the New Zealand nor the American data support the hypothesis that, as a deterrent, capital punishment is more effective than the long periods of imprisonment which take its place in abolitionist jurisdictions. It is equally important, however, to appreciate what this does not prove. In the first place, these studies relate to areas with relatively low murder rates. It is possible that other factors have reduced the rates in both abolitionist and retentionist jurisdictions or periods to a point at which further reduction would be very difficult to achieve. An analogy is the prevalence of tuberculosis, which is easy to reduce when it is high, but not at all easy to reduce beyond a certain low level. Although it sounds a paradoxical hypothesis, it is by no means unlikely that capital punishment is a more effective deterrent in countries with high murder rates.

Another assertion that is not supported by the data, even for countries with low murder rates, is that nobody is deterred from murder by the thought of the death penalty who would not be equally deterred by the thought of long imprisonment. All that the data suggest is that in countries with low murder rates such people are not numerous enough for their murders to be detectable among the fluctuations due to other factors.

THE BURDEN OF PROOF

Most important of all, such studies provide no justification whatsoever for the sweeping assumption that other forms of general deterrent are ineffective. This is due to a loose sequence of reasoning, which seems to go like this:

(i) we must not accept any statement unless and until it is supported by sound statistical evidence;

(ii) the only statistical evidence we have about general deterrents is the evidence about capital punishment, which suggests that its effectiveness in civilized countries at least is negligible;

(iii) we must not therefore act on the assumption that such measures as fines or imprisonment serve as general deterrents.

The main flaw in the argument is the way in which it begins by talking of 'accepting' statements and ends by talking of 'acting on' them. If the first assertion means that it is desirable to question any important assumption until it is supported by statistically sound evidence, it is an excellent principle for the social scientist. But if it means that we should not base social policy on that assumption until the scientists have pronounced it confirmed, this is contrary to commonsense. It would be rational only if we were faced with a choice between courses of action, knowing only that one course was beneficial and the other detrimental, but not knowing which was which. In matters of social policy this is hardly ever the situation. Almost always we have some grounds for predicting the outcomes of our choices. At worst these grounds consist of our own experience and self-knowledge, as when we say 'Well, I know that I am deterred from illegal parking by the thought of a stiff fine'. More often we have the benefit of the experience of others, although not in a statistically satisfactory form. In this situation it is certainly desirable that some social scientist should try to find a way of appraising this experience statistically, or of testing our belief in an experimental situation. What is not reasonable is to allege that until he does so we have *no* grounds for acting on our own prediction of the outcomes of the choices. To use a lawyer's phrase, if a social scientist sets out to undermine a belief which is at present based on crude experience, then the burden of proof lies on him.

What the social scientists have done is to question effectively the time-honoured belief that capital punishment keeps down the murder rate. So far as societies with low murder rates are concerned they have succeeded in shifting the onus of proof on to those who, for some reason, wish to cling to the belief. But murder is one of the rarest of crimes. To what extent can these conclusions be applied to other sorts of offence? It is not unreasonable to apply them to offences of serious personal violence, since many of these occur in the same situations as murders, spring from the same motives, and indeed often differ from murders only accidentally – for example, because the knife or the bullet missed an artery, or because the victim reached hospital in time for a blood transfusion or cranial surgery.

What is unreasonable is to apply the same conclusions to other types of offences such as bad driving or theft, which have nothing in common with murder beyond the fact that they are committed by human beings and are triable by criminal courts. One might as well argue that because few chess-players bet on their games few card-players probably do so. The Illinois experiment supported the commonsense assumption that taxpayers respond to the threat of sanctions. The impossibility, however, of applying the same technique to other everyday offences, such as theft, is obvious, and it must be plain from the preceding discussion how unlikely we are to find sound evidence of the efficacy of deterrents in routine statistics. Failing this, we are entitled to consider what can be learned by other methods.

A SURVEY OF YOUNG MEN

One is the interviewing of potential offenders. An interesting example of this is the subject of a recently published report by the Government Social Survey (Willcock and Stokes, 1968). Since young males in the second half of their teens and early twenties are the age-group with the highest rates of serious crime, the Home Office asked the Government Social Survey to interview a sample of youths whose ages ranged from fifteen to twenty-two. This was done in 1963, and the sample obtained was 808. Sixteen per cent had been in court, accused of an offence of some kind, serious or trivial; three out of four had met someone to whom this had happened. Whether or not they had been brought to court for it, 17 per cent admitted at least one theft[6]; 20 per cent admitted having taken part at least once in vandalism or gang fighting, and 84 per cent admitted traffic offences. Although these percentages are no doubt smaller than they would have been if every member of the sample had been completely frank, it is clear that these males at a delinquency-prone age were a mixture of the deterred and undeterred.

Factual information apart, what someone says in response to a questionnaire or interviewer may not be a reliable indication of the way in which he will think and act when faced with a real situation of the kind which he is talking about. Consequently what these 808 young males said about the considerations which would or would not deter them from offences cannot be accepted without reservations. Nevertheless, this is a case where some information – so long as it is obtained with care, as this was – is better than no information.

Although Mr Willcock's sample were questioned about a

6. Including taking and driving away a motor vehicle.

fairly wide range of offences[7] let us for the moment at least confine ourselves to one type of crime, of a kind which is usually attributable to a rational motive, and which can hardly be committed without a deliberate decision to attempt it, so that anyone contemplating an attempt at it might be expected to take any deterrents into consideration. Shop-breaking is an obvious choice. It is one of the commonest forms of acquisitive crime, and appears to be especially attractive to young men of the age-group represented in Mr Willcock's sample. It has the additional advantage of being separately dealt with in the published Criminal Statistics, so that objective, if rough, estimates can be made of the probability of detection and its consequences.

Consider the young man of twenty-one to whom it has occurred to break into a shop. One likely possibility is that he would decide against doing so for reasons which are not connected with deterrents. He might be restrained by what is sometimes called 'conscience', sometimes 'super-ego', sometimes 'self-image' and sometimes by the deliberately vague term 'internal restraints'. In Mr Willcock's sample 43 per cent gave a reason of this kind which, they said, would hold them back or at least worry them. (Another 2 per cent seemed simply to lack confidence in their ability to commit a competent break-in.) A roughly equal percentage (47 per cent) seemed to be more concerned about the consequences of being identified as criminals, although – as we shall see – it was not necessarily the official consequences which they had in mind.

How high did they rate the chances of detection? Objectively the published Criminal Statistics show that only about one third of shop-breakings are 'cleared up': a phrase which almost always means 'traced to a suspect', although this does not always imply prosecution.[8] In other words, the general risk of detection in a single shop-breaking is something less than one in three: and for certain sub-groups – such as the young man of normal intelligence – it must be lower still. Among Mr Willcock's sample, however, estimates of the risk varied widely. Most of them thought that their chances of 'getting away' with burglary

7. 'Starting a punch-up', 'breaking into a private house', 'stealing from a large store', 'stealing from a small shop', 'breaking into a lock-up shop', 'taking and driving away a car', 'stealing from a coat' and 'picking up a wallet'.

8. For instance, the suspect may be let off with a warning. Many crimes are 'cleared up' because the accused is advised to ask for them to be taken into account to avoid being charged with them on a later occasion. Consequently the actual probability of being detected is less than the clear-up rate.

were less than fifty-fifty; some were very pessimistic indeed. Less than a quarter gave anything like a realistic estimate. In other words, most of the sample greatly over-estimated their chances of being caught.

There was some evidence, however, that the more experience a youth had of committing offences the more optimistic he tended to be about the chances of getting away with them. And of course in the case of the sort of offence which we are considering optimism meant realism. The point is important, because one of the commonest platitudes on the subject of law enforcement is that the best hope for improving it lies in increasing the probability of detection. So far as shop-breakings (and most other acquisitive crimes) are concerned this is a visionary's hope. The clear-up rate is so low that it is *over*-estimated by all but a small minority. To alter the estimates of the realistic minority would require an enormous increase in police efficiency; and to raise still further the over-estimates of the majority seems almost out of the question.

On the other hand we do know that a sudden and well publicized lowering of police efficiency can lead to a sharp increase in some types of offence. For seven months in 1944 the Danish police force was under arrest by the German occupation troops, with the result that robberies and larcenies multiplied in a spectacular way (while crimes such as fraud and embezzlement did not!) (Trolle, 1945, and Andenaes, 1966). In England the strike of the Liverpool police in 1919 was accompanied by widespread looting; and there are similar accounts of the effects of police strikes elsewhere (for example in Melbourne).

Detection does not, of course, mean automatic conviction. It is true that most acquisitive offenders plead guilty, especially if by doing so they can make it likely that they will be sentenced by a magistrates' court, with its limited sentencing powers. If, however, they plead not guilty before a jury their chances of an acquittal are by no means negligible (a police survey of jury acquittals in 1965 showed a probability of about 30 per cent where the charges involved breaking and entering premises). Mr Willcock's sample were not asked for their estimates of the probability that detection would lead to conviction, but it seems likely that the more experienced they were the higher they would rate their chances of an acquittal.

What they were asked about were the assumed consequences of appearing in court. They were shown, in random order, eight cards each describing a possible consequence, and were asked 'Which of these things would worry you most about being found out by the police?', after which each youth sorted the cards into his order of importance. Table 2 shows the result.

TABLE 2

	Mean rank	Percentage placing item first
	%	%
1. What my *family* would think about it	2·38	49
2. The chances of losing my job	2·96	22
3. Publicity or shame of having to appear in court	3·88	12
4. The punishment I might get	4·40	10
5. What my *girl friend* would think	4·72	6
6. Whether I should get fair treatment in court	6·07	2
7. What my *mates* would think	6·08	1
8. What might happen to me between being found out and appearing in court	6·20	2

There are several striking features in this table. 'What my family would think' is far and away the most important consideration. Next is the possibility of losing one's job. Considerably less important was public exposure in court, and slightly less important than that was the official penalty. The other items were relatively negligible.

We cannot, of course, conclude that the operative deterrent for about half of the sample was the thought of their families' reaction. For we must remember that almost as many (43 per cent) had said that they would have been held back from law-breaking, or at least worried, by 'conscience' or some other form of internal restraint. And since the sort of family which reacts strongly against law-breaking is also the sort of family which is likely to have sons with strong internal restraints, many of the youths who put their families' reactions at the top of their lists of deterrents must have been youths who would in fact have been held back by internal restraints. Nevertheless, Willcock found that even youths who had committed a wide variety of offences seemed to rank these disincentives in much the same order as did their more innocent colleagues, giving top place on the whole to the same unofficial consequences of detection.

(In passing, it is worth noting that one of the most powerful deterrents – if this table is of any value at all – is one which is being deliberately weakened. It is fashionable to dissuade employers from dismissing employees merely because they have been convicted of offences. The case for this is strong, since loss of job makes it more difficult for the offender to live honestly. But Mr Willcock's table suggests that if this campaign is success-ful – or more precisely if its success is made known or exag-gerated – an important deterrent will be undermined.)

We must, however, pay some attention to the deterrents which are within the power of the courts to impose. Not surprisingly, the great majority (81 per cent) of Mr Willcock's sample ranked prison as the penalty which they most feared. Borstals were ranked first by a much smaller percentage (13 per cent), and next came approved schools and detention centres. What was surprising was that a fine seemed to be regarded as a less for-midable deterrent than probation, although this is certainly not the assumption upon which courts or probation officers make their decisions. Yet when one looks at the choice from the point of view of a young man, it is not difficult to understand how the prospect of two or three years' supervision by someone whom he regards as representing authority (and rightly) is more unpleasant than the loss of one or two weeks' wages (few of the youths expected the fine to be more than £25, and some expected much less).

That is by the way, however: we must get back to the custodial penalties which were at the top of the list. We cannot infer from this that they operate as the most powerful deterrents unless we know that potential offenders consider them probable results of being convicted. Mr Willcock's sample were asked what was the 'worst' penalty which they expected someone to get for offences such as shop-breaking or joy-riding in an unknown person's car: they were told to distinguish between someone with no criminal record and someone with a bad record. Since a custodial sentence of one sort or another is not only a possible penalty in both cases, but is actually imposed on a minority of first offenders of this age-group (and of course more often still on offenders with previous records) it was interesting to see that over 60 per cent of the sample gave a fine or a probation order as their answer. It hardly matters whether they really meant that a custodial penalty was out of the question; for them it was not a serious possibility.

Since a fine or a probation order are in fact the most likely outcomes for 'first offenders', it is difficult to argue that these respondents were being over-optimistic, still less that by ensuring that they were better informed we should ensure that they were better behaved. In other words, only a sharp and well publicized increase in the frequency of custodial sentences for a 'first offender' could conceivably render them effective as general deterrents for potential but inexperienced offenders. This would be so directly contrary to present ideas on the sentencing of first offenders, which are not without some rational foundation (as we shall see), that the case for it would have to be overwhelming before it could seriously be advocated.

Where offenders with previous convictions are concerned, the probability of a custodial sentence is already considerably higher, as most of Mr Willcock's sample recognized, although there were substantial minorities (14 per cent in the case of shopbreaking) who still thought that probation or a fine were the worst that could be expected in such cases. We do not know how high it really is after the second, third or nth conviction; still less how high the experienced shop-breaker thinks it is. The more knowledgeable he is, however, the more optimistic he is likely to be about his chances of escaping conviction. As we have seen, the general probability of escaping detection for this type of offence is over two in three, and when this is multiplied by the not altogether negligible chance of an acquittal if the shopbreaker appears before a jury, he does not have to be overoptimistic to regard the prospect of a custodial sentence as unlikely. (It is true that a probability of two in three for a single shop-breaking falls to four in nine for a couple of shop-breakings, to eight in twenty-seven for three, and so on, geometrically; but shop-breakers are not conversant with the mathematics of probability.) This being so, it would require a very considerable increase in the percentage of shop-breakers with previous convictions who receive custodial sentences to make any impression on them.

Indeed, it is doubtful whether anything short of a mandatory sentence of imprisonment – that is, one which the court are obliged to impose – would have much effect upon the experienced shop-breaker's calculation of risks; and mandatory sentences – even for offenders with previous convictions – are not popular with legislators, for reasons which will be discussed in Chapter 11.

EXEMPLARY SENTENCES

Courts sometimes try to escape from this *impasse* by what are called 'exemplary sentences'. A judge who believes that more severe sentences will influence potential offenders, but who cannot ensure that his colleagues will adopt his policy, will sometimes impose sentences which are markedly more severe than the norm for the express purpose of increasing their deterrent effect.

Thus although imprisonment is an exceptional sentence for a shop-breaker with a clean record, a court might impose it 'because shop-breaking is becoming too common in this town'. If imprisonment *is* normal – as it seems to be for male shop-breakers over twenty-one with previous records – the court might for the same reason exceed the normal range of prison terms for this offence – which for a higher court is from twelve to eighteeen months – and award an exemplary sentence of, say, three years.

Exemplary sentences are usually imposed in order to deal with a special type of offence which has suddenly become more frequent, or suddenly begun to receive more publicity, especially if this has taken place in a restricted locality. Their effectiveness is very difficult to assess, since the evidence for it is largely anecdotal. For example, the Cadogan Committee on the use of corporal punishment investigated five instances in which the use of flogging by the courts was said to have suppressed waves of offences, ranging from the London garrottings of the 1860s to living on immoral earnings in Glasgow and Manchester in this century. The Committee found that in some cases the statistics were not consistent with this hypothesis, while in others they were consistent with it but also with other explanations, some of them more plausible (such as decreasing unemployment).

The example most often cited in recent years is the suppression of attacks upon coloured people in the Notting Hill district of London. In August 1958, following the distribution of an inflammatory broadsheet, there were a number of attacks by white men on coloured men or their homes. The first serious incident – according to the Police Commissioner's annual report – was on 23 August, and though it led to the arrest of nine youths it was followed a week later by incidents on five consecutive nights, and there were occasional affrays in the first half of September. On 16 September the nine youths – all of whom had pleaded guilty – were each sentenced at the Old Bailey to four years' imprisonment (which was at least double the normal sentence) in spite of the fact that all but one were admitted by the prosecution to be 'of good character'. It was clear from the judge's remarks that the sentences were intended as exemplary deterrents, and as such they were later upheld by the Court of Criminal Appeal. The trial was followed by others in which the offenders received lighter sentences. So far as can be ascertained from newspaper reports there were few further brawls in Notting Hill, although on 3 October, for example, a white man and a coloured man were taken to hospital after a stabbing.

This story illustrates how difficult it is to draw confident and definite conclusions from the reported occurrences. The facts are fairly consistent with the assertion that it was Mr Justice Salmon's four-year sentences which halted the racial violence, although there were examples of subsequent violence in the area. On the other hand, we cannot be sure that the broadsheets were not the most important factor, and that the dying down of the brawling was not due to the waning of their influence. Nor do we know how much to attribute to the undoubted increase in police vigilance and activity after the first incidents had taken them unawares. The mere appearance of more constables in the streets of Notting Hill must have been a deterrent. Finally, it is possible that those arrested during the first hectic week or two included at least some of the active fomenters of trouble, who were thus prevented from keeping the pot boiling.

In any case there is a difference between an exemplary sentence aimed at a local 'outbreak' of a certain type of crime and one which is intended to affect a more widespread trend. An individual judge who gives an unusually long sentence for, say, armed robbery, with the intention of discouraging potential robbers throughout the country, has to contend with the knowledgeable realism of criminals. He is only one of many judges: he cannot bind his colleagues to follow his example. If he presides over a particular court, it is easy to avoid coming within his jurisdiction. Even if – as happens under the English circuit system – he may unexpectedly turn up at some provincial assize court, an individual robber's chances of encountering him are small. Moreover, there is always the hope that the appellate court will reduce a sentence which is avowedly heavier than usual. A robber does not need to be more than mildly optimistic to dismiss the occasional exemplary sentence from his mind in this way.

LENIENCY

Less often discussed is the converse of the exemplary sentence: the occasional sentence of unusual leniency. Although the arguments with which sentencers justify these occasional decisions are interesting in themselves, what is relevant at the moment is the effect upon general deterrence. We cannot simply reason that if exemplary sentences make little impression because they are either avoidable or improbable the same must be true of lenient sentences. In the first place, if a recorder or bench of magistrates is known to have a tendency to leniency, the rational criminal can choose to operate in that jurisdiction. Even if – as seems to be the case – nearly all sentencers have a propensity for occasional and unpredictable decisions in favour of leniency it does not follow that these make as little impression on robbers as exemplary sentences seem to.

For one thing, the occasional act of leniency seems to be rather more frequent an event than the occasional act of severity; so that it would be more rational for a thief to be optimistic than to be pessimistic. Secondly, the thief who is leniently sentenced is likely to make a more vivid impression on his friends and acquaintances than the thief who is severely sentenced. The latter is 'out of sight' and 'out of mind' for a considerable time; the former soon rejoins his colleagues, to talk of how he 'got away with' probation or a short prison sentence.

TARIFFS

The point is important because of the controversy over what have been called 'tariff systems': that is, sentencing policies which prescribe fairly definite penalties (such as two years' imprisonment) for specific offences. Tariff sentencing is often dismissed as the product of nineteenth-century retributivism, as no doubt it is from a historical point of view. Yet even the pure reductivist must reflect that if the type of offence is one which is likely to be reduced by general deterrents, their effectiveness will be greater if their magnitude is more or less precisely known. Nor is a publicized tariff as inhumane as its critics suggest; for it need not preclude occasional departures from it in the direction of leniency, so long as these are not so frequent or so well publicized as to encourage optimists to *expect* leniency. This does not, of course, dispose of another argument – that tariffs reduce the effectiveness of penal measures in correcting the offenders to whom they are actually applied; but as we shall see in later chapters this is a very difficult point to substantiate.

MINIMUM SENTENCES

Opponents of tariffs – leaving aside those who altogether refuse to consider deterrents – must logically consider the alternative, which is the minimum sentence. Quite a number of sentencing systems prescribe minimum terms of imprisonment for serious offences, so that a sentencer has freedom to choose a term so long as it is not shorter than the minimum (and in most cases he is also limited by a prescribed maximum). In some other systems – such as the Californian – the sentencer merely pronounces the minimum and the maximum as prescribed by statute, and the exact term to be served is decided upon by the executive in the light of the prisoner's progress. The English sentence of borstal training, which means that in normal cases the young offender cannot be released from a borstal in less than six months (or more than twenty-four months), is a rather special analogy of this, with the difference that no court is ever *obliged* to impose borstal training.

Prescribed minimum sentences – whether they take the form of custody, of fines or of supervision – can be advocated on the grounds that they maximize whatever deterrent effect the sentence may have. There may also be other arguments in their favour: as we shall see in Chapter 9 the disadvantages of very short prison sentences from the corrective and administrative point of view are already recognized, and it is arguable that there should be a lower limit of six months. Whether a low minimum of this sort, however, would maximize deterrence is doubtful. The higher the minimum, on the other hand, the weaker the non-deterrent arguments for it become, and the stronger the objection that it interferes with 'individualization'; in other words, that it compels the system to deal more severely with some offenders than is necessary to correct them. I shall be discussing the concept of 'individualization' in Chapter 9; for the moment all that can be said is that if one believes both in individualizing sentences and in maximizing their deterrent effect one should prefer a flexible tariff system to one based on prescribed minimum sentences.

The supporters of either sort **of** system must of course meet the argument that complete uncertainty about the severity of the penalty is a more effective deterrent still. Whether this is so or not has never been scientifically investigated. In any case the argument can be disposed of at once by pointing out that *even if this were so* the necessary uncertainty cannot be achieved in practice. Potential offenders of the kind who are susceptible to deterrence are too well informed about current sentencing policy.

One final point, however, must be made. If it is unjustifiable to assume that there is no type of offence against which deterrents have any effect, it is equally unjustifiable to assume the opposite. The problem is not a choice between these two unreal assumptions, but something much more difficult. Whatever the offence, there is almost certainly a percentage of potential offenders who are restrained from it only by a deterrent. For some offences (such as murder and other degrees of personal violence) the percentage is probably smaller than for others (such as shop-breaking or embezzlement). An omniscient penologist would thus be able to say, in the case of any given type of offence, how much would be gained by maximizing the deterrent effect of the permissible penal measures. In the case of some offences the gain would be large enough to force us to take it into consideration: in others it would be so small as to be negligible. Since no penologist is omniscient, however, or indeed has anything like enough empirical information on this subject, it is necessary to reason more loosely.

Criminologists and forensic psychiatrists believe that there are several types of offence which in the great majority of cases are committed impulsively or compulsively, in states of mind which either prevent the offender from thinking of the consequences at all or else are so overwhelming that the thought of the consequences is powerless to halt him. Personal violence, for example, is usually impulsive. Indecent exposure is usually compulsive rather than impulsive; that is, the offender usually chooses circumstances which somewhat lessen his chances of being caught, but is nevertheless compelled by his pathological motivation to take considerable risks. The same seems to be true of homosexual importuning in public lavatories. Another sort of offence upon which deterrents are most unlikely to have more than a slight effect are those which are committed by negligence. Some – though by no means all – traffic offences are of this kind.

In short, there are some offences against which deterrents, though probably not totally ineffective, have so little effect that it is unnecessary to complicate sentencing policy by taking it into account. On the other hand, there are others against which it is perfectly rational to maximize the deterrent effect of sentences so long as this does not seriously conflict with other aims, such as humanity, economy and corrective efficacy. Obvious examples are acquisitive offences of the kind which are committed from rational economic motives, such as shop-breakings, wage-robberies and frauds. This is not to deny that sometimes these offences are committed irrationally, in states of mind which are immune to deterrence. Such cases, however, are not an argument against the maximizing of deterrents, but an argument for ensuring that the sentencing system is not too inflexible to deal suitably with them.

Chapter 5

Corrective Measures

Corrective techniques were defined in Chapter 3 as those which are intended to remove or reduce a known offender's disposition to repeat his offence – or, more ambitiously, intended to remove or reduce his disposition to break the criminal law in any way. As I pointed out then, it is difficult if not impossible to be sure whether such a technique is achieving its effect through deterrence or through reformation, so that it is best to use a term, such as 'correction', which does not beg this question.

In any case, there is little point in trying to decide how a technique achieves its effect until we are sure that it has an effect, and if so in which cases. As we shall see, this involves formidable difficulties. But before discussing them let us briefly consider the nature and problems of the main techniques which civilized countries nowadays employ on the assumption that they are efficient correctives. If we confine ourselves to those which are neither obsolescent (like capital and corporal punishment) nor applicable only to special classes of offender (such as committal to mental hospitals) we are left with five main sorts.

CUSTODIAL MEASURES
These deprive the offender of liberty, sometimes for years on end. This is usually regarded as in essence a deterrent measure, but there is an increasing tendency to combine it with techniques which are intended to reform the offender – for example, by teaching him a legitimate trade and the habit of steady work. In the case of institutions for juvenile offenders this tendency is carried to the length of denying that they are intended to act as deterrents, and claiming that their effectiveness is reformative; indeed, it is usually asserted that they are not penal establishments at all, but educational institutions. The fact that their inmates regard them as deterrents, and persist in talking about their 'sentences' is dismissed as irrelevant.

Regarded as an attempt at reformation, a custodial sentence presents two inescapable problems. One of these is the difficulty, under conditions so unlike those of real life, of telling whether, and if so when, reformation has been achieved. Conformity under the strict regime of a prison is no indication that the prisoner has become law-abiding. It is true that there are custodial institutions – especially for the young – where the regime is designed so as to test the offender's responsibility, self-control and other qualities that will help him to lead a law-abiding life outside; but the staff of such establishments are the first to admit that they are often wrong in predicting subsequent success or failure for individual inmates.

The other inescapable problem is the unwanted by-products of custody. The inmate loses his job, is separated from his family and is compelled to associate with other delinquents. Even in the best-run systems, prison work is seldom more than a way of reducing the economic burden which prisoners represent, and of weaning them from idleness: it is only in the exceptional case that the prisoner learns a trade which he afterwards takes up. Again, prisons make efforts to palliate the effects of separating the prisoner from his wife and family by allowing them to visit him; but this does not prevent many a marriage from breaking up during a long or even a medium sentence. As for the effects of associating with other delinquents, most prison systems have long since given up their efforts to counteract these by enforced segregation or silence. At most they separate the mature from the immature, and the recidivist from the first offender; but this still leaves plenty of scope for the contamination of the unsophisticated offender by the professional criminal.

These are hackneyed points: most of them were first made in the eighteenth or nineteenth centuries. They are not conclusive arguments against the use of custodial sentences, although they are sometimes used in this sweeping way. Nevertheless they are strong indications of the directions in which most custodial regimes need improvement. And – most relevant to this chapter – they are reasons why we cannot expect much in the way of reformation from custodial measures, especially when applied to adults. So far as adults are concerned the main function of custodial measures must always be to deter and to incapacitate.

SEMI-DETENTION

In an effort to minimize the unwanted by-products of custody some countries are developing types of sentence which are designed to restrict liberty without losing the offender his job or completely separating him from his family. The Belgian word '*semi-détention*' is a convenient generic term for such sentences, although they feature under different names in other countries, such as West Germany and New Zealand. They take two main forms: week-end custody, intended to deprive the offender of his leisure without interfering with his working week; and night custody, which allows him to go daily to work and visit his family after work but requires him to return to a prison or hostel to spend the night. Expedients of this kind have the additional advantage of considerably reducing the offender's contact with fellow-inmates: and although this contact cannot be completely eliminated he need not be so dependent on them for company and support as in an ordinary prison.

On the other hand, semi-detention is suitable only for the prisoner who can be trusted not to abscond: that is, roughly speaking, for the prisoner who values his job and his family, and is sufficiently self-controlled to resist the occasional impulse to seek complete freedom. It is obviously unsuitable for the man without job or family, for the man who makes a successful living by well-planned crimes, or for the man whose violence or sexual propensities make him a danger to others.

Nor should semi-detention be confused with what is called in England the 'prison hostel scheme'. This merely allows selected prisoners to spend the last few months of a fairly long sentence in a hostel from which they go out to work and are allowed to spend evenings and week-ends with their families. Prison hostels have their merits, and in particular help the prisoner to make the difficult transition back to normal life. But unless the prisoner spends the whole of his sentence in a hostel he has still lost his original job, been separated from his family and been thrown into the closest possible association with other delinquents. The essential point of semi-detention is that it is intended to avoid these side-effects. Genuine semi-detention in the English penal system takes the limited form of compulsory residence in a probation hostel for a maximum of one year as part of a term of probation; and it is only very recently that probation hostels have been provided for adults.

SUPERVISION

Supervision is a measure which can be used in two ways. It can be applied to an offender who has just been released from a custodial sentence, in order to assist and control him during the difficult transition to normal life. In this form it is known as 'parole' or – euphemistically – 'after-care', and is usually reserved for young offenders and adults who have served medium or long sentences. Alternatively, under the title of 'probation', it can be applied to an offender instead of a custodial measure. When it originated in nineteenth-century Massachusetts it was used for young first offenders, and the supervision was the task of dedicated amateurs: this example was followed when the Massachusetts idea was copied in England. Nowadays the supervision is carried out by trained, full-time probation officers, although in some countries their training is still rudimentary. More important still, although most probationers are still young first offenders, there is – in Britain at least – an increasing tendency to use the measure for adults, and for offenders with one or even more previous convictions.

Techniques of supervision vary greatly according to the personality and training of the probation officer, and his assessment of the offender. He may be authoritarian or sympathetic; he may concentrate on such matters as job-finding, proper use of leisure, and decent lodgings; or he may concern himself with the probationer's values, reactions and self-image. The training of the British probation officer lays great stress on 'case-work', a technique which seeks to establish a strong personal relationship between social worker and 'client' and to exert influence through this rather than by authority. The technique was originally inspired by the psychoanalytic treatment of middle-class neurotics with its emphasis on 'transference'; and the task of applying it to offenders, of whom only a minority are middle-class or neurotic, and most of whom are suspicious of and antagonistic to any person connected with the penal system, is probably its supreme test.

It is not surprising to find that in practice many probationers receive a less intensive and demanding type of supervision. In a sample of some 600 offenders on probation in Middlesex in the early 1960s it was found that a half had received supervision which the investigators classified as 'nominal' (Folkard, 1966). In some cases, no doubt, this was due to the unco-operative attitude of the probationer. In other cases, however, it was due to the preferences of the probation officer, for it was noticeable that older officers made less use of the more intensive forms of supervision. In many cases their policy seems to have been justified, for the success rate of the nominally supervised probationers was above average; and it is distinctly possible that these were probationers who were rightly diagnosed as requiring little or no supervision.

Important as it is to be able to identify such offenders, the central problem of the probation service is how to supervise the remainder effectively. These are, by definition, the offenders who are likely to offend again unless the probation officer can do something to prevent this. He may be able to do so by altering the offender's circumstances – for example, by finding him a job and a home away from his delinquent family and friends. Or he may, if he is both skilful and lucky, actually alter the offender's disposition, at least so far as law-breaking is concerned. What is certain is that he cannot really 'supervise' him. Except where probation or after-care is combined with residence in a hostel, he has only two important sources of information about what the offender is doing with his spare time. One is the offender and his family; the other is the police. The offender – and most offenders' families – are apt to censor what they tell the probation officer, while the police are a source of information only when the offender is clearly in conflict with the law again. This problem of information about the offender's actual behaviour during probation is ignored by most textbooks, but deserves more attention.

Another of the probation officer's problems, however, is the probationer or parolee about whom he does have information which suggests that the supervision is unlikely to be successful. Sometimes the offender is simply unco-operative, failing to keep appointments, giving up his job without consulting the probation officer, and so on. Sometimes he breaks the law in a minor way – for example, by drunken brawling in a public house. The probation officer is usually the person who has to decide whether to persevere with his supervision or to tell the court that he is failing. Most probation officers would regard the latter as a last resort, and would point to cases in which they had eventually been successful with offenders who were extremely troublesome during their first few months on probation.

A striking aspect of the English approach to probation is its purism. It is a measure which must not be combined with a penalty for the same offence. The explanation is partly historical, for probation originated in the practice of deferring sentence to see how the offender behaved: if all went well, he was not recalled for punishment. Modern legislation[1] therefore states that when a court makes a probation order it does so 'instead of sentencing' the offender, although it is worth noting that courts can, and do, combine probation orders with orders to compensate victims for loss or damage; and that if the offender is found guilty of more than one offence at the same court appearance he can be fined for one and put on probation for the other! The purists argue that probation is not compatible with a penalty, and will be less effective if the offender feels that he has been punished for the offence already. Some purists are even prepared to defend the present state of the law, and to argue that offenders appreciate the difference between paying a fine and paying compensation, or between a fine for the same offence and a fine for another offence. There is no evidence for (or, it must be granted, against) any of these assumptions.

Compulsory supervision, whether it takes the form of probation or of after-care, is nearly always for a specified time, which must not exceed the limits laid down by the law or by the court acting within the legal limits. In England there is only one exception – the released 'lifer', who is in theory under supervision and the threat of recall until he dies; and even this exception is theoretical rather than real, since eventually – if his conduct is satisfactory – the supervision is reduced to nothing. A probation order cannot last longer than three years, although of course another one can be made if the offender is reconvicted. Recently, it has been suggested that some types of offender – such as the chronic petty thief – might benefit from longer periods of supervision than three years; but such suggestions have not been taken very seriously.

It is important to appreciate that both in Britain and in North America the probation officer is not merely a supervisor but also an adviser of the court, whose task it is in many cases to investigate the offender's history, background and personality before the court decides upon its sentence. If the court chooses probation it is usually in accordance with his recommendation, although it is by no means unheard of for a probation order to be made against his advice.[2]

1. See s. 3 of the Criminal Justice Act, 1948.
2. It is remarkably difficult to find any estimate of the frequency with which courts disregard the probation officers' advice. At the Cornwall Quarter Sessions from 1955 to 1960, about 30 per cent of probation officers' recommendations in favour of probation were disregarded, while about 13

FINANCIAL PENALTIES

The commonest means of dealing with offences which are not regarded as serious – and especially with breaches of traffic or revenue laws – is the fine. Other forms of financial penalty are the order to compensate the victim and the order to pay the costs of the prosecution. Although strictly speaking the latter is not a punishment, it is often the most serious consequence of conviction for the offender, since 'costs' not infrequently exceed the fine.

Indeed, from the reductivist's point of view the distinction between a fine, compensation and costs may well be immaterial. I know of no research or other source of evidence which shows that the enforced payment of, say, £50 is more effective if the offender is told that it is needed to make restitution to the victim (or to meet the prosecution's expenses) than if he is simply told that it is a fine.

The two problems which financial penalties raise are the fixing of amounts and the enforcement of payment. The usual methods of enforcement are compulsory deductions from earnings, the seizure of goods, and the threat of incarceration. The last of these, which burdens custodial institutions with short-term inmates, is increasingly unpopular with penal administrators, and is regarded as a last resort, to be applied only when all else fails. Indeed, there is now a tendency to argue that the persistent fine-defaulter is an offender who should not have been fined; and certainly it is true that many fine-defaulters are either petty criminals who have lost their fear of imprisonment, or drunks whose money is compulsively spent on alcohol, or homeless migrants whose earnings and goods are impossible to trace. Nevertheless, in Britain at least the great majority of financial penalties are eventually collected.

The fixing of amounts is a problem which is partly technical, but partly of a more fundamental kind. The assessment of an offender's financial position, if it is to be done conscientiously, can be a complicated and protracted task, as income-tax authorities know only too well. The cost of a thorough investigation would often exceed the amount of the eventual penalty by a ridiculous margin. Even in Sweden, where the assessment of fines is done with some care, a great deal of reliance has to be

---

per cent of their recommendations against probation were disregarded (see Jarvis, 1965). But Cornishmen may well behave differently from Londoners, or Welshmen or Midlanders.

placed on the offender's own statements. In England, one of the most reliable sources of information about a man's earnings – the Inland Revenue Department – is ruled out by a protection as strict as that of the confessional.

Even if the information about the offender's earnings, however, is accepted as reasonably accurate, there remains the difficulty of deciding how much of these earnings to demand. The theoretical answer of the humane utilitarian is 'Just enough to make it unlikely that he will repeat his offence, and no more'. But how much is enough to deter a man earning, say, £15 a week? Or a man earning £150 a week? Obviously the answer will vary even for the same wage-bracket, according to the offender's financial commitments, and also according to his attitude to money. Equally obviously, one cannot arrive at the exactly correct answer for each individual. What the Swedes have done, with their day-fine system[3], is to adopt the rule of thumb that the fine must represent enough of the offender's daily earnings to make it necessary for him to practise strict economy. But this is only half an answer. How strict is strict economy for a film star or shipping magnate? For how long must he be forced to practise it? A week? A month? A year? The Swedes try to answer only the second of these questions, by saying that the number of day-fines depends on the gravity of the offence.

In other words, the day-fine system is essentially similar to other fining systems in that it ultimately relates the amount of the fine to the seriousness of what the offender has done or tried to do. This means that, unless an unlikely assumption is granted, the basis for fixing the amount is retributive rather than utilitarian. The unlikely assumption is that the 'graver' the offence the stronger the incentive to commit it, and therefore the larger the fine needed to deter the offender from a repetition. To see how unlikely this is one has only to compare illegal parking with running down a pedestrian on a crossing. If the horror of the accident is not sufficient to make the driver more careful in the future, it is unlikely that an increased fine will do so. Indeed, it could be argued, on these lines, that the fine for illegal parking should usually exceed the fine for causing death by dangerous driving, since illegal parking seldom has consequences which are themselves likely to cause terror or remorse.

3. It should be noted that the system does not apply to all fines by any means; for many offences fines are levied on what seems very like the usual tariff system.

This example illustrates the fundamental difficulty which any thoroughly utilitarian system for fixing fines must encounter: the deep-rooted feeling that the amount of the financial penalty should to some extent be related either to the moral wickedness of the offence or to its actual or possible harmfulness. In all systems known to me – including the day-fine system – the maximum permissible fine for almost all offences is clearly meant to be proportionate to the legislature's estimate of the harmfulness or wickedness of the offence. Only when the offence is itself a tempting financial proposition – for example, tax evasion, currency smuggling, or share-pushing – are legislators forced by sheer commonsense to abandon this principle, and allow fines large enough to deter even wealthy financiers.

NOMINAL PENALTIES

Finally a group of measures must be mentioned which has received remarkably little attention from penologists. These are what might be called 'nominal' measures, since their common feature is that they do not impose any form of restraint, treatment, supervision, or deterrence on the offender. In almost all civilized systems courts either are given express powers to refrain from imposing any positive measure, or, if the law appears to compel them to do so, find ways of circumventing it. Thus courts in nineteenth-century England would 'defer' sentence on some offenders, with no intention of actually punishing them unless they got into further trouble. Official measures of this kind take several forms. Courts may 'dismiss', 'admonish'[4] or 'discharge' the offender, who cannot then receive any punishment, compulsory treatment or supervision for his offence. Alternatively, the dismissal or discharge may be 'conditional', so that the offender can be brought back and sentenced if he offends again within a certain period. Sometimes this 'conditional disposal' takes the form of a suspended fine[5] or custodial sentence, which will take automatic, or more or less automatic, effect if the offender is reconvicted.

To the extent that nominal measures appear effective, they are

4. A Scots measure, consisting essentially of an oral reprimand, with or without a homily.

5. Systems of the French type allow both suspended fines and suspended prison sentences. The English system now has the suspended prison sentence, and the traditional power to bind an offender over with 'recognizances' (which involve the forfeiture of a specified sum of money if he is reconvicted) is very much the same as a suspended fine.

bound to appeal to the reductivist because of their economy and humanity. Indeed, it is sometimes straightforward reductive reasoning which inspires courts to use them. The offender's prospects of keeping on the right side of the law may already be so good and so obvious that no penalty or other positive measure which the sentencer can impose will improve them. The offender may, for instance, be a child on whom the process of arrest and trial has plainly made a deep impression. Or he may be a sufferer from a mental illness for which treatment has already been arranged, or an embezzler who has lost the position of trust which he abused, and is unlikely to find another.

Sometimes, however, the sentencer's reasoning is moralistic rather than reductive. For example, he may be compelled by the evidence and the law to find the offender guilty of the offence charged, although morally his act or omission may seem entirely or almost entirely excusable. In English law, for example, even the most extreme provocation is no defence to a charge of assault, and strictly speaking can be taken into account only when the time comes to pronounce sentence: in such cases courts sometimes choose the solution offered by a discharge. Another example is provided by offences of strict liability. These are offences whose nature makes it too easy for the accused to offer the defence that his act was neither intentional nor negligent, so that the legislature has enacted that he must be found guilty whatever his state of mind. The result of this policy of expediency is that courts are occasionally compelled to convict a person who had clearly done his reasonable best to avoid the commission of the offence, and is thus morally guiltless: again the solution is often a discharge. Although the courts' reasoning in such cases is retributive, the reductivist might well arrive at the same decision by reckoning that a more positive sentence would be unlikely to reduce the probability of a repetition of the offence, and might well do harm, especially if it aroused antagonism by an over-rigid application of the law.

The suspended penalty – whether it is custodial or financial – raises at least one special problem. Strictly speaking it is not so much a nominal measure as a focused deterrent – a threat addressed to an identified offender. The problem arises from the fact that by pronouncing a suspended sentence the sentencer must to a great extent deny freedom of choice to a later court if the offender is reconvicted within the specified period. In penal systems which embody the principle of judicial discretion in sentencing (as all modern systems do) the suspended sentence is sometimes regarded as a breach of this principle. It is argued that by the time of his reconviction the offender's circumstances may be so different that the automatic imposition of the suspended sentence would be objectionable. Sometimes the objection would be a moral one. For example, it is argued that a short prison sentence would not be excessive punishment for an unmarried thief without a job; but that if by the time it has to be imposed he has acquired a job and a family, it would be excessive to incarcerate him. The reductivist might argue in the same circumstances that the automatic imposition of imprisonment might have become unnecessary (and therefore unjustifiable) since a thief with a job and family is more likely to respond to a heavy fine than a thief without such responsibilities.

On the other hand it is argued that if the second court has complete discretion in its choice of sentence the effectiveness of the threat will be diminished. The usual solution seems to be a compromise, which allows the second court to disregard the suspended sentence only if it can produce a special justification for doing so, based on the circumstances of the case.

Yet even if the second court has no wish to interfere with the imposition of the suspended sentence, it is sometimes worried by the question 'What penalty should be imposed for the second offence, the one which brought the offender back to court?' This question is of course a much more awkward one for the retributivist than for the reductivist. The former feels uneasy if the offender is not made to atone for the second offence by having something added to his original sentence. The reductivist, on the other hand, sees no need for moral book-keeping of this sort, and merely asks whether the imposition of the suspended sentence is likely to be sufficient to prevent another repetition of the offence: a question which can be answered only by waiting to see!

PSYCHOTHERAPEUTIC TECHNIQUES

A deliberate omission from my list of corrective measures is the group of techniques which can be given the broad label 'psychotherapeutic'. Virtually all of them are descended from methods which were evolved in the treatment of the sub-division of mental illnesses known as 'neuroses', and one of the most interesting phenomena of the twentieth century has been the tendency to extend them, with or without important modifications, to the treatment of other aberrations of behaviour: to schizophrenia, to depression, to compulsive conduct, and of course to delinquency.

They include psychoanalysis in its various forms[6], Jungian analysis, existential analysis, 'Individual (i.e., Adlerian) Psychology', Roger's 'non-directive counselling', and Wolpe's Pavlovian 'behaviour-therapy'. Most of them can be practised either in tête-à-tête or in group sessions. An even broader definition would also include social case-work (which has been briefly mentioned in the section on probation) and 'milieu therapy', in which all the staff of an institution, whether hospital, children's home or custodial institution, are meant to play a part.

The effectiveness of these techniques in dealing with the forms of mental illness for which they were originally devised is still a matter for heated debate among psychiatrists and psychologists.[7] Their critics claim that their success rates are no better than the rate at which patients recover spontaneously if left untreated. Their defenders either claim higher success rates or argue that they would be higher if so many of their colleagues did not accept so many patients who were unsuitable for psychotherapy.[8]

This is not the place for a detailed review of all the evidence for and against the effectiveness of psychotherapy in treating offenders. From the point of view of this chapter the question is whether it can reasonably be regarded as a corrective with sufficiently general applicability to be considered along with custodial supervisory, financial and nominal sentences. This is a question which can be answered straightforwardly by making two points. The first is that very few psychotherapists claim success in treating mentally normal adult offenders, nor do I know of any sound evidence in support of those who do. There is more support for the claim that psychotherapy is beneficial for young offenders – and probably the younger the better. There is still more support for the claim that it is effective in treating offenders who are suffering from some – but by no means all – types of mental disorder.

The main point, however, is that even if we concede what

6. Including analysis which makes use of hypnotism or drugs as facilitants. For a brief survey of contemporary methods and their development, see my *Short History of Psychotherapy*.

7. See for instance Professor Eysenck's attack on them (1960).

8. This is not necessarily a reflection on the *bona fides* or competence of psychotherapists. Many patients come to them in desperation after unsuccessful treatment by other means, and are accepted out of humanity rather than over-optimism.

few supporters of psychotherapy would claim – that it can cure normal adult offenders – it would still be unrealistic to regard it as a corrective of general applicability. Not even the most affluent society can afford the cost of such a policy. What is more, not even the most psychotherapeutically-minded society – which is probably that of California – has enough psychotherapists to implement it.

It is more realistic to regard it as a special measure, to be applied selectively to cases in which the expenditure of so many costly man-hours is likely to yield returns. Moreover, if success is problematical and the offender's behaviour is a serious nuisance or danger, it makes sense to couple the treatment with one of the standard measures, whether this takes the form of custody, of supervision or merely of conditional discharge, so that if treatment fails the offender is still within the power of some penal agent, and does not have to be prosecuted all over again before he can be brought under control.

This, at any rate, is the approach of the English penal system to the treatment of the adult offender who does not seem sufficiently disordered to be handed over completely to the psychiatrist. It has its own difficulties. For example, a psychiatric probation order (which includes in-patient or out-patient treatment among its obligatory conditions) is said to introduce an element of compulsion which interferes with the relationship between psychiatrist and patient, and to assume a degree of co-operation between psychiatrist and probation officer which is not always achieved. Again, the psychotherapeutic treatment of prisoners is said to be impeded by the way in which they are handled by custodial staff, and also by the fact that the prisoners are artificially protected from the very strains and temptations of ordinary life to which the treatment is trying to immunize them. Special psychiatric prisons, where all the staff are supposed to understand and honour the principles of psychotherapeutic treatment, are an attempt to solve this dilemma.

Although these are real problems, it is possible to exaggerate them. Intelligent offenders – and many of those who are selected for psychotherapy are highly intelligent and articulate – are skilful at detecting and exploiting ideological weaknesses among those who are in charge of them[9], and it is not difficult to make a psychiatrist feel guilty, or to play him off against the custodial staff. Nevertheless, there is a case for arguing that so far as

9. As T. Mathiesen has so ably demonstrated (1965).

possible psychiatric treatment should take place outside the penal system; and Chapter 12 will discuss how far this is in fact possible and desirable.

In this chapter I have done no more than glance at the fundamental issues raised by those correctives which are of more or less general applicability. The precise form which they take varies greatly from one penal system to another; and one or two – suspended penalties and semi-detention – are no more than embryonic in some systems. It is impossible to discuss here the host of technical problems which each country tries to solve in its own way. The most important question of all, namely 'What can be said about their efficacy?' is the subject of the next chapter.

Chapter 6

The Efficacy of Correctives

The assessment of the efficacy of corrective measures is one of the central problems of penology. We have made a little more progress towards a solution of it than we have in the case of deterrents; but not much. Part of the difficulty, as we shall see, lies in the complexity of the problem, but part of it lies in people's attitude to it.

Before proceeding to consider what might be called 'direct evidence' on the subject we must briefly take note of a point which has been made by some psychologists as a result of in-direct inference from laboratory experiments. This is that, in so far as penal measures are intended to make the offender learn to refrain from repeating his offences, they are most unlikely to have any effect at all, because they are applied too long after the offences. Suppose, says Professor Eysenck (1964), that you are trying to create a 'conditioned reflex' such as a tendency to blink at the sound of a buzzer, which can be produced by subjecting the eye to a puff of air whenever the buzzer sounds. The best results are achieved if the delay between the buzz and the puff is a fraction of a second. In contrast, the delay between a crime and its penalty (if it leads to one at all) is measured in weeks, if not months.

Laboratory reasoning, however, can be almost as dangerous as armchair reasoning, and there are several weaknesses in this argument. Firstly, as Professor Eysenck himself admits, human beings have the capacity to re-enact their offences mentally, and are quite likely to do so when undergoing punishment, in which case the suffering and the recollection are brought close together in time. Secondly, as other psychologists have admitted, the deed may be followed by immediate anxiety at the thought of the penalty, and this may be effective. The weakest point of all, however, is the assumption that all human learning is of the same nature as eye-blink conditioning. In fact, psychologists recognize several different kinds of learning, governed by different laws. Children, for example, can acquire strong and ineradicable revulsions from violent, dishonest or sexual behaviour as a result of punishment which is so delayed that it can hardly operate by classical conditioning.

Finally, although the infliction of physical discomfort is a convenient subject for experiments, it is disappearing from civilized penal systems. As for other forms of deterrent, prison probably operates chiefly in this way, as has been suggested in the previous chapter, although nowadays it is intended to apply reformative influences as well. Probation cannot operate *wholly* as a deterrent, even if Mr Willcock's survey suggests that it can function in this way. Probably the only measure which cannot be anything but a mild deterrent is the fine. If so, it is worth noting that there is no direct evidence whatsoever to suggest that this is less effective than a reformative measure such as probation; indeed, *prima facie*, the opposite seems to be the case, as we shall see.

Before we turn to the direct evidence, however, there are ideological obstacles to be cleared up.

The most important of these is people's notions of what is evidence of correction. It is still possible, even at conferences of experienced judges and magistrates, to hear anecdotes of the form: 'I remember sentencing a man with twenty previous convictions. I put him on probation two years ago, and the probation officer told me the other day that he is doing well . . .'. It should not be necessary to point out either that the probation officer's report is not very strong evidence of permanent reform, or that, even if it were, a single case is not evidence in the scientific sense. I am not suggesting that the anecdote or the case-history are altogether valueless. If true, they can be used to *disprove* generalizations of the form: 'Men with twenty previous convictions will not keep out of trouble for even a year if put on probation'. What they cannot do is to form a basis for generalizations until they are multiplied many times.

Even then there are many inferential pitfalls. Before one starts trying to multiply instances, one must be clear what they are instances of. Are we to accept the recidivist as corrected because his probation officer says that he has responded well during his two years on probation? What if the police say that he has in fact been detected in one attempt at shop-breaking? What if the probation officer retorts that this was an isolated incident which occurred just after the recidivist had been sacked by an employer who had discovered his previous record? In this situation the penologist has a choice between what he calls 'soft data' and 'hard data'. 'Soft' means 'based on personal impressions, and liable to alter in shape when someone else's impressions are ascertained'. 'Hard' means 'objective, and unlikely to alter when someone else is consulted'. Penologists prefer hard data, for obvious reasons, but especially if the soft data are based on the impressions of penal agents who, quite understandably, would like to think that they are having some effect on offenders.

The only sorts of hard data which the penologist can collect in sufficient quantity are recorded instances in which an identified offender has subsequently been detected in a further offence: in other words, what are usually called 'reconvictions'.[1] Penologists, however, have to defend their reliance on reconvictions against strong ideological objections. Because the results of counting reconvictions are rather disappointing, they are sometimes criticized as 'misleading', on the grounds that a man may refrain from breaking the law and yet remain a most unsatisfactory husband, father and worker, while another man may undergo a real improvement in his character and yet lapse occasionally into crime. No doubt both these possibilities do occur: but they do not show that reconvictions are *misleading* unless we assume that such cases are typical. An assumption of this kind is most improbable; all the information which we have suggests that it is the more satisfactory husbands, fathers and employees who keep out of trouble with the law. If so, further convictions may be misleading in the case of the *occasional* individual, and so may be *imperfect* as a criterion of effectiveness; but when applied to a reasonably large sample of offenders they cannot be regarded as misleading.

There are of course practical issues, such as the minimum acceptable length for a follow-up period, or the number of further convictions which should be regarded as the criterion for 'failure' (most investigators classify offenders with one subsequent conviction as failures, but some prefer two, especially where young offenders are concerned). These, however,

---

1. Sometimes, of course, detection does not lead to reconviction, but to a police 'warning', or to an acquittal. But in practice penologists usually confine themselves to reconvictions, since the additional labour of doing otherwise would yield only a small gain in accuracy.

are merely matters which affect the reliance placed by penologists on the results of this or that investigation.

There is, however, one fundamental difficulty which has not yet been overcome. Suppose that our information about the subsequent records of a sample of ex-prisoners is comprehensive, accurate and in every way satisfactory; and suppose that by the strictest criteria 80 per cent have 'gone straight'. It would be fallacious to attribute this to the effects of imprisonment unless we had good grounds for saying that none of them would have gone straight if not imprisoned. Some would probably have gone straight if fined or put on probation. Some might have gone straight if discharged, perhaps because the mere experience of being detected and prosecuted had been effective. Some might even have gone straight if they had not been detected at all, either because the detection of one of their friends or acquaintances had frightened them, or for some more complex reason, such as marriage and steady employment. The notion of a 'spontaneous recovery rate' is by no means ridiculous: as we have seen (page 86), it is accepted as a fact by investigators of the efficacy of psychotherapy.

Unless we can estimate the spontaneous recovery rate, we cannot estimate what can be called the 'absolute efficacy' of any positive measure. And for obvious reasons it is unlikely that we shall ever be able to do so where offenders are concerned. We cannot, for example, accept the success rates of offenders who are convicted and discharged without a penalty as the equivalent of spontaneous reform rates, for two reasons. One is that the mere experience of detection and prosecution may have had a positive effect. Even if this is disregarded, in practice courts are very selective, as we have seen, in the offenders whom they discharge. Only if they could be persuaded to discharge a random selection of offenders whom they would otherwise have imprisoned, fined, or put on probation would the success rates of discharged offenders be useful information.

This does not spell complete defeat, however. What we can do is to estimate the *comparative* efficacy of sentences. The simplest situation from this point of view would be one in which courts had only two types of sentence – say imprisonment and fines – at their disposal. Suppose, too, that we could find enough criminal twins of the identical (monozygotic) type to subject half of each pair to imprisonment and half to fining. Then – other things being equal – we might be in a position to say that one sentence was more effective than the other. In fact the effectiveness of the other might be nil. It is even conceivable that both sentences might increase the probability of reconviction. But at least we should know which increased it less, and therefore which was preferable.

In practice, the situation is always more complex. Courts have at least four main types of sentence at their disposal for mentally normal adults, let alone children and the disordered. Identical twins are uncommon, criminal twins are rare, and criminal quadruplets unheard of. Courts are hardly ever willing to randomize their sentences for experimental purposes – a point of view with which one can sympathize when one imagines the public reaction if they did.[2]

THE 'LAWS' OF RECONVICTION

Fortunately, courts vary so much in their sentencing policies that there is a certain degree of randomness[3] in their sentences; and it is possible to exploit this if one can obtain large enough samples from different courts. As for the dearth of criminal quadruplets, this has to be remedied by making allowances for variables which are known to affect the probability of reconviction.

Reconviction studies have shown that at least five 'hard' variables are strongly associated with the probability of reconviction:

(a) other things being equal, females are less likely than males to be reconvicted after a given penal measure has been applied;

(b) other things being equal, the older an offender the less likely he is to be reconvicted after any given penal measure;

(c) other things being equal, the more previous convictions an offender has the more likely he is to be reconvicted;

(d) other things being equal, the more time he has spent in penal institutions on previous occasions the more likely he is to be reconvicted;

(e) other things being equal, the reconviction rate is higher for some types of offence (e.g. house-breaking) than for others (e.g. sexual offences), although this may well reflect little more

2. It is possible, however, that courts and public might be persuaded to accept randomization in the sentencing of some category of offender which does not arouse strong emotions – such as traffic offenders.

3. In the sense that, for no rational reason, similar offenders receive different forms of sentence from different courts.

than differences in the probability that an offence of the type in question will be reported and traced to the offender.

Any investigation, therefore, which aims at a comparison of the 'success rates' of penal measures must ensure that these rates are not distorted by uneven proportions of females, first offenders, older offenders and so on amongst the samples being compared. Fortunately there are statistical methods for coping with this difficulty. The most satisfactory investigation from this point of view (and from several other points of view) was carried out by Dr W. H. Hammond of the Home Office Research Unit (1960 and 1966). His samples consisted of the careers of some 4,000 offenders of all ages from the Metropolitan Police District and from Scotland. Eliminating female offenders from his samples, and making allowances for the other variables mentioned, he found that:

(a) in general, *fines* are followed by fewer reconvictions than other measures;

(b) *heavy fines* are followed by fewer reconvictions than light fines;

(c) in general, next to fines, the measure followed by fewer reconvictions seemed to be *discharge* (absolute or conditional). The exceptions were the older 'first offenders'[4] aged thirty or more who received a discharge; these tended to have an abnormally *high* reconviction rate;

(d) *imprisonment* was followed by more reconvictions than fines or discharges;

(e) but *imprisonment* compared better with other measures when applied to offenders with previous convictions than when applied to 'first offenders';

(f) *probation* was followed by more reconvictions than imprisonment;

(g) *probation* compared rather better with the other measures when it was applied not to 'first offenders' but to offenders with previous convictions (but was still the least often effective);

(h) for some reason, however, 'first offenders' convicted of house-breaking showed lower reconviction rates than any other kind of probationer when placed on *probation*.

It is possible to interpret these results in at least two ways. They can be taken at their face value, and used as a basis for a

---

4. 'First offender' is a misleading but time-honoured term for an offender convicted for the first time of an indictable offence. He may of course have committed many previous undetected offences.

fairly simple sentencing policy, on the following lines. If a man's circumstances make it reasonable to fine him, this is the choice most likely to be successful. If a fine is ruled out by his means, discharge him. Reserve prison for those whom you feel you cannot deal with in either of these ways – for example, because the offence itself was of the kind against which people need protection. Use probation only where you have a strong positive reason for doing so – for example, for a house-breaker who cannot pay a fine.

But the interpretation of the results needs more care than this. For example, we know that courts are very selective in using their power to discharge. Is it not possible that they are able to pick out those offenders who are unlikely to repeat their offences whatever is done to them? In the previous chapter I described the sort of considerations which persuade courts to discharge; and most of these are of a kind which might well operate in this way. If so, the low reconviction rates after discharge simply confirm the courts' skill at selecting 'good prospects', and are not evidence of the effectiveness of this method of dealing with offenders.

For the sake of brevity I shall call this sort of explanation 'selective'. It is equally plausible when applied to the low rate of reconviction of men who have been fined. We have only to suppose that the sort of man whom courts think they can correct by means of a fine is in the nature of things more likely to go straight whatever is done to him. This is not at all unlikely. The man who is regarded by sensible courts as worth fining is the man with a steady job, good wages and a fixed address: a better prospect than the intermittently employed man with 'no fixed abode'. The very nature of a fine makes it *less* likely to be applied to the men who are *most* likely to be reconvicted. Even the fact that larger fines are followed by fewer reconvictions than smaller fines is consistent with this explanation: the larger fines may well be levied on the men with the better jobs, who may well be less likely to be reconvicted anyway.

The selective explanation is not quite as plausible when it is applied to the disappointing figures for probation, which were consistently worse than the rates for fines and discharges, and for most age-groups worse than the rates for imprisonment. If we wished to put it forward, we should have to suggest that courts tend to use probation for the sort of offender who is least likely to go straight. This is not the way, however, in which courts seem to think they use probation, nor is it the way in which probation officers seem to advise them to use it. Both courts and probation officers seem to regard probation as the measure of choice for the offender who is not a sophisticated or hardened criminal, and whose circumstances offer some hope of reform without drastic penalties. This being so, the selective explanation is tenable only if we suppose that, by thinking on these lines, courts and probation officers are in fact achieving the opposite of what they intend, and are selecting the worst prospects!

If this seems contrary to commonsense, must we fall back on the straightforward interpretation, and conclude that a fine or a discharge is more likely to be beneficial than probation in *all* cases? Or should we consider the even more worrying possibility that probation is the best choice for some offenders, but actually *worsens* the prospects of others?

This is not as implausible as it sounds. Some investigators have suggested that techniques of treatment which have beneficial effects on offenders of one psychological type may not merely fail to benefit offenders of another type but even do them harm.[5] The evidence for this is far from impressive, but it is a real possibility. So far as imprisonment is concerned, it is a possibility which has worried penal reformers for over a century and a half; for they have constantly warned us of the risk that a prisoner who would otherwise go straight may be turned into a recidivist by association with more sophisticated criminals.

The line of reasoning which I have followed in this chapter emphasizes the complexities and uncertainties with which penologists have to contend. It is not surprising that they tend to take refuge at the end of the day in a plea for more careful diagnosis of offenders before they are sentenced; and that this is the stage of reasoning at which they stop. In the next chapter, however, I shall try to show that, from the sentencer's point of view at least, the problem may not be quite so complex after all.

5. See for example J. and M. Grant's important article (1959). Unfortunately the article does not define the criterion for failure.

Chapter 7

Diagnosis and Social Inquiry

The need for information about an offender who is about to be sentenced is recognized by all sophisticated penal systems, although the sheer numbers who have to be sentenced for common offences, such as careless driving, often mean that the need is ignored. In some systems courts are actually debarred from deciding on the disposal of certain categories of offenders before they have been given reports on them. For instance, except when dealing with trivial offences, an English juvenile court must have a report – usually supplied by a children's department or a probation department – on the young delinquent's character, health, home surroundings and school record. Since 1967, too, the Home Office has had powers to require any kind of criminal court to obtain a 'social inquiry report' before imposing a custodial sentence on whatever category of offender the Home Office may prescribe, although its present policy is to issue recommendations rather than directions.

Indeed, in some systems courts now expect not only information but also advice. Psychiatrists are expected to say whether the offender should receive psychiatric treatment; governors of prisons and other institutions are encouraged to report on the offender's suitability for certain types of custodial training; probation officers are now more or less officially encouraged to give their views on the offender's probable response to supervision and other forms of correction.

Quite apart from the actual value of the information and advice, this trend is healthy, because it means a departure in practice from the legal convention that the disposal of the offender is the sole responsibility of the persons who preside over the trial of his guilt. The origin and merits of this convention are discussed in Chapter 9. For the moment it is sufficient to point out that it is a convention which is gradually becoming a fiction.

The purpose of this chapter, however, is to consider the

extent to which it is reasonable to expect help from pre-sentence investigations and the advice of the investigators.

PSYCHIATRIC AND PSYCHOLOGICAL DIAGNOSIS

Let us begin with the sort of investigation which not only enjoys the most prestige but also – as I shall show – has to a great extent determined what we expect from other sorts: the psychiatric investigation. Obviously, this achieves its greatest value when the psychiatrist is able to diagnose a mental disorder for which there is a known remedy of proved efficacy. The shoplifting housewife who is found to be suffering from depression can usually be entrusted with confidence to the hospital or the clinic.

In other cases the psychiatrist may with equal certainty be able to diagnose a disorder, and be fairly optimistic about his ability – or his colleagues' – to treat it; but may be less confident that the result of the treatment will be to prevent the offender from repeating his offences. He may report, for example, that the elderly widow who started a dangerous fire in the flat where she lived a solitary and suspicious existence is suffering from delusions caused by poor nutrition, and can be treated with good hope of success. What he cannot guarantee is that when she leaves hospital she will not drift back again into the same condition. Much the same is true of many younger schizophrenics, whose disorder is controlled and rendered more tolerable by the phenothiazine drugs prescribed in mental hospitals, but who leave hospital and eventually cease to take their drugs. Sometimes it is by no means certain that the offender's offences are the result of his disorder; many a petty thief is successfully treated in a mental hospital but goes on stealing, this time from patients and staff.

Again, the disorder and its nature may be clear, but there may be little that psychiatry can do for it beyond the provision of care. An example is the mentally subnormal man who is behaving anti-socially. He will sometimes respond to careful and sympathetic training – especially if this begins early in youth. But the underlying defect of intelligence cannot be remedied, and if attempts at training begin too late it may prove necessary to keep him in an institution or colony indefinitely, especially if his behaviour is dangerous.

In all these cases, however, the psychiatrist can at least say with justifiable confidence what should be done with the offender.

He is less confident, however, when faced with what are some-times called 'behaviour disorders', sometimes 'character dis-orders (or neuroses)' and sometimes 'psychopathic' (or 'socio-pathic') behaviour. His difficulty is not merely that these are notoriously unresponsive to ordinary psychiatric techniques, nor that the people who suffer from them are serious nuisances in ordinary mental hospitals. A diagnosis of 'psychopathic' be-haviour raises other problems. Unlike most other psychiatric labels it does not hint at an explanation of the offender's conduct, but says in effect little more than 'He is the sort of person who does anti-social things like this', and 'He will probably not respond either to psychiatric techniques or to penal tech-niques'.

Indeed, it is much more logical to regard 'psychopathy', or equivalent terms, not as a psychiatric diagnosis at all, but as a psychological label. Psychology is primarily concerned with the behaviour of people who are not regarded as requiring psychiatry, although a minority of psychologists specialize in what are called the 'abnormal' or the 'clinical' branches of this subject. Never-theless, it recognizes very wide variations between individuals – and even in the same individual at different times – in conformity to rules, moral judgement, self-control, aggressiveness, honesty and other qualities involved in social behaviour. Forensic psychologists – who of course include psychologists in prisons, borstals and similar correctional institutions – are especially interested in the variables of personality which are associated with anti-social behaviour. Most of them would regard 'psychopaths' as people who, without necessarily[1] suffering from disorder in the psychiatric sense, are more than usually 'below par' in these variables.

This does not mean that psychologists are better than psy-chiatrists at identifying psychopaths, or more optimistic in recommending forms of treatment for them. Indeed, one of the 'symptoms' most likely to lead to a 'diagnosis' of psychopathy is failure to respond to the whole repertoire of correctives. In general, even where more normal individuals are concerned, forensic psychologists do not claim great expertise in predicting who will respond to what. The characteristics which do seem to be useful in distinguishing between offenders who will be

1. Although some 'psychopaths' are also found to be suffering from brain damage, thought disorder or low intelligence, to mention only a few possi-bilities, just as some diabetics also suffer from weak chests and rheumatism.

reconvicted and those who will go straight are not character-istics which are measured in interviews or tests; indeed – apart from the obvious *differentiae* of age and sex – they are not charac-teristics which are easy to assess in the artificial atmosphere of a remand centre, allocation centre or clinic.

SOCIAL INQUIRIES

They are in fact what can be called 'social', rather than psycho-logical, characteristics. Most follow-up studies seem to agree that for adult males at least the prognosis is poorer

(i) the more intermittent a man's employment record, and the more unskilled his jobs;

(ii) the fewer ties he has with a wife or a relative;

(iii) the more he has moved about the country;

(iv) the more time he spends in leisure pursuits such as drinking and gambling;

(v) the more members of his family and circle of friends have convictions;

(vi) the higher the conviction rate in the area where he works or lives.

This means that from the sentencer's point of view the most important information about an offender who is not mentally disordered will be found in the social inquiry report and not in the psychiatrist's or psychologist's notes. Two riders need to be added to this statement. The first is that I am talking about the needs of the sentencer (whoever he may be) and not those of the penal agent to whom the sentencer's decision may hand over the offender. Probation officers and custodial staff may very well find psychiatric and psychological classifications helpful in their treatment. The second rider is that it is often necessary for the sentencer to consult the psychiatrist or clinical psychologist in order to make sure that the offender is not disordered.

This poses a problem for designers of penal systems. The percentage of offenders who, after being given ordinary sentences, often more than once, are eventually diagnosed as disordered is not large, but it is large enough to make one wonder whether every offender should not be subjected to some sort of psycho-logical screening before sentence, or at least before his first sen-tence. On the other hand the total volume of offenders passing through courts makes this impossible; and in any case to insist on a psychiatric examination for trivial infringements of, say, traffic laws would provoke ridicule and even resentment (although in some systems the psychological investigation of repeated and dangerous traffic offenders is already a reality). The scarcity and costliness of psychiatrists and psychologists make it necessary to use them selectively. It is not difficult to suggest several categories of offenders which might be sensibly selected. For example:

(i) the mature person who, after years of steady, respectable living, is unexpectedly detected in some 'out of character' offence, such as embezzlement or assault; and, as an extreme case, any first offender over sixty years of age;

(ii) at the other extreme, the offender with a history of persistent anti-social behaviour which fails to respond to ordinary correctives;

(iii) the offender whose offences have an irrational quality about them, especially if they follow a stereotyped pattern (for example, the man who picks up and then assaults prostitutes, or steals only women's clothing);

(iv) the offender who commits serious violence against members of his own family;

(v) most sexual offenders, apart from those who have simply had intercourse with willing girls just under the age of consent.

The list is not exhaustive. Nor is it a list of categories in which *every* offender, or even the great majority, will necessarily be found to be disordered: simply a list of categories which, if psychiatric resources allow them to be examined, will yield enough positive diagnoses to justify singling them out.

Yet, although economic realities compel sentencers to adopt the assumption of an offender's normality in the great majority of cases, this assumption should not be regarded as a *pis aller*, which would be falsified if there were enough psychiatrists. The great majority of illegal parkers, thoughtless drivers, dishonest taxpayers and spare-time or full-time thieves, who make up most of the courts' lists, are not psychiatric cases, but act understandably (if selfishly) and respond more or less rationally to their estimates of the likely consequences of their actions. In their case a psychiatric report, however full of human interest, would be less relevant from the sentencer's point of view than a social inquiry report, and might even be a misleading distraction.

The social inquiry report, however, also has its limitations. It is important to realize that the information in it often makes it possible to predict with an accuracy a good deal better than chance that the offender will or will not be reconvicted, but that it does so *irrespective of the sentence*. In other words, it gives the sentencer grounds for optimism or pessimism, but hardly ever for a choice between sentences. Here again I must hastily add one or two riders. The first is that, if the offences involved are of the kind against which society needs protection (a problem discussed in Chapter 10), then a sentencer with grounds for pessimism will justifiably choose a sentence which, whether it corrects or not, will undoubtedly protect. Secondly, some social inquiry reports include, either expressly or by implication, psychological statements of the form: 'This man seems likely to be responsive to supervision'; and these statements sometimes prove correct. It is important to recognize, however, that they are based not on scientific psychology but on 'hunch', natural or acquired; and that the man who makes them must prove by results – and plenty of them – that he is right more often than he would be by chance. Thirdly, the statement that an offender is likely to respond to supervision is sometimes taken to mean that supervision offers the only or best chance of correcting him. For this there can be hardly any justification whatsoever. Probation officers do not have either the personal experience or any access to unpublished statistics which would enable them to compare the probabilities of reconviction for any sub-division of offenders after a measure other than probation. What they can legitimately say is that the offender seems quite likely to respond to probation; that a fine or custody would therefore be unnecessarily drastic; and that probation is therefore to be recommended.

I know of only one scientifically designed attempt to assess the value of pre-sentence reports. This was Dr Hood and Mr Taylor's comparison (1968) of the subsequent reconvictions of 300 males sentenced by the Sunderland magistrates, 200 of them after the introduction of a scheme under which reports were obtained in most cases, the remaining 100 before the introduction of the scheme, when reports were much less often requested. Although the obtaining of reports did seem to be associated with a better reconviction rate, the difference was slight.[2] If my arguments are sound, this is not surprising.

2. In fairness it must be pointed out
(i) that this is an interim report;
(ii) that it is not clear to what extent the magistrates did what the probation officers (and other reporters) would have wished in the way of sentencing.

PENAL HISTORY

There is one more sort of information, however, which must be considered: the offender's penal history. What sort of offences has he committed, in what sort of company, at what intervals? More important still, what sorts of sentence have been tried, and with what degree of success? (It may seem odd to ask 'With what success?' if, *ex hypothesi*, he is in trouble again: but it may be relevant to know how long he stayed out of trouble after a stiff fine, or whether he behaved himself *while* on probation if not *after*.) Psychiatric and social inquiry reports sound so much more sophisticated as aids to sentencing that we need to be reminded that one of the best and most reliable predictors of an offender's response to a penal measure is whether he has failed to respond to one in the past.

Moreover, whereas social information cannot, in the nature of things, tell us whether the offender's high (or low) reconviction-probability will be greater or less if, say, he is fined than if he is put on probation, the penal history can tell us what has so far been tried without success, and what has not. It is true that a man who was reconvicted after one spell on probation may keep out of trouble after a second spell; and probation officers will often recommend a second or even a third chance on probation for some recidivists. (It is a sign of our neglect of the obvious that we have no figures to show by how much the probability of reconviction increases after each unsuccessful probation order.) But it is a fair assumption that, if a man is reconvicted after measure X, it is rational to try an alternative measure before trying X again.

All this seems so obvious that it is at first sight rather difficult to understand how we have drifted into a position from which it has become lost to view. The explanation is probably to be found in what can be called 'the diagnostic fallacy'. The origin of the fallacy lies in the prestige of psychiatry, which has to some extent been earned, to some extent borrowed from the successes of physical medicine. (It is interesting, by the way, to speculate as to what might have happened had the profession developed out of psychology instead of medicine, with the result that psychiatrists would not have benefited from the social prestige of surgeons and physicians.) Psychiatry is visualized as a process of diagnosis, prescription and treatment; and although psychiatrists themselves would be the first to admit that this is an idealized picture of what is usually a less tidy process of trial and error, it has become a model for penologists, many of whom have a psychotherapeutic training or orientation.

I do not want to suggest that the diagnostic approach to sentencing is totally misconceived. But, if the point of a 'diagnosis' is to indicate the correct choice among several possible forms of treatment, then this is not usually what is needed by sentencers, although some of them may think so. My point may become clearer if we consider the logic of the sentencing situation.

Chapter 8

The Strategic Approach

Let us take the situation in which the court is dealing with an adult male first offender who is known or assumed not to be mentally disordered and in which it has at its disposal the four main choices open to the courts which Dr Hammond studied, namely discharge (including other nominal sentences), fine, probation and imprisonment.

Just how important is the choice which the sentencer has to make? His decision has of course both humanitarian and economic aspects: prison, for instance, costs more than a fine, and imposes more hardship on offenders and their families. I shall return to these aspects later. For the over-riding question is 'Which of the choices will result in non-reconviction?' Many sentencers – and penologists – proceed on the assumption that this question is as difficult as it could possibly be: in other words, that among the four choices there is only one right one. How likely is this?

Consider what is logically possible. Since we know that after any of the four sentences some first offenders go straight and some do not, we know that none of the sentences is universally effective. We can also be fairly sure that none of them is universally ineffective, although this ignores one awkward little possibility. An offender who is subjected to a given type of sentence may have been unaffected by it but have been turned into a non-offender by some other vicissitude, such as marriage to a stable and respectable woman. This is more than a theoretical possibility: penologists and penal agents believe that it does account for some of the successes which are attributed to penal measures. It is thus conceivable that all the apparent successes of one or more sorts of sentence are of this kind, and that they are really ineffective with any offender. But this is unlikely. The most that we can assume with confidence is that all success rates exaggerate the effectiveness of all forms of sentence.[1]

We can also be fairly sure of another assumption: that there are some offenders who will not respond to any of the measures at the courts' disposal, at least on a given occasion. For there are cases in which these measures are tried in rapid succession, without success. It is theoretically possible that on these occasions some measure other than the one tried would have been effective, and that by the time it was tried the offender's personality had so changed that it was ineffective. No doubt there are such cases; but it would be too strained to assume that they account for all the offenders who within a fairly short period fail to respond to any of the courts' choices. We need not assume that these 'universally incorrigible' offenders will remain so all their lives: merely that, on the occasion of their first encounters with the system, offenders include a percentage who will not respond to any sentence.

Are there also offenders who will respond whatever their sentence? The number of offenders who go straight after nominal sentences – and especially after absolute discharges – is sometimes cited as evidence that this is so. It is possible that the special criteria which courts tend to use in selecting offenders for nominal measures (see Chapter 5) are such that these offenders are more likely to respond to them than to supervision, financial penalties or custody; and no doubt there are a few who would feel that any such penalty was so excessive that they would become enemies of law and order if treated in this way. But to dismiss the evidence completely on these lines would be too far-fetched. Beyond serious doubt there are offenders who will go straight whatever the court does to them.

It is the other offenders who are more problematical: those in whose case the choice of sentence presumably does make a difference. It is natural to assume that they are what can be called 'selectively responsive': that is, that each would go straight if subjected to *one or more but not all* of the possible sentences. Theoretically, they could be of fourteen sorts: those who will

1. There is at least one other way in which they exaggerate it: for among every sizeable sample of sentenced offenders who have apparently gone straight there is an unknown percentage who have merely avoided detection. Dr West (1963) found that among a sample of fifty-nine recidivists who had apparently gone straight for at least four years, at least 40 per cent had certainly (from their own admission) or very probably committed offences for which they had not been convicted.

respond to *only* one of the four measures, those who will respond to *all but* one, and those who will respond to one of the six possible pairs. Some of these combinations seem more plausible than others: it is easier to believe in the existence of men who will respond to everything except a discharge than in the existence of men who will respond to discharge or imprisonment but not to a fine or probation. What is more important is that there is very little evidence for the existence of any of these types. Because courts tend to use fines and probation before imprisonment, and because some men seem to go straight after imprisonment who have not gone straight after less drastic measures, it is reasonable to infer that there is a group which responds only to prison. What is harder to find is evidence of the existence of a group which will respond only to a nominal measure, or only to a fine or only to probation.

If we assume for a moment, however, that all fourteen types exist, plus the universally incorrigible who respond to no measure and the universally responsive who respond to any, can a sentencer reasonably expect an answer to the question 'To which type does this first offender belong?' For the reasons given in the previous chapter he cannot. But if he were fairly sophisticated he might ask another sort of question: 'In what proportions are these types likely to be represented in any sizeable series of first offenders who come before me?' For suppose that the answer showed that the largest group in any series was that which responded to fines (whatever else they did or did not respond to): it would be rational for him (in the absence of any other information about them) to fine them all, since this would maximize the number of successful choices. On the assumption of selective responsiveness this is exactly what Dr Hammond's results suggest.

A REALISTIC MODEL
To visualize offenders as selectively responsive in this way, however, so that the choice of a given sentence is correct or incorrect, and could be seen to be such if the sentencer had sufficient diagnostic information, is not the only model[2] on which to theorize about the sentencing problem. It may be more profitable, and certainly it is more realistic, to recognize

    (i) that the sentencer's choices are not identical remedies, like the standard doses prescribed by a doctor, but cover a wide

2. For an explanation of this term, see Appendix A.

variety under the labels 'fine', 'probation', 'imprisonment' or even 'conditional discharge';

(ii) that differences between the 'success rates' of these choices may be due just as much to the indirect way in which they affect the offender's subsequent environment as to their direct effect upon his temperament. For example, the difference between the success rates of fines and imprisonment for first offenders may be due not so much to the failure of prison to deter or to reform as to the difficulties which it creates for them after release.

It therefore begs fewer questions to visualize sentencing not as the application of a set of uniform choices to a group of individuals of differing responsivity, but as the application of choices entailing different probabilities of reconviction to a group of individuals whose responsivity is assumed to be conditional and indistinguishable. This represents more realistically the state of knowledge, or rather ignorance, in which sentencers are obliged to operate. Because this line of reasoning is not only unfamiliar but also involves some mathematics, it is pursued in an appendix (A), which owes a great deal to Mr Willmer and Mr Carr-Hill, as well as to additional data and advice from Dr Hammond himself. The most interesting feature of the result is that – at least so far as the most numerous age-group of adult males is concerned – the data are reasonably consistent with a model in which

(i) the sentenced offenders are regarded as equally responsive in the majority of cases, but as including *either* a *smallish* minority of individuals who are unresponsive to any of the four measures, at least up to their fourth conviction, *or* a very *large* minority who are certain to respond to any of the four measures at the first application (or combinations of both types);

(ii) each of the four main sentences entails a probability of reconviction which does not vary greatly throughout the usual penal career (or more precisely, up to the fourth conviction);

(iii) a fine still carries the lowest probability of reconviction.

The most interesting of these three features of the model is (i). For it is extremely important to know whether we should assume a *small* minority of incorrigibles or a *large* minority of universally responsive offenders. It is a mathematical fact that the smaller a minority the harder it is to devise reliable criteria for identifying its members. If we could be sure that the only minority group, so far as responsiveness at the time of sentence is concerned, was very small, we might decide that diagnostic research had little hope of offering sentencers (or of course their professional advisers) reliable criteria for identifying it. On the other hand, if we could be sure that the minority was a large one, it would be more rational to press on with diagnostic research in the hope of eventually devising a practical guide.

Only a good deal of further research, analysing criminal careers in a way which has not so far been attempted, will tell which type of model is the most useful one for sentencers. Meanwhile the sentencer's best recourse is strategic reasoning, using the term 'strategy' in the sense in which it is used in games theory. A strategy is a rationale for making a choice or sequence of choices with the greatest probability of successful outcomes in a situation in which, because of the intervention of chance or other players or both, the chooser cannot make certain of the outcome. The essence of the argument in this chapter is that the sentencing situation is one in which the diagnostic approach is of little help and the strategic approach is the only practical one.

It leads to very simple conclusions. Sentencers need not worry about the extent to which universally responsive or incorrigible individuals are represented among the offenders whom they have to sentence; for in their case the choice makes no difference. As for the remainder, so long as Dr Hammond's data are the best we have, the strategically correct choice for an offender who has not yet been fined is a fine.

This does not mean that a fine would be the sensible choice in all cases. Strategic reasoning can be tempered with commonsense, and commonsense advises against fining the thief with no job, no savings and no fixed address, or the member of an organized gang of wage-snatchers. Nor should sentencers be discouraged from selecting the occasional offender for a nominal measure, since the statistics suggest that courts are able to select for this purpose with a certain amount of success. What the argument suggests is that unless the sentencer has some positive reason for choosing a nominal measure or a custodial measure (for example, the protection of society), he should choose a fine.

Fortunately this is a conclusion which will appeal also to the humanitarian and the economist. Fines are more humane than imprisonment, and less costly. They are less costly, too, than probation, not merely in financial terms but also in their demands on scarce manpower; and, as we saw in Chapter 4, they may even be less objectionable to the offender.

The suggestion that probation should not be regarded as the measure of choice for the first offender is of course contrary to the traditional assumptions of the probation service. Probation gives the first offender a second chance, before a positive penalty is applied. It would be more realistic, however, to treat a nominal measure as 'giving him a second chance', and to recognize that probation does in fact impose certain inconveniences upon him, which may be resented. Historically, too, it must be remembered that probation was devised as a 'second chance' at a time when courts either had no clear powers of discharge or were very reluctant to use them; a situation which has now changed. But this is a debating point; there are far stronger arguments for reserving probation until a later stage in the offender's criminal career. One is the economic fact that – in Britain at least – the probation service is over-loaded, and that a considerable part of its case-load consists of first offenders who – if they are responsive to any measure – may well be responsive to less costly ones. By reserving probation for the offender who has failed to respond to a fine or to a nominal measure sentencers can at least reduce the waste of probation officers' time.

They will also be ensuring that the probation officer is faced with probationers who have shown, by their failure to respond, that they are not easy cases. The very circumstances of their failures may be helpful. The modern probation officer's training is designed to help him to penetrate complex situations and personalities, and it is wasted on the delinquent offender who has been so impressed by his first appearance in court that he is already unlikely to reappear.

On the other hand, probation should normally be tried before imprisonment, which is costlier in both the economic and the humanitarian sense. In systems which allow a suspended custodial sentence, this too can rationally be tried before actual imprisonment. Some systems – for example that of France – allow suspended sentences to be combined with probation. Others – for example, the English – do not, on the assumption that a threat of this sort is incompatible with the spirit of probation (which in more concrete terms must mean that it reduces its effectiveness, an assertion resting on no evidence whatsoever).

Throughout this short outline of the notion of strategic sentencing I have used words such as 'normally'. Not only will there be cases – of which I have given examples – where common-sense suggests that a measure such as a fine would be useless.

There are also cases in which the aim of correction must give way to the aim of protection; for instance, in which a measure might well correct the offender but does not offer enough protection to likely victims if, while it is being applied, it does not work. Fines and probation are unsuitable for armed bank-robbers. What sort of offences are serious enough to make protection the over-riding consideration is a question which is discussed in Chapter 10. Meanwhile what calls for discussion in the light of my arguments about diagnostic and strategic sentencing is the fundamental assumptions which underlie our sentencing system, and most others.

Chapter 9

Assumptions of
the Sentencing System

To explain completely and in detail the assumptions upon which the modern approach to sentencing is based would require a good deal of history. This in itself does not mean that they are no longer justifiable; but it is a good reason for examining them critically.

Perhaps the most venerable and fundamental of them all is
(A) *That the sentencer can deal only with the offender.*
The judge or magistrate who has to sentence a convicted criminal may feel that others are equally or more to blame; but unless they too are successfully prosecuted before him there is virtually nothing he can do about it. Or he may feel that the crime was the product of a situation which will have to be remedied if there is to be any hope of preventing a repetition; but he cannot order anyone else to do anything about it.

There are minor exceptions. Magistrates who have been trying one of the participants in a brawl to which others have clearly contributed may bind them over, even if they have only appeared in the witness-box and not the dock. Similarly, in a Scottish salmon-poaching case a sheriff has been known to order the confiscation of the poacher's car although it was known to have been borrowed from one of the witnesses (a valid use of his statutory powers against which the witness had no appeal!). A judge who considers that the behaviour of a witness may have amounted to a crime can ask that the circumstances be reported to the Director of Public Prosecutions. Occasionally a judge has gone further and openly stigmatized someone connected with a case, although there was no question of prosecuting them. I have attended an assizes in which a young man who had pleaded guilty to carnal knowledge of a girl just under the age of consent was given an absolute discharge by the judge, who remarked that he was in no way to blame, but that the girl's parents had deliberately and culpably encouraged the commission of the offence. Judicial comment of this kind, however, is not regarded as good practice.

But these are trivial exceptions. Ironically, the cases in which courts do not intend to penalize others are those in which they often feel compelled to do so. Fining a man may mean that his wife's housekeeping money is cut. Imprisoning him may mean an even more serious decline in his family's standard of living, although the state may ensure that they do not starve. Sometimes the court tries to take this into account, for example by refraining from imprisoning the mother of a young family. In most cases, however, they feel bound to act on the principle that it is for some other agency to deal either with the situation which gave rise to the offence or with the situation created by the sentence. In a system which is based on the criminal trial it is not easy to see how it could be otherwise. In non-criminal proceedings juvenile courts are sometimes able to do better by conferring quasi-parental powers on children's departments; but nobody has seriously suggested that such powers should be extended to adult offenders, nor would they probably be very useful if they were.

Another traditional principle, although it has been considerably modified in this century, is

(B) *That the sentence is irrevocable.*

Once pronounced it cannot be altered, except in those rare cases in which the court changes its mind before the end of its session. Irrevocability has obvious advantages from the point of view of general deterrence, as the Medes and Persians realized. In English practice, however, the extent to which the sentence really was irrevocable has varied. When hanging or mutilation followed quickly on the sentence it was in the nature of things impossible to reconsider it. The extra-legal device of the royal prerogative, however, by which convicted offenders could be pardoned or their sentences commuted, soon became an expedient for interfering with the law, sometimes in the interests of justice or humanity, sometimes as a result of mere corruption. (In the eighteenth century Parliament tried to reduce the number of murderers whose death sentences were commuted by enacting that they should be hung within forty-eight hours!) Today the prerogative is still used to avoid the more obviously undesirable consequences of irrevocability. A pardon can be obtained if there is enough doubt about the justice of the conviction. A sentence can be commuted if it is causing excessive and unforeseen hardship: seriously ill prisoners are often released.

The prerogative, however, is used to remedy injustice or reduce a punishment which seems retributively excessive, and hardly ever to rectify a sentence because it seems mistaken from the reductivist's point of view. The same is broadly true of the modern device of appeal against sentence, which will be discussed in Chapter 11.

Although from the reductivist's point of view the principle of irrevocability has not been greatly affected by either of these institutional devices, it has been modified by other developments. The prisoner's right to remission for satisfactory conduct, and more recently the introduction of parole, with the possibility of recall to prison if it is abused, mean that the *length* of a prison sentence is no longer rigidly fixed at the time when it is pronounced, although the sentence still ensures that he goes to prison for a minimum period. Newer forms of penal legislation usually provide expressly for some sort of second thoughts. Probationers, for example, can be brought back to court not only for further offences but also for breaches of the requirements of the probation order, in which case the court can cancel the order and substitute a custodial sentence or some other measure. A fined offender can have his fine reduced, or be given more time to pay, or be put under supervision while he pays the instalments. Notice, however, that these modifications of irrevocability are still to a considerable extent controlled by the court. In its modern form the principle seems to be

(BB) *That once pronounced a sentence can be modified from the corrective point of view only in restricted ways, which are largely controlled by the courts.*

More will be said about this principle later. Meanwhile, another venerable one is

(C) *That the sentence must take one of the forms prescribed by law.* Although it was stated by Beccaria in protest against the arbitrariness of continental punishments ('. . . only the laws can decree punishments for crimes . . .'), it was recognized long before him in some penal systems, such as England's. Even the Bill of Rights of 1688, which declared that 'cruel and unusual punishments' were illegal, was merely expressing in statutory form what was felt to be the law.

The principle had several attractions. If a penalty was regarded as just retribution, the law should ensure that it was the same for all who incur it. Regarded as a deterrent, a penalty which was known in advance seemed more likely to be effective than one which was not. Even from the offender's point of view it had its merits, for it was a protection against arbitrary barbarities, of the kind which courts in some continental countries used to invent even in Beccaria's time.

Nowadays such inventiveness is almost entirely out of the question in civilized countries. When it is allowed, this is because the form which it takes is not more severe but more lenient than usual. A court may decide – perhaps for one of the reasons described in Chapter 5 – that to impose a custodial supervisory or financial measure would be inappropriate to the offender's case; and it may therefore discharge him or defer sentence on certain conditions. English courts sometimes discharge offenders from Ireland or Scotland on condition that they go back to their own country – an unofficial form of deportation which is of doubtful legality, but considerable utility. A Scottish court dealt with a litter-dropper not long ago by deferring sentence on condition that he swept the street for a few weeks. Some courts in the U.S.A. make bad drivers attend driving classes or work in casualty wards of hospitals.

Experimentation of this kind sometimes leads to the general adoption of an idea. The 'psychiatric probation order' which is used in order to ensure that some probationers receive psychiatric treatment is the result of the initiative of a London magistrate, William Clarke-Hall, in 1927. This raises the question whether, in a civilized and humane country, the principle that the sentence must take a form prescribed by law is still needed. May it not nowadays be an impediment to the discovery of new and effective measures rather than a protection against 'cruel and unusual punishments'?

It is not a complete answer to point out that there are still some sentencers who would like to impose penalties – such as flogging or hanging – which their society has discarded. Offenders could rely for their protection on an appellate court, an institution which did not exist in the days when the principle was established. Alternatively, if we are afraid that even an appellate court might uphold a barbarous sentence, it would be possible merely to prohibit certain types of punishment, leaving courts free to exercise their ingenuity within broad limits.

A sounder, though more prosaic, reason for preserving the principle is that sentences have to be carried out by penal agencies of one kind or another, and that these could not cope with large numbers of improvised sentences. It is only by stereotyped procedures that they avoid being swamped by the enormous volume of offenders who pass through the criminal courts. Thus, while more improvisation of a humane kind is desirable, too much would lead to a breakdown of the agencies who have to see that sentences are carried out.

Another point which needs emphasizing is that even in the twentieth century the control of sentencing by statute is an institution without which penal reform would be more difficult than it is. A great many changes in sentencing policy have been accelerated, if not actually initiated, by legislation which prohibited older forms of penal measure or permitted newer ones. The abolition of corporal punishment, the suspension of capital punishment, the step-by-step raising of the minimum age for imprisonment, and the suspended prison sentence are all examples. It is true that some bold sentencers have anticipated legislation either by abandoning a measure of which they disapprove or by experimenting more or less illegally with a new one; but without the legislation their example would not have been followed, or at least not so soon.

An interesting and important by-product of the statutory prescription of sentences is another assumption:

(D) *That the sentences at the courts' disposal should not vary from one area to another.*[1]

It is assumed that a summary court (or higher court) sitting in Manchester should have the same choice of measures as its counterpart in Devon. Admittedly, exceptions have been forced on us. While detention centres for young male offenders were being set up centre by centre, courts in some areas were allowed to use the limited vacancies in them while courts in others were not, although this was accepted because it was a temporary state of affairs. Attendance centres are not available to most rural courts, simply because the small number of boys who could be sent to them would make them very uneconomical.

Both exceptions, however, are limited to young offenders and dictated by economic difficulties. In general, and especially

1. Local Acts and bye-laws often include local prohibitions, backed up by penalties which courts can impose, so that, for example, you can be fined for flying a model aeroplane in the parks of some cities. The penalties, however, must be of the same scale and nature as those allowed by general Acts, and in practice almost always consist of fines.

where adults are concerned, it is felt that the law should not allow offenders to be at risk of different measures merely because they happen to be sentenced in different parts of England (although we seem prepared to tolerate *de facto* differences resulting from variations in courts' sentencing policies). This has at least one unfortunate result: that it is very difficult to experiment with new measures before they are made available to courts in general. It is true that experiments are not unheard of, for the Prison Department have been allowed to run experimental attendance centres for young men of seventeen to twenty-one in two areas, which were available only to courts in those areas. In contrast, however, the suspended prison sentence was introduced by a general Act of 1967 after twenty years of argument about its merits and demerits, but with no attempt to test it in a selected area.[2] In Chapter 11 I shall suggest a remedy which would allow local experiments without making too wide a breach in the principle.

On the other hand, paradoxical as it seems at first sight, it is the same principle that the sentence must take a form prescribed by law which is responsible for the fifth fundamental principle of modern sentencing:

(E) *That the sentence should be chosen by the person or persons responsible for presiding over the trial of the offender's guilt.*[3]

For until recently, so far as serious crimes were concerned, the judge's function was not to make a choice but merely to make an announcement – of the penalty provided by law. You may wonder what I mean by 'recently'. After all, in England it is over three hundred years since it began to be possible to substitute transportation for hanging. But for a long time any such mitigation of the sentence laid down by law – and especially a death sentence – was regarded as the function not of the court but of the crown. The judge would advise the king to grant a conditional pardon, and eventually judges were allowed more or less to anticipate the king's decision, and commit him to it.

But transportation, and the penal servitude which took its

2. And apparently no more than superficial attempts to appraise its effectiveness in countries which had been using it for some time: see, for example, Appendix D of the report of the Advisory Council on the Treatment of Offenders (1957).

3. Like some of the other principles I am discussing, this has been slightly modified. A *remanded* offender will not necessarily be sentenced by the judge, recorder or magistrates before whom his guilt was established. Some offenders, too, can be remanded by lower courts for sentence by higher courts.

place in the nineteenth century, were imposed in accordance with what has been called a tariff system, so that judges regarded themselves as more or less bound to impose certain periods of detention, within narrow limits, for certain types of offence. This is clearly illustrated by the trial of William Hilliard in 1899 for the attempted murder of his wife. Hilliard, who was not represented by counsel, pleaded guilty; but the judge suspected that he might not be sane, and sent for the prison medical officer, from whom he elicited the view that Hilliard was not of sound mind at that moment, and had probably been even less so at the time of the crime. All this sounds very enlightened of the judge. At this point, however, he seems to have reasoned that as Hilliard had pleaded guilty he had no alternative to sentencing him to penal servitude, and for five years; and that the most he could do to help Hilliard was to bring his case to the attention of the Home Secretary, so that the latter, as the sovereign's adviser, could consider whether to interfere with this sentence!

Whether the court is the best body to choose sentences is a question which will be discussed in Chapter 11. Meanwhile, Hilliard's case emphasizes that the conception of the court as an authority whose function is to think flexibly about the disposal of an offender is a comparatively recent development.

Like all such developments, it has had an underlying philosophy, which can fairly be called 'the philosophy of individualization'. In so far as this can be summed up in a single sentence, it is that

(F) *The penal measure imposed on an offender should be chosen and adjusted with his particular circumstances in mind.*

Like so many other features of our penal philosophy, this can be traced back to Bentham, who thought that the amount of suffering imposed on an offender in order to discourage him from repeating his offence ought not to exceed the minimum which was necessary for the purpose. Consequently it ought to vary according to his capacity for suffering. Bentham then enumerated no less than thirty-two variables – ranging from sex, age, physical and mental health to climate, religion and lineage – which affected one's capacity for suffering: an astonishingly modern piece of writing for an eighteenth-century penologist.

Apart, however, from an increasing leniency towards women and children, nineteenth-century legislators paid little attention to this idea of Bentham's, and it was not until late in the century that there was serious talk of 'individualizing' the punishment of adult males. The word itself seems first to have been used in this sense by German prison administrators and to have been adopted by French penologists, who gave it a retributive rather than a utilitarian interpretation. To 'individualize' the penalty meant to adjust it according to any circumstances which mitigated the offender's culpability. In England, where the term was introduced, rather diffidently and self-consciously, by Ruggles-Brise (the Prison Commissioner) in connexion with the borstal system, it seems to have been interpreted more or less in Bentham's utilitarian way: the penalty should be individualized so that it was as nearly as possible what was needed to correct the offender. But the convenient ambiguity of 'individualization' as a battle-cry makes it possible for the retributive as well as the reductively minded sentencer to claim that he is loyal to it.

What we must now do is to examine the meaning and implications of the utilitarian version, which seems to be that

(FF) *Sentencers should be free, and should do their best, to choose for each offender the measure most likely to correct his tendency to break the law as he has done (or, in a more ambitious version, to break the law in any way at all).*

In some cases it is necessary to add 'and which will protect society while he is being corrected': but protective sentencing is a subject which is being reserved for Chapter 10. A reductivist who is also an economist and a humanitarian would also add 'within the limits imposed by our resources and by humanity'. But these are minor points.

It is obvious at once that FF is a statement of an ideal which cannot possibly be realized in practice. For one thing, the corrective measure with the best chance of success may be out of the question, at least for a court to impose. To take an example, Dr West investigated a sample of rather inadequate, but persistent, thieves who had some curiously long gaps in their series of recurrent convictions. In quite a number of cases the gaps seem to be due to the fact that the offender had been living with some motherly and law-abiding woman, either in matrimony or in what some people would call sin, although in their case the result seemed to be virtue. When this association broke up they resumed their careers of crime. Unfortunately matrimony is not recognized as a permissible sentence by our criminal law.

Ridiculous as this example may sound, it does draw our attention to the conflict between the principle of individualization and the principle of control by the law. Under the latter, the sentence of a court must be something which can reasonably be defined in words, prescribed in advance and enforced in practice. The sentencer must not improvise, but must use one of the choices provided by the official system, knowing – as far as possible – what its practical effects will be. Since his choices are circumscribed in this way he cannot possibly suit them to the individual offender.

Supporters of individualization will say that I am being unfair to them, and that they do not mean anything so ambitious as my interpretation. What they mean is

(i) that the assortment of measures open to the courts should be as wide and varied as possible;

(ii) that there should be flexibility in their application (for example, it should be possible to extend the time for payment of fines, to shorten a fixed sentence of imprisonment, to alter the conditions of probation); and

(iii) that from measures of this sort the courts should make the choice most likely to correct the offender.

This sounds much more convincing. But it glosses over, or at least blurs, the central issue, which is

'To what extent should individualization be attempted by adding to the choices of the courts, and to what extent by increasing the discretionary powers of penal agents in putting the courts' decisions into practice?'

The point can be illustrated by considering the problem which would confront British legislators if they wished to add semi-detention – as described in Chapter 5 – to the existing range of penal measures for adults. Should it be introduced as a distinct alternative to imprisonment, to be applied only to those offenders for whom it is ordered by the court? Or should it be treated as one form which a sentence of imprisonment can take (as, for example, allocation to an open prison is treated)? Or should it be treated as a special development of probation, resembling as it does the probation order with a requirement of residence in a hostel which is imposed on some young offenders?

The disadvantage of making semi-detention a separate form of sentence rather than a discretionary variant of imprisonment or probation (or both) is obvious when we consider the possibility that the offender might after all be quite unresponsive to this measure. For if it were a sentence, the principle of irrevocability (BB) makes it impossible to substitute another measure, at least until he is convicted of another offence. It is true that semi-detention might be treated as being like a probation order, so that the offender could be brought back to court for breach of the requirements of the order, and another form of sentence substituted. A similar result, however, could be achieved in a less cumbersome way by making semi-detention a form of prison sentence, so that the offender who failed to conduct himself properly could be transferred to an ordinary prison, just as if he had misbehaved in an open prison or a prison hostel.

It is possible to foresee two dangers in a system of this sort. The more important of these is that the prison service might allow semi-detention with less regard for public safety than would the courts. Whether this is so is debatable; but in a system which already allows the prison service complete discretion in allocating offenders to open prisons or to prison hostels it would be inconsistent to argue that they could not be trusted with this decision. The other danger is that the prison service would be more restrictive than the courts in selecting prisoners for semi-detention, or might take so long over the selection that the offender would have lost his job. A compromise which would meet both criticisms would be a system in which the court ordered semi-detention but the offender could be transferred to ordinary imprisonment at the discretion of the prison service (perhaps with provision for some sort of appeal).

In whatever form semi-detention is eventually introduced into the British system, it illustrates the central problem of 'individualization' as it is defined on page 119. As soon as individualization ceases to be a retributive objective and becomes a corrective one it ceases to be something which the court can achieve by itself, and indeed becomes something which can really be achieved only by penal agents. In an ideal system in which penal agents could be trusted completely to act with efficiency, humanity, regard for public safety and psychological understanding of the offender, the greatest flexibility could be attained by complete delegation to them of the choices between corrective measures. (Something approaching this degree of delegation is attempted in some systems so far as juvenile delinquents are concerned.) Since we are far from trusting our penal agents to this extent – at least where adult offenders are concerned – the courts have an important function. If my argument is sound, however, this function should not consist of making choices so much as of controlling them. More precisely, 'controlling' means 'ensuring that the choices which penal agents make in the name of correction are not excessively inhumane, uneconomic, inefficient or dangerous to the public'.

The gradual transition from choice to control which seems to be taking place is most obvious and important where custodial sentences are concerned. 'Life' sentences apart, the nominal length of a term of imprisonment has always been prescribed by the court. In practice, penal servitude (which meant at least three years, and often much longer) could be shortened by remission of one quarter for industry and good conduct; later, imprisonment (which meant two years or less) could be shortened by one sixth for the same reason. During the Second World War remission for all sentences[4] was increased to one third; and nowadays remission is a right of which the prisoner can be deprived only as a result of a breach of discipline and formal proceedings before the prison governor. Nevertheless, courts are not supposed to take remission into account when prescribing the nominal length of a sentence.[5]

The courts' power to determine the period of actual custody has now been further weakened by the introduction of parole, which in Britain means that the prison service is not merely obliged to release a properly behaved offender for the final third of his sentence, but also able (though not obliged) to do so for the middle third, provided that this does not prevent him from serving at least a year inside. Consequently, a court which pronounces a sentence of, let us say, three years is guaranteeing only that the offender will be a prisoner for the first third of that time. It is true that release on parole is sparingly granted, and is subject to control by a Parole Board on which sentencers are represented; but it is not controlled by the courts.

SEMI-DETERMINATE SENTENCES

Some systems have gone much further than this. In California, for example, the law lays down the minimum and the maximum period of imprisonment for each type of felony. Except for certain crimes the judge need not necessarily impose imprisonment,

4. With an exception for very short ones: remission must not reduce the period below thirty-one days.

5. Although a recent decision by the Court of Appeal (Criminal Division) now regards it as proper to do so if the purpose of the sentence is 'treatment or reform' (see *R.* v. *Turner* (1966) 51 Criminal Appeal Reports, 72). It would be more logical to make an exception where the purpose was the protection of society.

but, when he does, all he can do is to name the minimum and maximum prescribed by law. Within these limits the actual period served by the prisoner is determined by the Department of Corrections and the Parole Board. Other systems compromise by fixing the maximum period by law but allowing the court to fix the minimum – an expedient which is sometimes abused by judges who set the minimum not far below the maximum.

In England the system of borstal sentences for young offenders between their seventeenth and twenty-first birthdays is approaching this pattern. Provided that the offence is of a kind for which an adult can be imprisoned, a higher court can impose a sentence of borstal training, which means that the offender must serve not less than six months[6] and not more than two years, the date of his release being determined by the Prison Department. A borstal sentence is thus one in which the court has no say in the time to be served. It is based on the assumption that since the object of the sentence is wholly reformative, it is for the penal agent – in this case the borstal staff – to say when this objective has been achieved.[7]

This raises the question whether prison sentences which are intended as correctives for adults should continue to have their lengths even partly determined by courts. Can we assume, however, that any such sentence is intended purely as a corrective? May it not also be meant to protect the public? I shall argue in Chapter 10 that the protective function of the great majority of our prison sentences must, because of their shortness, be negligible. As for their function of general deterrence, it has already been pointed out in Chapter 4 that this is more likely to be weakened than strengthened by the way in which courts individualize their custodial sentences. If so, we can proceed to consider the lengths of corrective sentences, and the way in which they should be fixed, without these distractions.

To illustrate the point, consider for a moment the lengths of the sentences imposed on adult men in England and Wales for house-breaking, an offence which has been selected because an adult house-breaker is always dealt with at assizes or quarter

6. But the Home Secretary can authorize earlier release in special cases (which are rare).

7. In contrast, since a period in a detention centre is intended as a mild deterrent, and is short in comparison, it is assumed that there is no point in minor variations in its length. If so, it would be more logical still to provide for only one period of detention, such as three months; and this in fact is what the Scots have done.

sessions, who can thus exercise their discretion without the limitations imposed on lower courts. The maximum sentence allowed by law for this offence is seven years, but fourteen if an offence such as theft or assault is committed in the course of it. In practice, as Table 3 shows, sentences of more than five years

TABLE 3
PRISON* SENTENCES FOR HOUSE-BREAKING† BY MALES
IN ENGLAND AND WALES, 1964–6 (SOURCE: FIGURES
SUPPLIED BY HOME OFFICE STATISTICAL BRANCH)

Nominal length‡	Percentage of all sentences
3 months or less	2·3%
4–6 months	9·9%
7–9 ,,	13·4%
10–12 ,,	19·0%
13–15 ,,	4·7%
16–18 ,,	18·8%
19–21 ,,	1·6%
22–4 ,,	12·6%
25–30 ,,	2·6%
31–6 ,,	9·2%
37–48 ,,	3·0%
49–60 ,,	1·9%
61–72 ,,	0·1%
73–84 ,,	0·4%
85–96 ,,	0·4%
97–108 ,,	–
109–20 ,,	0·1% (all four of these were imposed in 1966)
ALL LENGTHS: 5,078 =	100·0%

* Including corrective training and preventive detention, but not borstal.

† Adult house-breakers are invariably sentenced at assizes or quarter sessions, so that the limits which apply to magistrates' sentences have not affected the lengths of any of these sentences.

‡ Including the combined length of consecutive sentences. Of two or more concurrent sentences only the longest is counted. Remission is ignored.

are very uncommon, and in many cases consisted of sentences of preventive detention imposed on recidivists with long penal records. What is worth examination is the striking variation in lengths within the five-year range. There seem to be about five fashionable lengths of six, nine, twelve, eighteen, twenty-four, and thirty-six months, which in practice usually meant incarceration for two thirds of these periods: parole had not then been introduced.

At least 15 per cent of sentences, however, and probably more were of odd intermediate lengths.[8] What purpose is served by this variety? Certainly not general deterrence: if the argument of Chapter 4 is accepted, this would be better achieved by one or two standard lengths. Nor is the difference between a sentence of three years and one of, say, two years of any importance from the point of view of public safety, especially when it is reduced by remission to a difference of eight months. We can therefore concentrate on corrective efficacy.

There is very little scientific evidence on the subject of the comparative efficacy of custodial sentences of different lengths. Amongst a sample of male first offenders sentenced by Scottish courts, Dr Hammond found that sentences of six months or more were followed by lower reconviction rates than shorter sentences, even when differences in age and type of offence were allowed for. This accords with the views of prison staff who say that sentences of a few months are not only an administrative nuisance but often serve only to convince the offender that imprisonment is more tolerable than he had thought; and in some cases even introduce him to criminal associates for the first time.

The undesirability of sentences of six months or less – which in 1967 accounted for 72 per cent of all prison sentences – is beginning to be recognized in England.[9] So far as first offenders in summary courts are concerned, a sentence of this length must be a suspended one unless certain conditions are fulfilled. Admittedly these conditions are quite often satisfied; and, in any case, many a suspended sentence later becomes an actual one; but, half-hearted as it is, this provision is a step towards the abolition of the short sentence. Its abolition would not necessarily mean a corresponding reduction in the numbers of offenders who were sent to prison. Post-war statistics suggest that the

8. It is not possible to be precise because of the way in which lengths are grouped in the Home Office's computer system. We have to assume – not unjustifiably – that most sentences in the range of, say, twenty-two to twenty-four months were in fact two-year terms; but one or two may have been for twenty-two or twenty-three months, the result, for instance, of adding a consecutive sentence of ten months to one of twelve months.

9. While this book was in proof the West German Bundestag and Bundesrat approved a bill which will, *inter alia*, prohibit sentences of imprisonment of less than six months, except where the court considers such a sentence necessary and sufficient for individual deterrence (thus ruling out, for example, short sentences for petty recidivists whose careers demonstrate their unresponsiveness to such sentences). I am indebted to Mr L. Malz, of the Maximilianeum, Munich University, for this information.

trend away from short sentences has in many cases meant longer sentences, although in others it has meant a fine instead.

What is needed now is evidence about the comparative efficacy of longer sentences: i.e. terms of one, two, three, and four years. In the days of corrective training – the special reformative sentence which was designed for recidivists in their twenties – it seems to have been assumed that from two to four years was required for this purpose; for these were the limits specified by legislation. In fact, this assumption was not based on any scientifically collected information. Nor is it easy to find reliable evidence from other countries[10] to show how the duration of custodial sentences is related to their success as correctives.

Perhaps the best evidence is provided by an inadvertent experiment which was forced upon penal administrators by the decision of the United States Supreme Court in the Gideon case. The effect of the decision (which related to the right of the accused to be defended by counsel) was that large numbers of prisoners were discharged from penitentiaries earlier than they would normally have been. In Florida Dr Eichman (1966) managed to match[11] 110 of these prisoners with 110 prisoners who had served their full time, and to follow them up for slightly more than two years during which neither group was under supervision. Although there was a considerable overlap between the lengths of time served by the 'Gideon group' and those of the others[12], the difference in mean time served was substantial. Yet after two years only 14 per cent of the Gideon group, compared with 25 per cent of the others, had been reconvicted. It would be unjustifiable to conclude that shortening periods of incarceration in this way would always *improve* success rates; but not so unjustifiable to infer that at least it is unlikely to make them worse.

Until we have more evidence of this kind, what is a rational policy? One possible solution is to give prison staffs even more discretion than they have at present in deciding the prisoner's actual date of release. This could be achieved either by a com-

10. For example, Professor D. Glaser's statistics for Federal Youth Correction Act parolees in the U.S.A., which suggest that for some categories success decreases with longer incarceration, are undermined by the likelihood that prisoners with better prospects were released earlier (Glaser, 1964, page 302).

11. Using criminal histories and other significant factors as criteria for matching.

12. Sixty per cent of the Gideon group had served less than eighteen months, compared with 47 per cent of the others.

pletely indeterminate type of sentence – that is, one with no predetermined minimum or maximum – or by a semi-determinate one, with a maximum and a minimum.

The completely indeterminate sentence is a rarity in almost all penal systems. In Britain it takes the form of the so-called 'life' sentence[13], which is confined by law to murder (for which it is mandatory) and to a few serious offences, most of them involving personal violence or sexual molestation; and so far as these are concerned in practice it is even more sparingly used by the courts, who tend to impose it only on offenders whose offences or previous histories show that they are mentally unstable and likely to repeat their offences.[14] Its effect is to place the date of release entirely in the hands of the Home Secretary, and, although he invariably consults the Lord Chief Justice and the trial judge (if he is available) before releasing a lifer, and may consult the Parole Board, he is not bound by their advice. Some lifers – such as mercy killers – are released very quickly; a few are detained for twenty years or more.

There is no obvious theoretical reason why the indeterminate sentence should not be used for ordinary offences, such as theft or assault; but there are practical dangers. One is its possible use for political purposes. This cannot be prevented simply by prohibiting indeterminate sentences for political offences, since this can be circumvented by charging political offenders with offences such as theft or assault. Even if one is confident that one's own system of law enforcement could never be abused in this way, there are other dangers. For example, an offender who has misbehaved in prison, or merely antagonized the staff, might be kept longer than was justified. However tolerant the staff, men and women who are not prone to violence in ordinary life can give way to it under the frustrations of a closed and disciplined institution, so that they can be regarded as 'bad risks' by officers who do not appreciate that conduct inside is not a good indicator of conduct outside.

Unless these dangers seem quite unreal, we must ask 'What advantages would be lost by setting limits to all sentences which are intended primarily as corrective?' One answer might be

13. I am ignoring the very small number of juveniles found guilty of 'grave' offences who receive indeterminate custodial sentences under s. 53 of the Children and Young Persons Act, 1933.

14. See the remarks of the Court of Appeal (Criminal Division) in *R.* v. *Hodgson* [1968] *Criminal Law Review*, 46.

'maximum deterrence'; but if we reason on the lines of Chapter 4 we shall realize that the deterrible and knowledgeable criminal is too well-informed about actual practice to be impressed by indeterminacy, while the deterrible but ignorant over-estimates the severity of the penalty. A fixed and known maximum is quite likely to be regarded by the ignorant as the *probable* duration of a sentence, while the knowledgeable optimist will expect the norm whether there is an upper limit or not. Provided that the maximum is not absurdly low, it is unlikely to mean a real sacrifice in deterrence.

What should the maximum be? We have no scientific information that is relevant to this question. If we had, it might enable us to fix different maxima for different types of offence or offender.

The most that can be said at the moment is that there is a case, on strategic reasoning, for fixing a lower maximum for the prisoner who is serving his first custodial sentence[15] than for one who has already served a previous sentence. The principle is crude but not unsound: try a shorter one before trying a longer one. If six months is accepted as a sensible minimum for any prison sentence, then a maximum of the order of two years for a first such sentence gives scope for some discretion on the part of prison staff, but not too much. In 1967 three quarters of sentences by our higher courts were of two years or less; and of the remaining quarter an unknown but considerable number involved offenders with previous custodial sentences. Ninety-seven per cent of the sentences were of five years or less, so that a maximum of five years for offenders with previous sentences would not be out of scale with present practice.

Within these limits how should the prison service 'individualize' the prisoner's sentence? It would probably argue in the first place that there must be a system of automatic remission for the well-behaved prisoner, since forfeiture of remission is the most powerful disciplinary sanction left. There is at least one other good argument for retaining remission and distinguishing it from parole: that this helps staff to distinguish between conduct inside and prospects of success outside.

On these proposals, a well-behaved 'star'[16] prisoner could

15. Probably a previous borstal sentence should count, but not a stay in a juvenile institution. This is open to argument, however.

16. Convenient terms used in the prison service to distinguish prisoners who have not served a previous prison sentence ('stars') from those who have ('ordinaries').

count on being released between his sixth and sixteenth[17] months (on the assumption that remission remains at one third of sentence). If (but only if) he had forfeited all his remission he could be kept for the full twenty-four months, although – as at present – this would not debar the prison service from paroling him earlier. If he was an 'ordinary'[16] prisoner he could not be kept longer than forty[18] months (unless he forfeited remission) and his minimum period of detention would be determined by the time which he had previously served. If it were made the rule that he must serve at least six months more than he served previously, this would mean that the duration of an ordinary's sentence must be at least a year[19], and of course in many cases more. It should by now be clear that these proposals would not allow prison staffs enormous latitude for arbitrary decisions as to the actual date of release. In the case of the well-behaved star the range of choice would be ten months; in the case of the well-behaved ordinary, twenty-eight months at most, and in many cases much less. This is not so very different from the range of choice which the present system of parole and remission allows.[20]

This does not tell us how prison staffs are to decide when the prisoner has 'had enough' from the corrective point of view. Some governors and senior officers claim to be able to tell when a prisoner or borstal trainee is 'ripe' for release. What these claims are worth we do not know: they have not been tested. The sceptic is apt to point out that most borstal boys are said to be ripe for release when they have been inside for whatever is the average period for the borstal in question; but this too is an impression rather than a documented fact. One can at least argue, however, that a decision taken by people who have been in close contact with the offender for months is slightly more likely to be correct than one taken before he has begun to serve his sentence by someone whose contact with him is limited to the court room. Moreover, if the decision is to release on parole, it is one which can be used experimentally, and revoked if it proves premature; whereas a fixed sentence cannot.

The only important innovation in the system proposed is the

17. i.e., two thirds of two years.
18. i.e., two thirds of five years.
19. i.e., the minimum of six months plus the extra six months.
20. The chief differences are that some well-behaved stars could be re-leased at six months instead of twelve, while some ordinaries could not be released quite as early as at present.

idea of upper limits for a corrective prison sentence which are determined neither by the court nor by the law dealing with the offence, but by the offender's previous custodial experience. It is therefore important to emphasize what is *not* being proposed:

(i) it is not intended that prison staffs should ignore differences between offences in deciding dates of release, or in allocating offenders to different sorts of prison;

(ii) it is not implied that offences which are not punishable by imprisonment should incur imprisonment; whether an offence should be 'imprisonable' or not is an independent issue;

(iii) it is not implied that this system is sufficient to protect the public against dangerous offenders (precautionary sentences are discussed in Chapter 10);

(iv) it is not claimed that the maxima should be precisely two and five years. Now or later there may be considerations pointing more clearly to other maxima.

It may also be necessary to point out that maxima of two and five years do not represent increases in the existing legal maxima for most offences, but *decreases*. For most forms of dishonesty the upper limit is ten years or more; for most forms of serious violence seven years or more. On the other hand, the proposed maxima need not in practice mean a reduction in the average length of sentences, for, as we have seen, very few sentences exceed them (and many of these would probably be justifiable as precautionary sentences: see Chapter 10).

Finally, similar arguments could be applied, *mutatis mutandis*, to probation orders. It is not easy to see why courts should decide at the outset, and before probation has been tried, whether the order should be in force for one, two, or three years, especially when, in cases of good conduct, orders can be terminated by the court before they expire. There is a strong argument for providing that all probation orders should be of a standard length, on the understanding that supervision can be terminated earlier if the offender's progress seems to justify this, or, if necessary, extended. Two years is by far the most frequent duration specified by courts, and it might well be made uniform. If so, there seems to be no case for seeking the court's authority to terminate supervision early when a probationer is doing well, although it is obviously desirable that courts should be responsible for ordering extensions beyond two years; and of course for substituting some other measure when probation is obviously a failure.

Chapter 10

Protecting Society

In the preceding chapters I have deliberately postponed any discussion of that very important complication, society's demand for protection against identified offenders. My reasons for doing so were that I wanted to work out what a rational system of sentencing would be like if this consideration were left completely out of account, and then to see what modifications might be needed in order to meet this demand.

For, while correction is an objective which we seriously consider in the case of any sort of offence, it is not every sort against which we demand protection; demand, that is, a measure which is not merely likely to deter or reform the offender, but is certain to incapacitate him from repeating his offence. The reason is that incapacitating measures are usually extremely drastic. Death, the amputation of a hand or foot, the castration of sexual offenders, exile, transportation, are measures at which humanitarian societies look askance because of the distress imposed on the offender and his family, and which are usually regarded as too high a price for certainty.

It is true that the nature of some offences makes it possible to aim at a less drastic, although also less efficient, form of incapacitation. The reckless or careless driver can be disqualified. Children who are maltreated by their parents can be taken away from them, either with their consent or by an order of a court. Sadistic or paederastic teachers can be black-listed. Although there are well-known loopholes in all these measures, they are essentially incapacitating, and yet are not regarded as unnecessarily inhumane.

PRECAUTIONARY IMPRISONMENT

It is the use of imprisonment as an incapacitating technique which gives rise to most controversy. Imprisonment is the most conveniently ambiguous of all penal measures, since it can be claimed that it functions as a general deterrent, an individual deterrent, an opportunity for reformation, a reinforcer of social stigma, and an efficient form of temporary elimination. In its eliminatory capacity it is, of course, less economical than, say, castration or disqualification from driving, but superior to them in certainty and in the variety of offences against which it gives protection. Few prisoners escape; there are few offences which they can commit inside; and their victims are usually their fellow-prisoners or custodians. The only incapacitator which is superior to imprisonment (as to all other measures) in universality, efficiency and economy is the death penalty.

Conditions of imprisonment in civilized countries have undergone enormous improvements in the last quarter of a century. Even maximum security prisons are less grim than they used to be.[1] At the other end of the scale, open prisons and hostels are being used for an increasing percentage of the prison population. Nevertheless the deprivation of liberty is still costly both in terms of resources and in terms of unwanted side-effects on the offender, and there is an increasing tendency to ask 'When is it justified as a means of protecting society?'

Several trends are combining to make this an increasingly acute question. As retribution and general deterrence become unfashionable justifications for imprisonment, the emphasis shifts to correction and protection. And when the corrective efficacy – at least of long sentences – begins to be questioned, the only safe ground left is protection. Parallel with these trends can be seen a change in the conception of protective sentences. In the nineteenth century, when most prison sentences were by our standards very long, it was unnecessary to devise special precautionary sentences. As they shortened, a demand was created for longer ones in the case of certain offenders, who were defined either as habitual criminals or as being likely to commit certain particularly objectionable crimes. Some countries, notably Germany and Britain, adopted a 'double-track' system under which offenders who were designated as requiring preventive detention first served the term which seemed to the judge to be appropriate retribution for their crime, and then went on to serve the prophylactic part of their sentence. But it requires an extremely retributive philosophy to sustain so

---

1. Curious barbarities, however, are preserved in unlikely places. For example the rule of silence is still enforced for long-term prisoners in some Swiss prisons.

artificial a piece of logic, and today the double-track system is rare, although still in force in Western Germany.

Other countries, including Britain, simply allow their higher courts to pass longer sentences than would otherwise be permissible in the case of certain carefully defined minorities of offenders. Sometimes these sentences are determinate, sometimes indeterminate, as in Sweden, sometimes semi-determinate, with maxima and minima fixed by statute or the court, as in California. The British 'extended sentence' is semi-determinate, since its length is fixed by the court (within the statutory maximum of five or ten years, according to the nature of the offence), but the offender becomes eligible for parole after one third of it.

In most penal codes the definitions of those eligible for prophylactic sentences contain at least one common element: there must be evidence that the offender is unlikely to respond to ordinary penal measures. In England the latest definition – in the Criminal Justice Act of 1967 – is an elaborate one:

(i) the offender must have been convicted on at least *four separate* occasions of *any* offence punishable with two or more years' imprisonment;

(ii) the convictions must have occurred *since his twenty-first* birthday;

(iii) they must have taken place *in a higher court*[2];

(iv) the custodial sentences imposed must have added up to not less than *five years*, and included at least *one* of three years or more or at least *two* of two years or more;

(v) the offence for which the precautionary sentence is imposed must have been committed *within three years of his last conviction* or release from custody for an offence punishable with at least two years' imprisonment.

Some of these requirements date back to the Criminal Justice Bill of 1938; others are refinements introduced by the Act of 1967. Their common objective, however, seems to be to ensure that the offender is incorrigible. He must have been convicted often, failed to respond to substantial terms of imprisonment, relapsed soon after his last sentence. Even the requirement that the convictions must have occurred since he attained his majority is probably intended as another assurance of incorrigibility, for it can be based only on the assumption that youthful conduct is not a good indication of what one will do as an adult.

Usually – though not everywhere – some attempt is made to

2. With certain permissible exceptions.

give such prisoners better living conditions than those serving ordinary sentences. They are sent to different institutions, or at least to separate wings of ordinary prisons. Although incorrigibility, or more precisely a failure to respond to ordinary penal measures, is the one characteristic which their inmates are supposed to share, these institutions usually make some effort at correction. Since it is assumed, with some justification, that these prisoners do not respond to individual deterrence, the only hope is reformation, and by subtler processes than those employed in ordinary prisons. In Denmark, this process of reasoning has led to a system in which dangerous recidivists are assumed to be cases for psychiatry, and their two main institutions for such prisoners are under the direction of psychiatrists.

Indeed, the hope of correcting the apparently incorrigible springs so eternal in the humanitarian breast that one of the criticisms levelled at the English system of preventive detention in recent years has been the high rate of reconviction among ex-prisoners who have undergone it (about three in every four were reconvicted of an indictable offence within three years of release). It would be more logical to regard this reconviction rate as confirmation of the courts' assumption that they were unlikely to respond to imprisonment, and as an index of what society was being protected against. A somewhat sounder criticism would have drawn attention to the one man in four who was not reconvicted, and would have asked

(i) whether he had in fact 'gone straight' for three years, and not merely avoided conviction for an indictable offence;

(ii) if the former, whether he continued to go straight after the three years;

(iii) if the answer to both these questions was 'Yes', whether it would not have been possible to identify this sub-group in advance so that it was not subjected to such long detention.

In fact, however, the only attempt to provide a prediction formula of this kind (Hammond and Chayen, 1963) showed that the best that could have been done with the available hard data would merely have separated the sample into those with one chance in three of not being reconvicted from those with one chance in five!

In other words, the attempt to protect the English public against these prisoners was founded on the not unreasonable assumption that, if at liberty, they would be committing indictable offences. Nor was the attempt unsuccessful, for the rate of successful escapes by prisoners, and especially by preventive detainees, is very low.

The soundest objection to preventive detention, at least as it was used by English courts, was that the offences of most of the preventive detainees were not really of the sort against which society demands, or should demand, a degree of protection which cost so much in terms of resources and unwanted side-effects. The same study by Hammond and Chayen of men sentenced to preventive detention in 1956 showed that among the offences which had led to their sentence, 45 per cent involved 'breaking and entering' homes or other buildings; 25 per cent were thefts of various kinds; 11 per cent were frauds. Only 4 per cent were offences of personal violence, and only 2 per cent were sexual offences. Thus four out of every five were acquisitive offences. Of these, a few (4 per cent) had involved property worth more than £1,000: but in three quarters of cases the value was under £100. As for their subsequent offences after release, most of these were relatively petty thefts, frauds and burglaries, involving on average £50 worth of goods. The cost of maintaining a man in a high-security prison at that time was nearly £500 a year, and probably exceeded by a small margin the annual cost of their depredations.[3]

In purely financial terms, it would have been more business-like to accommodate the less competent of these acquisitive offenders in supervised hostels; to find them work so that they could pay for their keep; to accept a fairly high rate of absconding and petty dishonesties; and to compensate their victims. A commercial calculation of this kind, of course, ignores aspects which cannot be included in a balance-sheet. Examples are the fear and distress of the elderly widow who encounters one of these petty burglars at his work, or the impossibility of replacing some unique piece of private property. The petty thieves and frauds whom we are considering, however, were not violent robbers or stealers of Goyas and Rembrandts.

THE CRITERIA FOR PRECAUTIONARY IMPRISONMENT

It is time, however, to face the general issue as squarely as possible. By what criterion should society decide whether an offence is sufficiently serious to justify secure custody purely as a means of prevention?

It is interesting to look again at the thirteen sorts of offences

3. Making an allowance for offences not traced to them.

which I distinguished in Chapter 2 and to see which are likely nowadays to earn long sentences. It is true that in England, for example, any offence punishable with at least two years' imprisonment can – if the other conditions are fulfilled – qualify the offender for a preventive sentence. In practice, however, whether in England or elsewhere, it is a rather shorter list of offences against which courts seem prepared to use this drastic weapon. It is also true that some offences qualify for long sentences for retributive or deterrent reasons, so that we cannot be sure when prevention is the main objective. What we can do, however, is to draw attention to the offences which never, or hardly ever, qualify for long sentences.

Perhaps the best way in which to review the thirteen groups is in a series of antitheses. We seem prepared to use long sentences:

(1) against intentional harm (actual or attempted) to the human person, but *not* against unintentional harm, for example by bad driving, or harm to animals;

(2) against sexual molestation which harms or seriously distresses adults, and against sexual advances to the immature, but *not* against mere solicitation of adults, public indecency or obscenity, and to a decreasing extent against acts which are 'unnatural', but do not involve immature or unwilling victims, such as 'gross indecency' between adult males;

(3) against conduct which harms the state, such as espionage or sedition, but *not* against the creation of public disturbances or attacks on religion;

(4) against dishonesty involving private property or the coinage, but *not* against the evasion of revenue-collection.

Finally, there are whole classes of offence against none of which we seem prepared to use long sentences:

(5) offences against social institutions; bigamy hardly ever earns more than three years' imprisonment in present-day England;

(6) the refusal of compulsory benevolence, such as failure to send one's child to school at the required ages;

(7) interference with the enforcement of the law, such as perjury, tampering with juries or assisting escapes.

This is a description of English practice, and no doubt it would be possible to find important differences in other countries. What would be more profitable, however, would be to see whether any rational justification can be read into the distinctions which are drawn between offences which do earn long sentences and offences which – occasional exceptions apart – do not. We must not expect complete rationality, for much of our sentencing law and practice is still determined by traditional, usually retributive, thinking.

With these exceptions, it is possible to make some sense of the antitheses by supposing that they are based on a distinction between intentional conduct which leads, or is likely to lead, to serious harm, and conduct which is either unintentional or unlikely to lead to serious harm. Certainly the rationality of this distinction is open to question. Why should we not use long sentences to prevent serious harm which is the result of recklessness, negligence, incompetence or even accident-proneness? Historically the answer lies in the emphasis which is placed on culpability: someone who did not intend to do what he did cannot be blameworthy enough to justify long imprisonment. A completely non-retributive penal philosophy must of course reject this answer as insufficient, although it might have to admit that, because the public in general, and more particularly juries, think in this way, it would be politically unwise to impose long prison sentences on typhoid-carriers, negligent surgeons and accident-prone drivers.

Fortunately, it is usually possible to argue that we can have some degree of protection against such people at much less cost. Typhoid-carriers can be prohibited from serving the public with food. Negligent surgeons sooner or later cease to be shielded by their profession, and have to practise some less hazardous form of medicine. Accident-prone drivers can be disqualified (although the driver who persists in driving after disqualification is a problem which – in England at any rate – has still to be solved). On the whole it is not altogether irrational to assume that the man who does not intend what harm he does can be prevented from doing it again by a less drastic expedient than incarceration. Usually he himself is anxious to avoid doing more harm, although there is a degree of negligence which seems to amount to a disregard of obvious danger to others (and which, under the label of 'recklessness', we are sometimes prepared to treat as almost as culpable as intentional harm).

What raises more difficulty is the distinction between 'serious' and other harm. All penal codes seem to rely on some such distinction, but none seem to define it. The English code, for example, talks of 'grievous bodily harm'. This used to be defined in judges' charges to juries as any harm which 'seriously' interfered with 'health or comfort'[4], but 'seriously' was not defined, and now even this half-hearted attempt at a definition is discredited.[5]

Must so important a distinction be left entirely to the interpretation of individuals, from the prosecutor who selects the charges to the judge who presides over the trials? Is it impossible to provide some objective guidance of a rational kind?

For example, should we rely on some sort of opinion poll, of the kind used in a recent American attempt to construct an index of crime? Professors Sellin and Wolfgang asked samples of policemen, university students, and juvenile court judges to consider a large number of different offences in which the harm done was described, and to rate the 'seriousness' of each. From the results they were able to propose a formula for assessing the 'seriousness' of a given offence in such a way that the assessment would be more or less independent of the prejudices of the individual making the assessment. The formula at which they arrived was open to the criticism that it should have been based on the ratings of rather different sorts of people, although how they should have selected their groups is itself a highly debatable question. What is more, they were not trying to divide offences into those which justified a drastic penal measure and those which did not, but were merely offering a way of comparing their seriousness. No doubt a procedure of this kind could be devised so as to reflect, not too misleadingly, the degree of protection demanded by a given group of people against a given sort of offence. It would always, however, be open to the criticism that the group chosen was too specialized, or biased, or ignorant, and that at best the result would simply reflect the prejudices of that group at that particular date.

THE KIND OF HARM

We need more objective criteria than a plebiscite, however sophisticated, can be expected to provide. At first sight this appears an impossible demand. How can the 'seriousness' of an offence be distinguished from the attitude of a community, or a section of the community, towards it, any more than the pleasantness or unpleasantness of cigar-smoke can be distinguished from

4. Ashman's case (1858) 1 Foster & Finlason 88.

5. In Smith's case ([1961] A.C. 290) the House of Lords said that 'bodily harm' needs no explanation, and 'grievous' means no more and no less than 'really serious'. But what is 'really serious'? Is it more serious than 'serious'?

the sensations of those exposed to it? The solution is to forget about that artificial concept called 'seriousness' or 'gravity', and remember that we are trying to answer a more limited and practical question:

'Against what sort of offences is it rational for a reductivist to demand a high degree of protection?'

This is the sort of question to which, *mutatis mutandis*, we provide rational answers in everyday life when we are not distracted by the emotions and superstitions which surround crime and punishment. When we are forced to decide between troublesome or costly precautions against some harm, we ask two other questions:

'How difficult would it be to undo the harm if it happened?' and

'How likely is it to happen?'

Since a protective sentence is simply a precaution against future harm from the behaviour of an identified offender, these two questions are surely the most relevant ones which we can ask. To take the argument a stage further, the first question from the reductivist who is anxious to prevent future harm at the minimum necessary cost in resources and unwanted side-effects on the offender should be:

'If he repeated his offence, how difficult would it be to remedy the harm?'

And only if the answer were 'Impossible', or 'Probably impossible' or 'Very difficult' would he consider so drastic a precaution.

This would not of course be his only consideration. He would also ask:

'How likely is the offender to repeat his offence?' and if the answer were 'Very unlikely indeed', he would decide against a purely precautionary prison sentence.

Of course both questions raise obvious difficulties. Some kinds of harm, such as the death of a human being, are clearly irremediable, just as others, such as the theft of a handbag, are easy to remedy, either by restitution or by compensation. There are kinds of harm, however, which are not so easy to classify, especially psychological harm. Sexual offences provide good examples. The psychological effects of rape or forcible sodomy are clearly unlikely to be completely effaced by the most skilful psychiatric treatment. At the other extreme, the shock or annoyance (if any) which is caused by indecent exposure or soliciting are almost always transitory. But what about a sexual advance, not involving any violence or abduction, to a child of twelve?

I have chosen this example because, although it demonstrates that the reductivist's distinction is not without its problems, it also shows that the solution need not be dependent on the subjective reactions either of a judge or of the respondents in a plebiscite. The effects of early sexual experiences on children is a subject which has received some attention from psychiatrists and psychologists. The reductivist would ask for an opinion by more than one expert as to whether the sort of advances which the offender in question had made to children were likely to have permanent ill-effects. In some cases the answer would be a unanimous 'Yes', in others a unanimous 'No'. (If there were disagreement, it would be advisable to give the offender the benefit of the doubt.)

Another point must be made here. The reductivist would ask not merely what harm had been *done* by the offence in question, but also what harm was *likely*, even if by good fortune or otherwise it had not actually resulted on this occasion. If a man armed himself with a loaded firearm to commit a robbery the reductivist would consider that, whether he had fired it or not, his behaviour was of the kind that was likely to result in irremediable harm. He would say the same of dangerous driving, whether or not it had resulted in actual injury.

It will be noticed that the examples of irremediable harm which I have given have consisted either of personal injury or of sexual molestation. Most cases of irremediable harm would in fact fall into one or other of these categories. Occasionally, however, the courts have to deal with other sorts. The harm may be done to the state instead of an individual; the obvious example is espionage. Or it may be done to a work of art by theft or deliberate damage. (It is arguable that since stolen works of art are in theory – and often in practice – recoverable, it is only damage to them which should be regarded as irremediable; but the way in which they are stolen often damages and nearly always endangers them.)

Works of art apart, however, it is difficult to think of other crimes against property which are likely to cause irremediable harm. It is true that harm of this sort is a likely consequence of large-scale robberies, but because of the personal violence which the robbers are prepared to use, and not because of the sums of money involved, which hardly ever mean a substantial loss to an individual. Even the fraud or confidence-trick which deprives someone of most of their source of income is not in theory irremediable, although in practice we do not yet have satisfactory arrangements for compensating the victims.

THE PROBABILITY OF REPETITION

Perhaps the most difficult questions for the reductivist, however, would be:

'How do you estimate the probability that the offender will repeat his offence?'

and

'What degree of probability would justify a precautionary sentence of imprisonment?'

These are not unanswerable questions. To the first criminologists are beginning to provide answers based on empirical investigations. An interesting feature of these answers is that for once they support rather than undermine the approach of most penal codes to this problem. One of the indications of future behaviour on which legislators have relied heavily for this purpose has been previous convictions; and criminological research does in fact confirm that these are among the most reliable and powerful predictors of future convictions. The more previous convictions a man has, the more likely he is to be reconvicted, irrespective of the penal measure to which he is subjected.

To this extent the English requirement that the offender must have been convicted on at least three previous occasions (and have failed to respond to substantial periods of detention) is unexceptionable. What is open to considerable criticism is the absence of any requirement that the convictions should have been for similar offences. Any offence carrying a maximum penalty of at least two years' imprisonment is enough to qualify. A man might become eligible for an 'extended sentence' as a result of one conviction for shoplifting, two for blasphemy and one for carnal knowledge of a girl just under the age of consent. And if it is argued that an English court would be too sensible to impose precautionary imprisonment for this last offence, it is worth recalling that in 1962 a court did exactly this, and was upheld on appeal.[6]

6. See *R*. v. *Crehan* [1962] 1 All E.R. 608. Crehan's previous convictions (of which there were fourteen!) were all for petty dishonesty of one sort or another, but the crime for which he received preventive detention was sexual intercourse with an apparently willing girl of fifteen.

Leaving aside for the moment the question whether the harm done in any of these cases is irremediable, they do not suggest that the man is likely to repeat any of them. At most they suggest that he suffers from a general disregard for the law, and to that extent is more likely than a man with a shorter record to be reconvicted: but they do not indicate what his next offence is likely to be.

Contrast my imaginary case with another in which a man is convicted of carnal knowledge. In this case it is his first appearance before a higher court (so that he would not be eligible for a precautionary sentence). But investigation shows that

(i) the victim was only thirteen years old;

(ii) there was evidence that he had used his position as her school-teacher to frighten her into submitting, although the charge of rape was not proceeded with;

(iii) he had, under an alias, been twice previously convicted by a magistrates' court of inducing young girls to commit indecent acts with him against their will;

(iv) he persisted in applying under various names for posts as a teacher in which he would have charge of young girls.

This offender would not satisfy the requirements of the English law governing preventive sentences, yet he would seem to a reductivist a better case for such a sentence than the other man.

In short, the reductivist would want to use not only information about the offender's official penal history, but also any other information which would indicate whether the offence in question was part of a consistent pattern of dangerous behaviour or an isolated incident. If it were objected – for example, by lawyers – that this would open the door to a great deal of unprovable statements from police, social workers and psychiatrists, he could point out that sentencers accept such statements in considering less drastic measures, so that it is illogical to rule them out of consideration at this point. It is true that if the court is considering whether to impose a long sentence for a petty theft there is something objectionable about doing so on the basis of diagnostic statements; but since the reductivist has in mind only protection against irremediable harm this is not the situation. Mental health legislation allows patients with no criminal records to be detained in hospitals for long periods on the basis of psychiatrists' statements that the safety of the public would otherwise be endangered.

The other crucial question which has to be faced, whatever

one's views on the sort of harm or the sort of evidence that justifies precautionary sentences, is

'What degree of probability would justify such a sentence?'

The first point to be made is that in the present state of penological knowledge there are very few offences in the case of which we can state the probability in a statistical form. There are several quite thorough follow-ups of offenders' subsequent careers, but very few distinguish between the types of offence which they commit. Most studies of ex-prisoners, for example, are studies of samples consisting very largely of thieves, with a sprinkling of frauds, men of violence and sex-offenders; and most of their subsequent offences (even in the case of the minorities) seem to be petty dishonesties. If it is conceded – as it should be – that such offences do not justify precautionary sentences, this information is irrelevant. What is required is information about the probability that a man who commits an offence of personal violence will commit another such offence; that a man who sexually molests children will do something of the same sort again; and so on.

It is rather startling to find how little we have in the way of estimates of such probabilities. As regards sexual offenders, the Cambridge Institute's four-year follow-up of a sample of men convicted of such offences in England in 1947 yielded some interesting information. Of men convicted of heterosexual offences, those with two such convictions were reconvicted in 29 per cent of cases; those with three such convictions, in 48 per cent of cases. For homosexual offenders the corresponding percentages were 27 per cent and 55 per cent. Unfortunately in these published figures the heterosexual offences include indecent exposure, and the homosexual offences include importuning, both of them fairly trivial but compulsive types of behaviour whose inclusion would artificially raise the reconviction rate of the group as a whole. The most that can safely be said at present is that the more previous convictions one has for a sexual offence, the greater the probability that one will sooner or later incur another.

As for personal violence, a study of the careers of a sample of Scottish adult males which I carried out recently with the assistance of Dr Hammond and Mr D. J. Steer (1967) suggested that with each successive conviction for violence (excluding trivial assaults and sexual violence) the probability of a further conviction for violence rose as follows:

after the 1st conviction ... 12 %
after the 2nd conviction ... 35 %
after the 3rd conviction ... 40 %
after the 4th conviction ... 67 %

Although the numbers involved were not as large as we should have liked, the results suggested that, with each conviction for violence, one can be increasingly confident that one is dealing with an offender who is in some way predisposed to resort to violence, either for its own sake or as a means to attaining some other end.

With a greater expenditure of money and labour it would be possible to improve on these figures, and produce more reliable estimates for more refined sub-groups. If, however, we accept them for the sake of the argument as not too unreliable (and they are certainly more reliable than the subjective estimates of psychiatrists or probation officers), at what point does the probability become large enough to be accepted as justifying a precautionary sentence? And what about the offender of whom the psychiatrist and the probation officer can say only that there is a 'considerable likelihood' that he will repeat his offence, or words to this effect?

A forthright, if arbitrary, solution to both difficulties would be to accept only probabilities greater than 50 per cent, and to ask the psychiatrist or probation officer 'Do you mean that he is *more likely than not* to do this again?' There is no argument, however, that will point decisively to this or that level of probability as acceptable. What is certain is that the level which we are willing to accept will become lower as

(i) our dislike of the harm in question increases;

(ii) the hardships of the custody decrease.

In other words, if we insist that the harm must be irremediable, we can and should accept lower probabilities than if we do not. We should also be readier to accept lower probabilities as the regimes of precautionary custody become more tolerable.

THE NATURE OF PRECAUTIONARY DETENTION

This last point requires elaboration. The conditions under which long preventive sentences are served in this and most other countries are only slightly better than those of shorter corrective sentences. Indeed, in some countries there is no practical difference. In England we allow long-term prisoners some extra 'privileges', such as private radios; but their lives in secure prisons are much less tolerable than those of men serving what are meant to be corrective sentences in open prisons.

In the past this state of affairs has been defended on grounds that were partly practical, partly doctrinal. The need for a high degree of security (which was in any case exaggerated in the case of the petty thief) was said to require confinement in small compact buildings, with very restricted space for exercise, carefully supervised contacts with visitors from the outside world, and many other inconveniences. The financial economy with which prisons are administered has prevented other improvements. The idea of using islands for communities of long-term prisoners was discredited for the illogical reason that Alcatraz and Devil's Island were barbarously administered.

Practical difficulties of this sort, however, can be overcome in affluent and technically ingenious societies if people are convinced of the need to overcome them. The reasons why there has been no real recognition of the need are doctrinal. If the life of a long-term prisoner is made too comfortable, he will not be atoning for his crime: an argument which a non-retributive penologist must of course disregard. Another objection is that the general deterrent effect of long-term imprisonment would be weakened. It is true that there is an institutionalized group of habitual prisoners who seem to find quite long sentences tolerable even under present conditions. These are usually, however, petty thieves rather than the sort of offender for whom precautionary sentences seem necessary, and it is very doubtful in any case whether many men of violence and dangerous sexual offenders are deterred by the difference between comfortable and less comfortable detention.

A third doctrinal argument, however, is that too comfortable a regime would not correct the offender. This brings us to the heart of the confusion which surrounds the expedient of the precautionary sentence. Because it developed out of ordinary imprisonment we have failed to acknowledge its different function and accept the practical consequences. Since it is intended for, and justified only in, cases where the prospect of correction is poor, it is illogical to model its conditions on those of sentences which are intended to be corrective. Indeed, it is undesirable that precautionary and corrective sentences should be served in the same establishments, and there is a strong case for prohibiting this.

Our failure to draw a sharper distinction between precautionary and corrective sentences of imprisonment is also bound up with a failure to think clearly about their relative lengths. It is by no means uncommon for a judge or recorder to put forward 'the protection of the public' as a partial – sometimes a complete – justification for sending a man in his twenties to prison for twelve, fifteen or eighteen months, a sentence which will incapacitate him for only a negligible fraction of his active life, even if he earns no remission.[7] So temporary a protection is hardly worth consideration, except in two sorts of situation. One is the situation in which the sentencer can be assured that correction will be achieved within that period: an assurance which is hardly ever reliable, unless in the case of a few well-defined mental disorders, which, in any case, are more likely to be treated in hospital than in prison. The other is the situation in which time will rapidly reduce the danger which the offender represents. Examples are the senescent sexual offender; the incestuous father whose daughters will soon grow up and leave home; the jealous husband or lover whose enmity will cool; the political offender[8] whose cause will soon be won or lost without him.

With rare exceptions of this sort, it is unrealistic to regard a custodial sentence as serving a precautionary function unless it is of substantial length. In Chapter 9 I argued in favour of a general upper limit of about five years for sentences which were meant to be corrective; and I now suggest that the normal minimum for a precautionary sentence should be slightly longer than the maximum for a corrective one. There is no strict logic in this; but it would help to preserve the distinction between the two sorts of sentence, and would compel sentencers to make up their minds which they were imposing.

Unlike the limits for a corrective sentence, however, neither the maximum nor the minimum for a precautionary one can be determined scientifically. In strict logic, a society which confines precautionary detention to offenders likely to cause irremediable harm and unlikely to respond to further correctives, and which has rendered the conditions of precautionary detention as tolerable as possible, should be prepared to accept very long periods indeed. Even the most humanitarian of penal reformers would

---

7. Several instances of this were found in a sample of sentencers' justifications collected by Mr Robert Purves of Wadham College, Oxford.

8. I am not assuming that imprisonment for political offences is justified: what I have in mind is the person who commits violence or other offences for political reasons.

hesitate to say when it would be justifiable to release sadistic violators of children.

What is difficult to justify is the practice (in Britain and some other countries) of allowing sentencers to determine even the approximate date of release years in advance. This could be justified only where there are grounds for distrusting the commonsense and humanity of prison administrators. If the administrators are suspected of a tendency to release dangerous offenders too early, there is a case for allowing the sentencer to fix a minimum period of custody, although this could as well be done by statute or subordinate legislation. If, on the other hand, the administrators are suspected of excessive caution in the matter of release, this could be better controlled by a procedure for periodic review of every long sentence by an independent authority. (Some countries have judicial or non-judicial tribunals for this purpose; in England the Home Office periodically reviews every 'life' sentence with considerable thoroughness.)

Few if any of the arguments against indeterminate corrective sentences are relevant to precautionary custody. If, as seems advisable, their minimum length – whether determined by legislation or by the court – is known to be substantially longer than the maximum for corrective imprisonment, this would leave no scope for optimism on the part of the deterrible offender. As for the humanitarian argument that indeterminacy imposes an unnecessary strain on the offender himself, this is more cogent if the alternative is a short or medium-length sentence. If the alternative is a long fixed sentence, it is arguable that indeterminacy gives him more scope for optimism, whether well founded or not. The extent to which ordinary courts should have a say, however, in the imposition of precautionary sentences is a question which is better discussed in the next chapter.

Chapter 11

Controlling Sentencers

This chapter discusses a problem at which earlier chapters have merely glanced or hinted: the extent to which it is practicable and desirable to control sentencers.

All civilized systems impose some form of control. Courts are debarred from using some penalties – such as imprisonment – for offences which seem too trivial, or on offenders who are under a certain age. Fines may not exceed certain amounts; supervision may not be ordered for more than so many years; prison sentences are usually subject to maxima, and sometimes to minima. In some cases the sentence is mandatory: the court is compelled to order the death sentence or life imprisonment for murder, and to disqualify motorists in certain circumstances. Let us consider the various devices which have been used or suggested, beginning with mandatory sentences.

MANDATORY SENTENCES

These are rare, and are invariably the result of a fear that courts will be too *lenient*. In some systems the death sentence is discretionary; but it is more usual to make it obligatory for a small number of offences, such as murder and treason, and so to relieve the sentencer of a controversial and distressing decision. At the other end of the scale, experience has shown that lower courts are too easily dissuaded from imposing disqualification on incompetent, negligent or reckless drivers, so that in England for example disqualification is discretionary in some circumstances but mandatory in others. For a period, too, imprisonment was mandatory for driving while disqualified; but this provision proved so unpopular that it was later repealed.

Mandatory sentences, being safeguards against leniency, are assumed to maximize the deterrent effect of penalties, and are seldom advocated for corrective reasons. Unless the offence in question is one which is unlikely to be committed in a state of mind which is responsive to deterrence – examples were given in Chapter 4 – it is difficult to challenge this assumption. The chief argument against mandatory measures is that they must often compel courts to pronounce sentences which are unnecessarily drastic from the corrective or precautionary point of view, and are therefore uneconomical, and possibly inhumane. This argument is at its strongest when applied to capital punishment and life imprisonment, and much weaker when applied to a measure such as a fine or disqualification. It would not be difficult for example, to draw up a long list of offences which could be committed only by people who were in a position to pay a fine (not necessarily a large one): offences against revenue legislation are an obvious example.

Nor need a mandatory penalty be obligatory in *all* circumstances. English courts are freed from the necessity of disqualifying a motorist if they can find 'special circumstances' in the nature of his offence; and experience shows that they often try hard to do so for compassionate reasons. In England even a suspended sentence which is followed by a further conviction within the specified time-limit does not have to take effect if the court finds that it would be 'unjust' in view of all the circumstances which have arisen since the sentence was passed. Sentences of this kind might more precisely be called 'semi-mandatory'.

Could a mandatory or semi-mandatory sentence be justified on precautionary as well as deterrent grounds? It is no answer to say that our higher courts seem only too ready to impose long sentences in the name of public safety. This may be so, although we have seen in earlier chapters how rare in actuality are custodial sentences which are long enough to be effectively precautionary. Even if it were so, however, it would be more relevant to consider how often courts refrain from a precautionary measure in circumstances in which one seems clearly required. That this does happen is strikingly illustrated by Simcox's case:

Christopher Simcox, who had been divorced by his first wife for physical cruelty, murdered his second wife in 1948. Fortunately for him, Parliament was debating capital punishment when he was condemned to death, and like all death sentences at that time his was commuted to 'life' imprisonment. After ten years he was released on licence, settled down to a job in the Midlands, and married a third wife. This marriage, too, was an unhappy one, and his wife left him to live with her mother. He seems to have been a man of strong resentments, for in September 1963 he forced his way into his mother-in-law's house and threatened them both with a pistol.

He was charged with house-breaking with intent to murder, and with unlawful possession of a firearm. As sometimes happens, he pleaded guilty to the latter charge, and the prosecution dropped the more serious one. The judge had received reports from a prison medical officer and a probation officer, whom he questioned closely in court. He was clearly anxious not to impose further incarceration on a man who had already spent ten years inside, and he eventually said to Simcox: 'Although there is a risk in my keeping you out of prison now, it is a risk I am entitled to take, and I am very anxious to take it.'

Mrs Simcox does not appear to have been asked whether *she* was prepared to take it. Although neither the probation officer nor the prison medical officer had sounded very sure of Simcox's reliability, the judge put Simcox on probation for three years, on his undertaking to go nowhere near his wife.

Eleven days later Simcox shot his wife and her sister, and the sister died. (He shot himself in the stomach almost immediately afterwards, but recovered sufficiently to be convicted of capital murder. He was reprieved because after sentence he was still too badly injured to walk to the scaffold.)

It is difficult not to sympathize with the judge's attempt at individualization, however retributive its reasoning and however unfortunate its results. Nevertheless the story illustrates the fact that, just as some magistrates cannot be relied upon to use the mild precautionary measure of disqualification from driving, so sentencers in higher courts sometimes lose their judgement when faced with a case for precautionary imprisonment. It is possible that these sentencers would be less hesitant if they could pronounce a sentence of indeterminate custody which did not bear the forbidding title of 'life imprisonment'; but that is a mere speculation.

So far as personal violence is concerned, it would not be impossible to draft a definition of the circumstances in which a precautionary sentence could be made semi-mandatory. For example, the elements of the definition could be

convictions on a minimum number of occasions (at least two) for offences of the following types:

murder;

the offences of personal violence defined in Section 18 of the Offences Against the Persons Act, 1861;

robbery;

> the use or possession of firearms in the circumstances defined in Section 23 of the Firearms Act, 1937;
>
> attempts, threats, incitement or conspiracy to commit any of these offences.

An escape clause should be provided for

> (a) cases of mental disorder (for which, however, a hospital order with restrictions on discharge might well be the mandatory alternative);
>
> (b) cases in which the previous conviction (or finding of guilt) had been incurred at an early age, and the offence for which the offender is being sentenced had occurred after a considerable period;
>
> (c) cases in which the offence for which the offender is being sentenced was committed under severe provocation[1];

and perhaps for other definable situations.

If the escape clause were satisfied, a precautionary sentence could be either prohibited or made discretionary, but should probably be prohibited. *Mutatis mutandis*, it would be possible, but more complex and tedious, to draft a similar provision for sexual offences which are likely to cause irremediable harm. There would remain, of course, situations in which the mandatory clause was not completely satisfied – for example, because the offender did not have the minimum number of previous convictions – but in which the court could be given discretion to choose a precautionary sentence. I shall be making a more radical proposal later in this chapter; but so long as the only body which can impose imprisonment is a court the semi-mandatory sentence seems the best solution to the problem of precautionary custody.

This brings us to the question whether a semi-mandatory sentence could be justified on purely corrective grounds. From what has been said in earlier chapters, and especially in Chapters 7 and 8, it must be obvious that there is only one measure which could be seriously considered from this point of view, and then only with many reservations. This is the fine. If the strategic argument in Chapter 8 is accepted, a fine could be made obligatory for a first conviction. It would be necessary to give courts a very wide escape route, which would admit offenders who were unlikely to pay, who seemed likely to respond to a nominal measure, who were too disordered in mind or who were too dangerous.

---

1. An exception which can sometimes be justified on reductivist grounds: see Chapter 12, and especially page 166.

The amount of the fine, and the time granted to pay it, would have to be left to the court, within the usual limits. A semi-mandatory fine for first convictions would almost certainly lead to a slight increase in the number of right choices from the point of view of economical correction. It could not lead to an enormous increase in success rates, for many first convictions are already dealt with by fines, while most of the remainder lead to probation, which is quite likely to succeed with offenders who would have responded to a fine. Perhaps the strongest argument for it is that it would reduce the waste of probation officers' time; but this does not amount to an overwhelming case.

THE PROHIBITED SENTENCE

The converse of the mandatory sentence is the measure which is prohibited in certain circumstances. Imprisonment is not permissible for a host of trivial offences; for some others it is permissible only for a second or subsequent conviction. Young offenders are protected against it. Magistrates' courts are debarred from imposing it on an adult first offender, although the Act of 1958 leaves them a wide escape route.[2] Until 1948 higher courts could not discharge the offender, and for some offences they could not fine him.

Whether precautionary sentences should sometimes be semi-mandatory or not, I hope that Chapter 10 has shown convincingly that they should be prohibited for all but a minority of offenders. This prohibition, however, could be effective only if the maxima for corrective custody were substantially less than the norm for precautionary custody, since otherwise courts can use custody ambiguously.

General prohibitions apart, should penal agents or administrators be allowed to prevent courts from using a measure in individual cases? At present, this can happen only in rather special ways. A court can be prevented from making either a psychiatric probation order or a hospital order if no psychiatrist is willing to say that the offender's mental condition justifies this, or even if the necessary evidence is given but no psychiatrist, clinic or hospital is willing to take the offender as a patient. The situation in which an offender is diagnosed as needing psychiatric treat-

2. The First Offenders Act, 1958. They may imprison the 'first offender' (as there defined) if they state reasons for their opinion that no other measure is 'appropriate'; and the 'gravity' of the offence seems to be a sufficient reason: see *Vassall* v. *Harris* [1964] *Criminal Law Review*, 322.

ment or care but cannot get it is usually due to an administrative shortcoming, such as the scarcity of units which accept psychopathic or adolescent patients; and there have been analogous administrative situations in the penal system proper. Because of the time which it took to provide detention centres for males, it was not until recently that every court in England was able to make a detention centre order more or less whenever it wanted to.

What is of considerably more importance is the question whether a penal agent, like a psychiatrist, should be able to say to a court 'I am afraid that this offender does not seem to me a suitable case for the sort of measure which I have to carry out', with the result that the court could not order that measure. So far as adults are concerned, there is only one sort of penal agent at present in whose case this should be seriously considered: the probation officer. Should he be able, in effect, to prohibit probation in individual cases? His position is much the same as that of the psychiatrist. His training and experience are meant to qualify him not only to treat offenders but also to make the preliminary investigations which are supposed to tell him whether they are likely to respond to treatment. Like the psychiatrist he may or may not be the person who will have to be responsible for the offender during treatment.

Those who find the idea of giving a veto to a probation officer too startling will argue that there are all-important differences. The psychiatrist is allowed to veto a measure which would remove the offender totally from the penal system[3] whereas a probation officer would be vetoing one of a set of measures which are within the penal system, and would thus be limiting the court's freedom of choice: if probation proves a mistaken choice he can always bring the offender back to court, whereas the psychiatrist cannot. The distinction can be granted for the sake of argument, although it is valid only so far as hospital orders are concerned, and not where psychiatric probation orders are involved.

The fact, however, that the analogy is not exact does not mean that the idea should not be considered on its merits. The similarity is close enough to show that a veto by a professionally trained penal agent is not unthinkable. The reason why it has not so far been considered is historical: probation officers, penal

3. A point which will be discussed in Chapter 12, where the relationship between psychiatric and penal measures is more fully examined.

administrators and penal reformers were anxious that courts should make *more* use of probation, and the possibility of its being over-used did not seem important. Indeed, it is only those who are worried about the overloading of the service, or who reason as I have done in Chapter 7, who find it worth concern.

If the suggestion is considered on its own merits, the soundest argument against it would be that the probation officer who vetoes probation would too often be wrong. What is the evidence on this point? In the Cornish sample mentioned on pages 80–81 n., the 336 reports by probation officers to Quarter Sessions can be sub-divided as in Table 4.

TABLE 4

Cases in which	Cases in which the probation officers' report		
	(i) was in favour of probation	(ii) was against probation	(iii) made no specific recommendation
a probation order was made	137	135	64
	97	18	16
probation was *not* successful	19	9	0

The criterion for success or failure was simply a further finding of guilt while on probation, and was thus not ideal for our purpose. It would have been better if it had been a further finding of guilt while on probation *or during a subsequent follow-up period*. Nor are we told explicitly whether the recommendations against probation were always made because the officers believed that probation would not keep the offender out of trouble, and never because they thought that he would go straight without supervision (in which case a 'success' would not have proved them wrong). We can therefore say only that these officers were right *at least* half the time. Nevertheless, the high success rate for the rest of the sample shows that the probability of their being right as often as this by pure chance was very low.[4]

What would worry most sentencers, however, would be the cases in which, notwithstanding the probation officer's recommendation against probation, the probationer had after all kept

4. Less than one in 100.

out of trouble while on probation. The sentencer would point out that if the court had been forced to accept the probation officer's advice a mistake would have been made. On the face of it, this is a strong argument, especially if it is assumed that the result of a veto on probation would have been an unnecessary prison sentence.[5]

It is not a complete answer to this argument to point out that if probation officers knew that this would be the result of their veto they would exercise it more sparingly, and presumably with fewer 'mistakes'. For the essence of the argument is that, unless we can assume that the veto would never be mistaken (a quite unrealistic assumption), its effect would be to increase, however slightly, the number of unnecessary custodial sentences. By allowing the courts to exercise discretion in such cases the number of unnecessary prison sentences is slightly reduced. Put in this way, however, the argument is subtly fallacious; for it assumes that it is only the courts' discretion which can reduce the number of unnecessary imprisonments in this way. This is very unlikely, for it implies either that courts have information which probation officers have not or that they are better at using the same information predictively – neither of which is at all plausible. In all probability, the same reduction in unnecessary imprisonments would have been achieved by randomly disregarding the probation officers' advice in the same number of cases. But since their advice does seem to be right oftener than it should be by chance, it would be more sensible to allow the reduction to be made by getting a 'second opinion' not from sentencers but from another probation officer.

In short, there seems to be a strong, though not overwhelming, case for allowing probation officers to veto probation, especially if the veto is endorsed by two officers (one of whom might well be required to be of senior rank, in order to guard against the possibility of a veto by two young and inexperienced colleagues).

APPEALS

Another form of control over courts is the appeal against sentence, which was briefly mentioned in Chapter 8. This not only allows individual sentences to be altered, but also means that sentencers' policies are affected by what they believe to be

5. This is probably a fair assumption; it is not easy to imagine circumstances in which a nominal or financial measure would probably be successful and yet a probation officer is likely to advise against probation.

the views of the appellate court. In England, however, the value of this institution is limited by at least two of its features.

One is the fact that only the sentenced offender can appeal against his sentence, and if his sentence is altered as a result the alteration can only be in his favour. The prosecution cannot appeal against a sentence which seems to it inadequate to correct the offender, deter potential imitators or to protect the public. Nor can the victim: Mrs Simcox had no opportunity of arguing before a judicial body that the risk which the judge was willing to accept was not one which *she* should be asked to take.

The one-sided nature of our system of appeal against sentence is another of our historical accidents, although like so many of them it has since been white-washed. It was created by a piece of legislation (the Criminal Appeal Act, 1907) which was prompted by the scandal of Adolf Beck's conviction and imprisonment on very questionable evidence of identification. The Act was therefore almost wholly designed for the protection of the accused, and the provisions allowing him to appeal against sentence were simply an extension of those allowing him to appeal against conviction. It is true that the appellate court was given power to increase as well as lighten his sentence, but only if *he* appealed against it, and the only object was to deter offenders from overloading the court by too many appeals of this sort! Consequently no power was conferred on anyone to appeal against a sentence which seemed too lenient. By the 1960s, however, it had become doubtful whether the power to increase sentence was in fact discouraging hopeless appeals, since the Court of Criminal Appeal felt obliged to grant legal aid when it was contemplating an increase of sentence, and with this plain warning the appellant would usually abandon his appeal.

The Donovan Committee, whose report in 1965 led to changes in the constitution and powers of the Court of Criminal Appeal, discussed this provision rather superficially. They conceded that if 'justice' required the reduction of a manifestly excessive sentence, it also required the increase of a manifestly inadequate one:

... if the doing of justice is the principal reason for the power, then it would seem that the prosecution ought to be able to bring before the Court cases where, in his view, the sentence was so inadequate that justice had not been done.

So far so good. Substitute 'rationality' or some such word for 'justice' and a reductivist would applaud their reasoning. But the

Committee were in fact heading in quite the opposite direction. To introduce such a provision would be a 'complete departure from our tradition that the prosecutor takes no part, or the minimum part, in the sentencing process'. And since the power to increase sentence was no longer – for purely procedural reasons – effective as a deterrent, they recommended its abolition. In effect they were saying 'This does not work as it was meant to. It could be made into a more effective and "just" institution by giving the prosecutor a right of appeal. But that would be contrary to tradition. So let us give up the idea altogether.' Their recommendation was accepted.

Consequently our system of appeals against sentences is almost wholly one-sided, and can be operated only by the offender and only in his interest.[6] It may be argued that in practice the judiciary seldom err on the side of leniency, so that in practice there would be few cases in which the prosecution would think it worth while to appeal. It is not difficult, however, to produce examples of sentences which would almost certainly have been the subject of a successful appeal by the prosecutor. One is that of Simcox.

THE REASONED SENTENCE

Another factor which reduces the effectiveness of any system of appeal against sentences is what Stephen (1874) called their 'ambiguity': the fact that most forms of sentence can be justified – if one is prepared to accept a little special pleading or looseness of reasoning – on retributive, deterrent, corrective or denunciatory grounds. Often, of course, the pronouncement of the sentence is accompanied by a statement or homily from the sentencer which explains, intentionally or inadvertently, the reasoning by which he arrived at his decision. Quite often, however, it is not; and in such cases the appellant and the appellate court must fall back on assumptions and speculations.

There seems therefore to be a strong case for requiring sentencers to state reasons for their choices: a case which has already been ably argued by Mr D. A. Thomas (1963). His proposal, however, is that *every* sentence should be accompanied by a

6. It is worth noting, however, that if quarter sessions are hearing an appeal from an accused person against a conviction or sentence in a magistrates' court, they are still permitted to increase the severity of the sentence (because they are retrying the case); and this power is occasionally used.

reasoned justification, and this raises difficulties unless one is prepared to accept a very simple justification in the great majority of cases.

For in most cases the justification – if the sentencer is honest – can only be that the sentence is in accordance with some norm. The norm may be based on retributive or (preferably) reductive assumptions. Sometimes it has been expressly agreed upon. Quite a number of magistrates' benches have drawn up a table of fines for motoring offences. Sometimes there is a looser consensus, so that the Court of Appeal's Criminal Division is able to say '*x* years is not excessive for . . .'. Whatever form it takes, a sentencer must have *some* norm in mind for the *majority* of his sentences. Consequently the justification for each of these sentences must be the general justification for the norm. It is only the departure from the norm that calls for and is capable of a justification which is based on consideration of the individual case.

The most cogent argument for requiring sentencers to state a reasoned justification for their sentences is that when this is done appeals against sentence become more rational transactions.[7] Both the appellant and the appellate court have some foundation on which to build their arguments. A modified form of Mr Thomas's proposal – that sentencers should be required either to say that their sentence is a normal one[8] or to justify its abnormality – would achieve this objective, without forcing sentencers to devise artificial justifications for every one of their sentences.

It is worth adding that neither the right of appeal by the prosecution nor the obligation to justify sentence are by any means unheard of. The former is commoner than the latter; but at least one country has incorporated both into its criminal law. This is Norway, where the result is that about 10 per cent of sentences are the subject of appeal, the prosecution being responsible for about a quarter of this number.[9] There is therefore little ground for fearing that these innovations would produce an enormous increase in the volume of appeals in this

7. Mr Thomas (1963) gives some good examples to show that this is so. His other arguments are less convincing, at least to a reductivist.

8. In which case of course the appellate court could be asked either to declare that the sentence was not, or should not be, normal or to say that there was a case for an abnormal sentence.

9. I am greatly indebted to Professor Johannes Andenaes of Oslo University for providing me with these estimates, based on a study of the year 1959.

country. In 1967 the English Court of Appeals received 5,189 applications for leave to appeal against sentence[10], which represented 14 per cent of sentences imposed at higher courts[11]; but only 400 of these applications were judged worthy of a hearing. If we assume from Norwegian experience that appeals by the prosecution would add about one third to this 400, the increase in the volume would not be totally unacceptable. In fact, since Norwegian sentences seem to be much more lenient than ours, English prosecuting authorities would probably appeal against a smaller percentage of sentences than their Norwegian counterparts. In Norway the 'success rate' of appeals by the prosecution seems to be about 70 per cent, which suggests that the prosecution chooses such cases with care but also that the appellate court does not automatically accept the prosecution's point of view. A transcript of a judgement by the Norwegian Supreme Court in 1962 which illustrates the conscientiousness with which the trial judges' reasons and the prosecution's arguments are examined will be found in Appendix C.

A SENTENCING AUTHORITY

Finally, it is time to consider the most radical proposal of all: that the task of sentencing should be transferred from the people who preside over the trial of guilt to some other kind of body, composed of people with special expertise of various kinds.

To suggest that no sentences should be passed by the courts which convict offenders would of course be quite impractical. If all the trivial cases of illegal parking, bad driving, non-payment of radio and television licences and so on had to be remitted for sentence to a special authority, the cost of the penal system would be enormously increased, without any appreciable increase in the effectiveness of the resulting decisions. For in most of these cases the sentencing authority would decide to do just what the magistrates do: to fine the offender. It might take more care in deciding the exact amount of the fine, and might slightly reduce in this way the numbers of offenders against whom action had to be taken for non-payment; but this would not necessarily reduce their chances of reconviction. The gain (if any) would not justify the expense of time and trouble.

A realistic question, however, is whether there are definable

10. Including applications for leave to appeal against conviction as well.
11. It is uncommon for a sentence imposed by a summary court to reach the Court of Appeal.

categories of offenders or offences which would benefit from being remitted to a sentencing authority without being too numerous for its resources, or, more precisely, for the resources which could reasonably be allotted to it.

Before this can be answered, we must consider the ways in which the decisions of a sentencing authority might be better than those of courts. Obviously, for example, it would be possible to ensure – by the selection of its members and in other ways – that its reasoning was less retributive. This would make it more suitable to deal with offenders whose crimes arouse strong emotions, for it is clear that some very long prison sentences – such as the forty-two years imposed on Blake the spy – were at least partly retributive in their aim. Such sentences could, of course, be remedied if we had an appellate court which had committed itself against retributive sentencing and if we also had a system obliging sentencers to declare their reasons for very severe sentences; but at present we have neither.

The hope, however, which has inspired most proposals for a sentencing authority is that its decisions would be more often right from the corrective point of view, and that it would be better able to review and alter them in the light of the offender's progress. The second of these objectives is easier to be sure of than the first. There is no doubt that a sentencing authority could be created which would be more efficiently organized than courts are to keep offenders' progress under review, more likely to ask the right questions of penal agents, and better at evaluating their answers.

A more difficult question to answer is whether, from the corrective point of view, their initial choices would be right much more often. Given the present rather limited range of measures for adult offenders, and given courts which pay a reasonable amount of attention to social inquiry reports and penal histories, it is not easy to be sure that this would be so. Unless one believes that a substantial percentage of the offenders with whom they could be asked to deal consists of those who will respond only to one or two measures, and that these can be selected *diagnostically*, one cannot be confident that a sentencing authority would do very much better than courts; and Chapters 7 and 8 must have undermined these beliefs to some extent.

What could be claimed with more confidence is that a sentencing authority's choices, without being right *less* often, would probably be more *economical* and *humane*, as would happen, for example, if they adopted a strategic approach of the kind suggested in Chapter 8.

It is true that this might weaken the general deterrent function of the sentencing system, at least so far as knowledgeable and deterrible offenders were concerned. This would be so, however, only if the sentencing authority had the reputation of being more lenient than the courts, and if it dealt with ordinary thieves, house-breakers and wage-snatchers. Whether it would in fact impose less drastic sentences in such cases is not certain. This would depend partly on the outlook of its members, partly on the reasoning underlying its policy. If it adopted the sort of reasoning outlined in earlier chapters of this book its sentences would not be noticeably less drastic than those of the mass of quarter sessions, and would certainly be more uniform and less liable to the unpredictable acts of exceptional leniency which (I have suggested) encourage optimism in the experienced offender.

In any case, the proposal to confine the sentencing authority to special categories would rule out such offenders. There would be little point in burdening the authority with a large number of cases for which there is at present no real alternative to imprisonment. This observation suggests, however, at least two categories which it *would* be sensible to refer to a sentencing authority:

(A) *Offenders who*

(i) *have failed to respond to the normal sequence of penal measures – financial, supervisory and custodial; and*

(ii) *appear on investigation to be suffering from some form of mental disorder or abnormality, although not such that they are thought likely to benefit from ordinary psychiatric treatment or care.*

An example would be what is sometimes called the 'passive inadequate offender', so vividly described by Dr D. J. West (1963):

Both [the passive inadequate and the active-aggressive deviant] have in common a generalised instability, a failure to cope with ordinary frustrations, but whereas the aggressives respond by hitting back at the environment the inadequates tend to collapse into passive resistance and querulous dependency. Inadequates tend to be typically feckless people, grossly lacking in drive and initiative. They are always complaining and demanding help from authorities, without exerting any effort themselves. They tend to form one-sided, parasitic relationships with whoever will put up with them. They never seem able to fend for themselves. Their spinelessness and sloth suggest that they have found social demands too much for them, and have contracted out of the system altogether, so that they no longer bother to try to do the things expected of a normal citizen. . . .

Prison staffs and probation officers are familiar with this sort of petty offender, who seldom responds to either form of corrective, but whose offences are not usually so harmful as to justify a precautionary sentence (although quite often an exasperated court will impose one).

(B) *The offender for whom some new type of measure seems to offer some prospect of success.*

In other words, the case in which there is a genuine choice to be made between accepted measures and some new alternative. A defect of our present system which has already been mentioned (pages 116–17) is that it makes it as difficult as possible to experiment with a new penal idea before legalizing it, but that if legalized it is then open to courts throughout the country. The existence of a sentencing authority with the function of testing new measures would make it possible to legalize these measures for use only by that authority until such time as it had reported their merits and difficulties. This would, for example, be the sensible way to introduce semi-detention.

A sentencing authority might even be given power to test not only new measures specified in legislation (or by the Home Secretary) but also measures of its own devising. If this seems to open the door too wide to inhumane experimentation, it would be easy to define limits: for instance, to prohibit corporal punishment and surgical or pharmacological techniques to which the offender's consent had not been freely given.

Another category which might be remanded to a sentencing authority is

(C) *The offender who seems to a court to require a precautionary sentence.*

This proposal could take several forms. In its extreme form it would completely transfer the power to impose precautionary sentences, leaving courts with nothing but the negative power to refrain from remanding the offender to the sentencing authority and to content themselves with shorter periods of custody of a corrective nature. In a less radical form it would allow courts to impose precautionary sentences where they felt certain that they were justified, but would permit them to remand doubtful cases. Neither form would be inconsistent with semi-mandatory precautionary sentences for some offenders (on the lines suggested earlier); but those who dislike that proposal might be prepared to accept precautionary sentencing by a body with more expertise than could be expected of a single sentencer. From the point of view of simplicity, flexibility and safety the best system would be one which

i. debarred criminal courts from imposing precautionary sentences (and any other custodial sentence of greater length than the standard periods suggested in Chapter 9); but

ii. permitted them to remit to the sentencing authority any offender for whom they considered a precautionary sentence advisable; and

iii. obliged them to remit to the authority any offender who on two or more separate occasions had been convicted of an offence which carried a serious risk of inflicting irremediable harm (such as those listed earlier in this chapter); but

iv. allowed the sentencing authority either to impose an indeterminate precautionary sentence or in exceptional circumstances to choose some other form of sentence, provided that in the latter event they stated a reasoned case for their choice.

There are many subsidiary issues which would have to be decided before a sentencing authority could be set up. Its membership is important, and should include not only experienced penal agents and psychiatrists but also representatives of the judiciary and the police, to make sure that it keeps in mind the non-corrective aspects of law-enforcement. There should be some way in which the offender could put his point of view to it, both in writing and in person; this might mean a system of local 'hearings'. Its decisions in individual cases should presumably be subject to appeal by the offender – if not the prosecution – to an appellate court: for although an unsympathetic Court of Appeal could do a good deal to sabotage the work of a sentencing authority it seems advisable to have this safeguard.

None of these issues is unimportant; but they are subsidiary. What is being discussed here is the central question: 'What tasks could be given to a sentencing authority with a reasonable expectation that it could perform them better than the courts?' My list of three such tasks is perhaps rather crudely defined, and certainly not exhaustive; but I hope that it illustrates how such an authority might function usefully without usurping the normal sentencing functions of courts.

Radical as it may sound, this chapter in fact repudiates two extreme approaches to the control of sentencing. One of these is based on the assertion that sentencing is an 'art', which seems to mean not that its products have aesthetic merit but merely that it is an incommunicable skill. On this view, sentencers, like other craftsmen, should be allowed a free hand, within wide limits of economy or humanity or retributive justice. The philosophy of individualization, whose shortcomings were discussed in Chapters 7, 8 and 9, lends itself to this view. At the other extreme is the belief that sentencing can be reduced to a set of rules – admittedly complex – which would choose penal measures more effectively than human sentencers. This approach has more in common with the first extreme than appears at first sight. Both seem to be based on a fallacious medical analogy which assumes that sentencing must be a process in which diagnosis is followed by choice of remedy. Indeed it is in the field of physical medicine that we seem to be within sight of diagnosis by computer. No doubt 'computerization' would be of help in some areas of sentencing, such as fixing the amount of fines. But if, as was suggested in Chapter 8, the strategic approach is sounder than the diagnostic, the rules for deciding between measures become rather simple, and the difficult task becomes the detection of cases in which exceptions should be made.

Exceptions are – or at least should be – exceptional: considerably less frequent, that is, than the case which is dealt with according to rule. They also tend to be heterogeneous. These two characteristics are drawbacks from the computer's point of view. No doubt over a considerable period of time it could amass data from enough instances of each sort of exception to give its advice or predictions some value; but the longer the time over which the data have to be collected the more likelihood there is of changes in social conditions or the penal system itself which will invalidate the advice or prediction (as has happened for example with the Mannheim-Wilkins formula for predicting the reconviction of borstal boys).

If we reject both these extremes, the problem is, and will continue to be, how to design a sentencing system that will on the one hand make it difficult for sentencers to choose irrationally without on the other hand making it impossible for them to cater for really exceptional circumstances. The solution I have suggested is to remit certain sentencing functions to a body of highly selected sentencers; but so far as everyday sentencing is concerned to develop several safety-devices which have already been invented, if not fully used: the semi-mandatory sentence, the advisers' veto, the reasoned departure from the norm, and the two-way appeal.

Chapter 12

Mitigation and Exemption

A feature of all penal systems is that they treat certain characteristics of offenders or their offences as reasons for modifying the penalty or exempting the offender from all penal measures. Fines are suited to the offender's means; old men may receive shorter prison sentences; mothers with many convictions but young families are often excused imprisonment altogether; sentences are sometimes lightened for men with good war records and motorists who suffer for their own carelessness. Children under a certain age are declared incapable of being found guilty. Provocation is a defence to a charge of murder.

Usually the reasoning which underlies these and similar practices is retributive. The careless motorist is said to have been 'punished enough' by his wife's death, or by his own injuries. The logic of this reasoning is questionable, since punishment in a retributive sense is something which is deliberate, not accidental, and is adjusted to the moral gravity of the offence. Nevertheless, with all its weaknesses the reasoning is essentially retributive. More logically retributive, perhaps, is the exemption of very young children on the ground that they could not have acted with a criminal intention, or the shortening of an old man's prison sentence on the ground that it would otherwise occupy too much of his remaining span of life.

Sometimes the sentencer's reasoning can only be described as sentimental or superstitious. During and immediately after wars, offenders who have taken active parts in battles – and especially those who have been wounded – can often expect lighter sentences from judges or magistrates who seem to be trying to express their country's gratitude. The judge who put Simcox on probation[1] seems to have been influenced by the length of time which he had already spent in prison: certainly it is difficult to

1. See page 150.

think of a logical justification, whether retributive or reductive, for his decision.

An example of superstitious exemption was the medieval institution of sanctuary, which protected criminals who could reach certain consecrated places before their pursuers could seize them. As for another medieval practice, the selling of pardons – sometimes in advance – it is difficult to categorize this by any other label than 'expediency'. Modern parallels are not easy to find; but the immunity allowed to diplomatic staff in foreign countries, or the exchange of imprisoned spies, seem to be examples of expediency at work.

Many examples, however, which are retributive, sentimental or superstitious in origin can be justified on reductive grounds. The careless motorist who has seriously injured himself or one of his family is likely to be so impressed with this experience that the imposition of a corrective is unnecessary: and the fact that in a few unpredictable cases this is not so does not weaken the argument, since they can seldom be identified in advance. An ageing offender is much less likely to commit troublesome offences than a younger one. Imprisoning the mother of young children will result in some very undesirable side-effects (unless, as is sometimes the case, she is such an unsatisfactory mother that her family ought in any case to be looked after by others). The man who is provoked to violence is less likely to repeat it than the man who commits an assault in cold blood.

The main purpose of this chapter and the next, however, is to discuss the rationality, from the point of view of a reductivist, of the way in which civilized penal systems deal with the two most important examples of mitigation and exemption, the immature and the mentally disordered offender.

In many ways our approach to both categories is similar. Extreme cases – the very young child or the very disordered adult – are excused even from conviction, a practice which is traceable to Roman law, but which has survived and become firmly established because of its retributive appeal. For the actions of the very young and the very disordered are regarded as lacking in one or other of the necessary conditions of culpability, such as ability to tell right from wrong or awareness of the natural consequences of one's act. At the other extreme, an offender's 'youth' (even if he is officially an adult) or a moderate degree of mental disorder may persuade a court to modify its sentence, although they are not regarded as grounds for excusing the offender altogether. There are also intermediate cases. For the offender who is between the minimum age for official proceedings and the age at which he is, for the purposes of the criminal law, an adult, or who is disordered enough to be regarded as a case for treatment, though not enough to be excused conviction, there are special procedures by which he is subjected to measures designed for his age-group or mental condition.

NON-PENAL MEASURES

In both cases, too, we are apt to assume that these measures are not part of the penal system. In England offenders who are sufficiently disordered in mind to be excused conviction or to be committed to mental hospitals become the responsibility of the National Health Service. Most of them go to ordinary mental hospitals. Even the special hospitals which are reserved for dangerous patients accept men and women who have not been accused of crimes. Moreover, the decision to release the patient is a matter for his psychiatrist, unless the court has expressly subjected the offender to the requirement that the Home Secretary's agreement must be obtained before he can be set free. Only the offender who receives psychiatric treatment while on probation or in prison is regarded as within the penal system.

A similar distinction is in process of being established where young offenders are concerned. Not only are those below a certain age immune from any criminal charge: the intermediate age-group which has been mentioned is also dealt with by procedures which are becoming more and more foreign to the criminal law as it is applied to adults, and by measures which are supposed to be different in kind from the sentences imposed on adults. In some countries offenders in this age-group are not 'tried' in the adult sense (although the public prosecutor has the right to insist on trial if the offence is very harmful). If they are subjected to official correctives these are administered by special authorities, often those responsible for the welfare of the young in general; and the correctives themselves are less deterrent and more reformative in their conception, often to the extent of being labelled measures of 're-education'.

The corollary is that the types of measure which are peculiar to penal systems are diminishing in number and importance. Capital punishment is becoming rare, and so is corporal punishment (which in Britain is now permissible only for enforcing discipline in certain institutions for delinquent boys). Secure custody is considered necessary not only for some offenders but also for some of the mentally disordered, although in both cases for decreasing percentages. Supervision of one kind or another is applied not only to probationers and ex-prisoners but also to unprosecuted juveniles and discharged mental patients. The only measure of numerical importance which is peculiarly penal is the fine.

This being so, an interesting question arises. We seem to draw two distinctions: one between people who have and people who have not been identified as offenders by the operation of the criminal law, and another between measures which are and measures which are not part of the penal system, with the result that offenders may be dealt with in any of three ways:

(i) some are dealt with non-penally without being officially identified as offenders in the eyes of the law[2];

(ii) some are officially identified as offenders, but handed over to non-penal agencies to be dealt with;

(iii) some are not only identified officially as offenders but are dealt with by penal agencies.

And all these groups include offenders who need special treatment or care because of their immaturity or their mental disorder.

Is this tripartite division unnecessarily complicated? Obviously the distinction between those who have and those who have not been officially identified as offenders is inevitable, and we must continue to rely on non-penal agencies to deal with the latter. Sometimes, indeed, it is only as a result of the offender's becoming a patient at a clinic or hospital, or being taken into care by a children's department, that he is found to be an offender: a situation which creates an awkward problem in professional ethics for doctors or social workers if his offences are very harmful.

But is the distinction between the other two groups really useful? Why should we not simply redefine the penal system so as to include any measure that can be provided for an offender by the order of a criminal court? Or would this tidiness sweep away something of value?

It would be naïve and out-of-date to argue that what we now call penal measures cannot provide the sort of treatment or care that is needed by immature or mentally disordered offenders.

2. Although they may be unofficially identified in the eyes of agencies of law enforcement, such as the police.

For example, prisons can and do provide psychiatric treatment. They may do so less often and less well than they should, but that is a defect which can be put right. As for the argument that 'a prison cannot be a hospital', this is a cliché which rests on no evidence. Again, custodial measures *can* be modified to meet the needs of juveniles, although those which are run by penal agencies attract more criticisms (rightly or wrongly) than those which are not.

A more fundamental argument for preserving the distinction is that what we now label as non-penal measures are designed primarily for non-offenders, and their agents (whether psychiatrists, social workers or institutional staff) are trained to think not merely of the anti-social behaviour of the people in their charge but of their other failings, and indeed of their welfare in general. It is true that this is a description of non-penal agencies as they are supposed to be rather than as all of them are; and it is also true that it is the aim of progressive penal agencies, and in particular of probation departments, to approach offenders in the same way. Moreover, people with whom psychiatrists, social workers and welfare institutions have to deal include a substantial number who have committed offences without being legally identified as offenders, and their behaviour in hospitals, hostels and other residential establishments often presents exactly the same problems as the behaviour of identified offenders. Yet no matter how closely penal agents model their objectives on those of non-penal agencies, and no matter how often non-penal agents are forced to adopt the security and discipline of penal agents, the fact will remain that the primary function of the latter is the reduction of law-breaking, and that the primary functions of non-penal agencies are different.

Unless, therefore, we are prepared to argue that there should be no difference between the aims and functions of penal systems and those of other social agencies, there is some practical point in distinguishing between offenders who are to receive special treatment or care within the penal system and those who are to receive this from non-penal agencies.

This does not tell us, of course, how to draw the distinction in practice. What sort of juvenile or mentally disordered offenders should be handed over to penal agencies for special treatment or care, and what sort to non-penal agencies? Although there is no obvious principle by which this should be decided, the distinction between offenders who do irremediable harm and others

seems to provide a sound basis. On the assumption that it is
these offenders against whom society needs protection – at least
until they can be said to have been successfully treated – the
provision of secure custody during treatment is important. It is
noticeable that secure custody is something which progressive
non-penal agencies both dislike and are inefficient at providing.
No doubt this is an inevitable consequence of their functions
and outlook, just as it seems inevitable that they should be less
concerned than penal agencies with the precise nature and seriousness of the offender's conduct. These are not necessarily characteristics which we should condemn: they may be inseparable
from effective treatment of the sort which the agencies provide.
If they are to be accepted, however, it follows that non-penal
agencies should seldom if ever[3] be entrusted with offenders who
are likely to do irremediable harm while under treatment.

EXEMPTION

What has not yet been discussed properly is a fourth group:
  (iv) persons who are officially identified as offenders but whom
    the criminal law regards as wholly excusable because of their
    immaturity or their disordered state of mind at the time of the
    offence.

English examples are the under-age child who commits what
in the case of an adult would be a theft, or the motorist who
disobeys traffic lights while in a state of automatism – as a
result say, of an epileptic fit. Both must by law be acquitted,
and the court cannot impose any penalty or other measure on
them.

---

3. I say 'seldom if ever' because it will be argued that there are dangerous
offenders who will respond only to treatment of a kind that cannot be given
in any penal institution, and not simply because the treatment is inconsistent
with the function and outlook of a penal institution. It is said, for example,
that there are offenders whose anti-authoritarian personalities prevent them
from responding to even the most tolerant of prison regimes. This is not
hard to believe. What needs proof, if their offences do irremediable harm,
is that they can be treated in non-secure conditions without a grave risk to the
community. When this can be demonstrated there will be a case for making
an exception to the rule. Until then, it seems necessary for the humanitarian
to swallow the unpalatable fact that, while there are a few offenders who
could perhaps be successfully treated by non-penal agencies, we are unable,
in our present state of knowledge, either to select them or to treat them without too much risk of further irreparable harm. The most that the humanitarian can justifiably insist upon is that the conditions of their custody
should be made as tolerable as possible.

The traditional justification for these exemptions is essentially retributive. The under-age child must not be found guilty because he is presumed incapable of knowing right from wrong (although nowadays the minimum age is so high that this presumption is highly artificial). The epileptic motorist must not be convicted because he could not help the collision.

The reductivist is bound to question this moralistic justification, and indeed the wisdom of having a completely exempted category at all. For his main concern is not to apportion blame but to prevent an identified offender from repeating his offence. Other things being equal, an under-age child who steals is more likely to steal in the future than one who has not so far stolen. A motorist who has an epileptic fit at the wheel may well have another. If all parents of under-age children were conscientious, upright and articulate, they could be relied on to correct their own child once they knew that he had stolen: but unfortunately some cannot. If all epileptic motorists were public-spirited they would voluntarily give up driving, or take their prescribed drugs regularly; but unfortunately some do not.

In fact, long experience of the dangers of complete exemption has led us to limit it as much as possible. If the child can be shown to have parents who are not bringing him up properly the court is allowed to subject him to the supervision and control of a social agency, such as a children's department. For persons whose offences are the result of their mental disorder all penal systems have special verdicts which exempt from ordinary penalties but allow, or even enjoin, committal to a mental hospital.

In Britain the increasing numbers of offenders who are recognized as disordered by the medical profession, but are not excusable under the restrictive rules of the law, have created a more or less utilitarian procedure whereby these offenders are found guilty by the court but are then disposed of by hospital orders or probation orders with a requirement of psychiatric treatment. Special verdicts are confined to higher courts, and even there are almost obsolete. Acquittals on the grounds of automatism are disliked and avoided wherever possible by courts, who prefer to convict and discharge on the understanding that the offender will undergo treatment, or take some other precaution.

From the reductivist's point of view this is a rational development. The total exemption of the insane from conviction belongs to a period in which the consequences of conviction were death or transportation. It began to be out-of-date as soon as society recognized the need to confine the dangerously insane whether or not they had been convicted.[4] Nowadays, when even the most open and permissive of mental hospitals accept convicted offenders, and when even the most secure accept unconvicted patients, the consequences of incurring or escaping conviction are less easy to distinguish. It is arguable that a schizophrenic offender should be spared the stigma of being found guilty; but this argument overlooks the stigma of being labelled schizophrenic and committed to a mental hospital, which in some social classes is greater than that of being labelled a thief and committed to prison.

But if the practical consequences of compulsory committal are more or less the same whether it is the result of a trial or simply of intervention by relatives and doctors, this raises the question 'Why bother to try the obviously disordered offender?' In fact we know that quite a number of persons who have been responsible for thefts, assaults and other offences are simply admitted direct to hospital, with or without their consent. (See, for example, Rollin, 1969.) Is this not a perfectly good way of disposing of them?

The answer is 'No', at least so far as patients who do serious harm are concerned. For the ordinary mental hospital which does not specialize in handling offenders is apt to lose sight of the harm which they do when they are outside. In particular, its records are often vague about the incidents which led to admission. The central index of patients is designed for statistical purposes, and not to provide psychiatrists with accurate or comprehensive case-histories. In this respect at least police records are superior. In England it is possible for authorized people to obtain from the Criminal Record Office a list of a patient's serious convictions. So far as really harmful behaviour is concerned, therefore, there is some point in a trial which results in a record of what the patient has done.

In this chapter I have dealt with what might be called the general theory of exemption, including the relationship of penal to non-penal agencies so far as offenders are concerned. I have also considered one of the main categories to which all penal systems accord a special position – the mentally disordered. Because it so obviously requires special measures, and because the medieval practice of according to it complete exemption is so obviously out-of-date, we have been driven further along

4. For the history of this subject, see Walker (1968).

the road to complete reductivism where it is concerned than we have in the case of the other main category, the young offender. This presents a more complex problem, with which the next chapter will deal.

Chapter 13

The Young Offender

So far as young offenders are concerned, penal systems fall into three groups:

(A) *Medieval systems.* In these, only children who have committed an offence can be made the subject of compulsory measures, and all these measures are penal. Usually, too, they are drastic, so that there is a strong incentive to find reasons for exempting children from them, in which case there is no alternative way of dealing with the children.

Modern systems, in contrast, recognize two sorts of reason for dealing compulsorily with children:

(i) that they have committed offences; or

(ii) that they are being brought up in a way which makes them likely to become criminal or anti-social in other ways (e.g., by begetting illegitimate children);

and such systems allow a choice between measures which involve penal agencies (although the measures are usually less drastic than their adult counterparts) and measures which are applied by non-penal agencies.

They fall however into two main groups:

(B) Those with a low minimum age of criminal liability (seven, eight, nine, or ten). In these, under-age children can be compulsorily dealt with only if it is clear that their upbringing is unsatisfactory, and not merely because they have committed an offence. Over-age children can be dealt with on either ground, up to the age at which they officially become adults (although even after that age measures such as imprisonment may be modified for certain age-groups, as in the borstal system). If dealt with for an offence, they are tried and 'found guilty'; otherwise the proceedings are 'non-criminal'.

Common-law systems are usually of this kind, although the tendency to raise the minimum age has meant that in many parts of the Commonwealth and the U.S.A. they approximate to type C:

(C) In these, the minimum age is high (usually fourteen, fifteen, or sixteen). Under-age children cannot normally be the subject of criminal proceedings[1], but can be the subject of non-criminal proceedings, *either* on the ground that their up-bringing has been unsatisfactory, *or* on the ground that they have committed offences. The measures which can be applied to them are in theory non-penal, and are applied by non-penal agencies, but include custody and other quasi-penal measures. Children over the minimum age are usually regarded as adults for penal purposes, although as in systems of type B penal measures may be modified in their application to younger age-groups.

Continental systems are of this type, and Scotland has just replaced a system of type B with one of type C.

In England, after a bold but unpopular attempt to substitute 'family councils' for juvenile courts, the Labour Government has now introduced a system in which

(i) children under ten will be subject only to non-criminal proceedings on grounds other than the commission of an offence – that is, broadly speaking, unsatisfactory parental care;

(ii) children between their tenth and fourteenth birthdays will be subject only to non-criminal proceedings, for which the commission of an offence can be the occasion, but must be associated with unsatisfactory parental care;

(iii) young persons between their fourteenth and seventeenth birthdays will be liable either to non-criminal proceedings on the same grounds as (ii), or to prosecution for an offence, provided that the prosecution is authorized by a magistrate, who must have regard to a number of prescribed consider-ations;

(iv) persons over seventeen will be liable only to criminal prosecution, although as before there will be special restrictions on the sentences which criminal courts can impose on those under twenty-one.

To the extent that the minimum age for criminal prosecution will henceforth be fourteen, and that the commission of an

---

1. Although in most systems of this type (including the English and Scots version) the public prosecutor has the right to insist on criminal proceedings if a child over the traditional age of criminal liability is suspected of a very grave offence, such as murder.

offence under that age is not by itself sufficient grounds for any sort of court proceedings, this is a system of type C.

THE AGE OF 'CRIMINAL INDEPENDENCE'

The modern preference for systems with high minimum ages needs a close and critical examination. It is sometimes based on the traditional assumption that under-age children are not as responsible for their conduct as adults are, in the sense that they are not fully aware of its wrongness or illegality, or are less able to withstand temptation. But the higher the minimum age the more artificial this assumption becomes. Only someone who has never had personal dealings with children could believe that a mentally normal boy of, say, twelve is unaware that theft is an offence or is unable to restrain himself from thieving, at least until he thinks he can get away with it. As for the moral wrongness of thieving, if he does not feel this at twelve he will not feel it as an adult.

Nor is it plausible to argue that a high minimum age protects the child against drastic penal measures. For even systems with *low* minimum ages protect over-age children against death or imprisonment; and as for modified custodial measures, even systems with high minimum ages impose these on under-age children.

A more realistic justification is that such systems protect under-age offenders against the stigma of being labelled as criminals[2], and that this is desirable because at that age the stigma does not act as a deterrent, and may even encourage further anti-social behaviour by alienating the child from his community. It has been argued that the label may even cause the child to regard himself as a criminal, and to behave accordingly. Although the English system has until now had a low minimum age, it has for long recognized the need to protect over-age children from stigma. Courts which tried children between their tenth and seventeenth birthdays were allowed to 'find them guilty' but not to 'convict' them. A finding of guilt before the age of fourteen must not be treated as a 'previous conviction' after he has become an adult at twenty-one. The public are not admitted to a juvenile court, and the news media must not report its proceedings in

---

2. With the paradoxical exception of cases in which the offence is regarded as so grave that the public prosecutor feels obliged to insist on criminal proceedings. In England the name of a child on trial for murder can be publicly reported.

such a way that the children who appear there can be identified.

On the other hand, it is questionable whether the stigma is
avoided, or even much lessened, if the child is the subject of
non-criminal proceedings. In so far as precautions of the kind
just described are effective in concealing his identity from the
public at large, they can be used whether the proceedings are
criminal or non-criminal. Where they fail is in concealing from
friends, neighbours, acquaintances and official agencies the fact
that he has appeared in court; and they fail whether the proceedings are criminal or non-criminal. For most friends, neighbours
and acquaintances the distinction between the two procedures
is not sufficiently clear to make any difference to their reactions.
For those whose minds are clearer on the subject, the stigma of
non-criminal proceedings may actually be greater, because of
the implication that the family situation is seriously at fault.
In other words, while being found guilty of a specific offence
undoubtedly involves stigma, it does limit the stigma in a way
which non-criminal proceedings may fail to do.

Yet there is at least one sound justification for drawing a
distinction between the proceedings of a court which is dealing
with a child and those of a court which is dealing with an adult,
even when both have committed very similar offences in full
knowledge of what they were doing. In the case of an adult
offender the court proceeds on the assumption that if anyone can
be held answerable for what he has done it is he himself (see
Assumption A in Chapter 9). The judge may well, in his
private thoughts, accept an explanation of the offender's behaviour which puts the blame on the latter's past upbringing,
or even on his contemporary associates; but the only workable
basis on which he can pass sentence here and now is the assumption that doing something to the offender himself will be beneficial.

In contrast, the assumption underlying the proceedings of
juvenile courts is that the possible target for its measures includes
not only the child but also his parents. In theory at least, it is
still possible to improve his conduct by influencing them. Even
when the court is satisfied that they have lost control of him,
or are so unsatisfactory as parents that there is no hope of acting
through them, it is allowed to provide what are – in intention at
any rate – substitute parents.

Admittedly it is highly artificial to assume that an offender's parents can be expected to help in correcting him up to, but not after, his seventeenth birthday, or whatever is the crucial age. If they had any influence over him at sixteen it will not vanish as suddenly as that. Nor is it realistic to adopt the same age as the watershed for all young offenders. But the system is not quite as crude as that. In effect it implies only that juvenile courts *must* consider whether the parents can help in correcting the child, whereas adults' courts are not obliged to. In other words, it neither compels a juvenile court to waste its time with parents who have no influence on their son, nor debars an adults' court from semi-officially appealing to parents who still seem to have influence.

If so, what has hitherto been called 'the age of criminal responsibility' badly needs a new name. Originally 'criminally responsible' meant no more than 'answerable to the criminal law', but with a gradual shift in the meaning of 'responsible' it has come to mean something like 'knowing what is criminal and able to decide rationally whether to do it or not'. In systems with low minimum ages this shift of meaning hardly mattered and went unnoticed, because the justification for exempting under-age children from being answerable to the law was that they were assumed to differ from adults, either in their moral sense or in their ability to take fully rational decisions. In a system with a high minimum age, however, this distinction would be ridiculous. It might be more precise to call it 'the age of criminal liability', but unfortunately most such systems allow children under that age – but over the traditional minimum age – to be prosecuted in exceptional circumstances (usually if they have committed murder or some other crime of serious violence).

If the justification which I have suggested for such systems seems a rational one, the least misleading term would be something like 'the age of criminal *independence*', meaning 'the age at which courts are free (though not obliged) to treat the offender as an individual who is independent of parental influence'. This does not, of course, tell us what the age should be. If a society has reached the stage of adopting a high minimum age, the question whether it should be fifteen, sixteen, seventeen, or even eighteen is a subsidiary one, but it is important that the answer to it should be based not on out-of-date moralistic assumptions about the 'responsibility' of teenagers, but on the rational justification for a high minimum age which I have suggested.

How should the crucial age be selected? Psychologists will

argue that it is quite as artificial to adopt a uniform age for this purpose as it was for 'knowledge of good and evil'. Just as some children are precociously responsible, so some teenagers are precociously independent of parental influence, while some men and women in their twenties are as dependent as school-children. Sociologists, however, would not be quite so discouraging. They would point out that the effectiveness of parental intervention at different ages is not entirely a matter of individual variation in personality, but is to some extent determined by the prevalent assumptions about the age at which young people become adults. These assumptions differ of course from one society to another, and from one generation to another; but while and where they are prevalent they are extremely influential. In a society, for example, which treats a sixteen-year-old as an adult it is more difficult for parents to exercise authority or influence over a son or daughter of that age than it would be for the same parents in a society which drew the dividing-line at a later age. Indeed in highly stratified societies there are differences between social classes. This does not mean that individual differences between families are negligible; but that their effect is somewhat reduced. Teenagers consult other teen-agers about their rights and obediences: parents consult other parents about their rules and degrees of permissions: and some consensus is the result. No family is an island.

Nor does this approach mean that a sensible age of criminal independence can be fixed only after a laborious and scientific social survey. No doubt this would be desirable, but there is probably a short-cut. If my sociological argument is sound, parental influence over children's behaviour is to some extent linked to the official status of children of their age in the society in question. For example, a child who is not yet free to leave school and become a wage-earner can hardly be regarded as independent of his parents, either economically or psychologically. It was probably reasoning on roughly these lines which led the Government, in its 1965 White Paper,[3] to propose sixteen as the terminal age for non-criminal proceedings. For it argued that

Sixteen will soon[4] be the upper age for compulsory school attend-ance. It marks a significant stage in the lives of many young people.

3. *The Child, the Family and the Young Offender* (Home Office, 1965, Cmnd 2742).

4. This was of course before the postponement of the raising of the school-leaving age was announced.

It is the age at which they begin to earn, at which many leave home, at which they may marry[5]. . . .

The proposals were unpopular, however, for this and other more fundamental reasons. The terminal age for juvenile court proceedings[6] had been raised from sixteen to seventeen as long ago as 1932, and the White Paper seemed to be trying to put the clock back.

The White Paper which superseded it in 1968 therefore conceded that seventeen should continue to be the terminal age. It must be admitted that the argument in the earlier White Paper did not prove that the age should be sixteen so much as that it should be *at least sixteen*. If the criterion is whether a teenager is still sufficiently likely to be susceptible to parental or quasi-parental influence to make this a justifiable basis for treatment, the argument does not show that this likelihood becomes too low after sixteen; merely that it must by then be on the decline. It is worth noting that the Latey Committee (1967) on the age of majority selected *eighteen* as a reasonable age for such matters as full contractual capacity, the right to marry without parental consent, and the powers of courts to make orders for custody and access[7]; and that even more recently the Seebohm Committee have recommended *eighteen* as the terminal age for non-criminal proceedings where behaviour problems are involved (1968).

EVIDENCE IN JUVENILE COURTS

Another aspect of juvenile courts needs discussion – the nature of the evidence which they should accept. The chief criticism of non-criminal proceedings in juvenile courts in the U.S.A. has been levelled by lawyers at the readiness of these courts to act upon evidence which would not satisfy a criminal court. Probably this is an inevitable feature of such proceedings, in which the child is not regarded as a defendant (and is not usually represented by a lawyer), and in which much of the information on which the court relies takes the form of reports by social workers on their impressions of the family.

5. But in England parental consent is required until the age of twenty-one.
6. With unimportant exceptions.
7. They were careful to say that their recommendations should not affect the criminal law 'since it is the irresponsible, the disturbed and the inadequate who become involved in anti-social behaviour and law-breaking regardless of chronological age'. Both the premiss and the inference from it suggest that the Committee had only a superficial acquaintance with juvenile delinquency.

It must be remembered, of course, that information of this kind is also taken into account by criminal courts, when they are deciding what to do with the offender, whether he is an adult or a juvenile. Because the offender has pleaded guilty, or has been convicted on the basis of carefully examined evidence, we tend to relax our standards of proof at the sentencing stage, and to accept uncorroborated and impressionistic reports from probation officers, psychiatrists, employers and even parents. The difference is that in non-criminal proceedings such reports are accepted as the basis not only for the decision as to the form which intervention should take but also for the decision whether intervention is needed.

If the grounds for intervention are that the child's circumstances, and in particular his home, are unsatisfactory it would be unreasonable to insist on the same standard of proof as we do in a criminal trial. To do so would make it so difficult to satisfy a court that intervention could not take place in many cases in which it is needed. (This is not to say that the reports of social workers should not be examined critically; or that parents should not have every chance of questioning their allegations.) But what if the ground for intervention is simply that a child from a satisfactory home has committed a theft or some other act for which he could have been brought to trial if he had been older? It must be realized that in the great majority of cases the child and his parents admit the facts. But if they do not, should he not have the right to have the facts established with the same care as they would be if he were an adult and had pleaded 'Not Guilty'?

The supporters of non-criminal proceedings can concede this without weakening their case. For it is not impossible to insist that a non-criminal court should apply criminal standards of proof to allegations of specific anti-social acts. Another solution, adopted by Scotland, is to allow the child or his parents the right to opt for a proper trial of his guilt if they deny the specific act.

It would be possible, however, to go even further, and to question the assumption that criminal standards of proof should be applied in such cases. For they have been evolved in order to protect innocent adults against extremely severe consequences of conviction. Indeed it is no exaggeration to say that in England and the U.S.A. a man on trial for an offence which carries a penalty of a few months' imprisonment at most, and for which he may well be let off with a fine, can demand to be tried with the same conscientiousness as a man on trial for his life, and that common-law rules of evidence which were painfully developed to save the innocent from the gallows are now being used to protect the guilty from probation.

It must be admitted that the care with which a man is tried should be related to the most drastic penalty that can be imposed on him if he is convicted, rather than the most probable penalty; and that imprisonment is drastic enough to warrant considerable care, if not quite as much care as the death penalty. In the case of children, however, what penalties are possible that would justify such care? A reasonable answer would be 'Any measure involving removal from home'. If so, a solution to the problem of evidence would be to insist upon a higher standard of proof before a court could order a measure of this sort. Indeed, it would be possible to insist that a higher standard of proof should be applied not only to the facts but also to the opinions of social workers and psychiatrists, by demanding that they be corroborated by a 'second opinion'.

THE DISPOSAL OF JUVENILES

Finally, what special considerations apply to the disposal of juveniles?

If the modern justification for distinguishing juvenile from adult offenders is that the former are more likely to respond to parental influence, it follows that the system should give that influence a fair chance to correct the juvenile before it resorts to more costly and drastic measures. To many parents the mere news that their child has been officially identified as a thief – whether by a shop, by his school or by the police – is by itself enough to cause them concern, and their concern may be enough to impress the child. (Indeed, there is even the danger that some parents will react with excessive anxiety or anger to what was no more than a thoughtless escapade.) For such families the police warning without prosecution – a practice that is becoming more and more frequent in the case of first offenders – is sufficient. Even if the parents are not entirely surprised to be told that their son is shoplifting, the fact that he has at last been detected may persuade them to take some action.

In areas where the police tend to prosecute even first offenders of this age, courts can still give the parents their chance by using a nominal measure. A more real problem is the parent who does not react normally and effectively to a police warning or to a court appearance. This calls for an explanation which a social inquiry report may well be able to give, and it seems a sound rule that no juvenile court should ever proceed beyond nominal measures until it has had a report which deals with this question.[8]

The possible explanations are, of course, so numerous and varied that they cannot all be discussed here; and in any case they belong to a textbook of social case-work. But they pose one or two special problems which must be mentioned. If the explanation seems to be that a parent who is capable of exercising authority or influence has not been stimulated to do so by his child's first appearance at the police station or in court, what steps should be open to a juvenile court? In England there were only two kinds of measure which juvenile courts could impose on parents. One was a fine (or damages or costs); the other was a recognizance (that is, a formal undertaking) to exercise proper care of the child, failing which the parent forfeits a sum of money – a measure which is in effect a suspended fine. As usual, we have no scientifically collected information about the effectiveness of these financial sanctions. The legislation of 1969 preserved only the recognizance to exercise proper care.

In practice, however, an order for supervision, although it is officially applied only to the juvenile himself, may give the social worker a sufficient opportunity to influence the parents as well. For this reason, as well as the more obvious ones, it should probably be the next expedient to be tried.

REMOVAL FROM HOME

What seems to awaken many parents to the seriousness of the situation when milder measures have failed is the prospect of the removal of their child from home. In England this can happen in three ways. The court may permit it (for short periods) when ordering supervision, but without interfering with the parents' rights and authority, except in so far as custody of the child is concerned. It may transfer the parents' rights and powers to a local authority[9] by a 'care order' which can last until the juvenile's eighteenth birthday; and this usually means that the local authority will remove him from home, although it may eventually return him experimentally or more permanently. Occasionally a local authority simply takes a juvenile 'into care' (as it has a duty

8. English juvenile courts are supposed to receive social inquiry reports when dealing with every offender; but an exception is made for 'trivial' offences, which are not defined.

9. Or other fit person.

to do if the parents are unwilling, unable or unfit to look after it) with or without a resolution assuming parental rights over him[10]; but this is rarely done as a result of delinquent behaviour.

Removal from home is undoubtedly the most drastic measure at the disposal of a juvenile court. Even a child who is used to periods at boarding-school or with relatives, or who is so estranged from his family that he wants to get away from it, is unnerved by committal to the care of strangers, however enlightened the institution or foster-home. There are few parents, too, who are so indifferent or antagonistic to a delinquent child – or at the worst so lacking in pride or possessiveness – that they are not deeply upset by his compulsory removal.

Unofficially, juvenile courts sometimes use the threat of a custodial measure or a fit person order in an attempt not only to correct the juvenile offender but also to stimulate his parents to action. Officially, English law makes no provision for 'suspended sentences' of this kind; but it seems reasonable to allow courts to utter such threats, especially if the result is to postpone actual removal by one more stage. Some people may argue that removal is either justified or not, and that in the one case it should be adopted forthwith, in the other not even threatened; but in real life the line between the justifiable and the unjustifiable is less obvious than these purists assume.

The most difficult decision for the court and the local authority arises from the case in which the family is less to blame for the juvenile's behaviour than his associates. The only way of severing his connexion with an older offender, or with a delinquent gang, may be removal to another area; and, since this is usually out of the question for the family as a whole, it may be necessary to remove the boy himself.

Too often in the past, removal has meant committal to a detention centre, approved school or even borstal. This is rightly regarded by most courts as a last resort. Quite apart from the immediate distress caused to the delinquent and his parents, there is a considerable danger than an institution of this kind will increase his chances of becoming a chronic delinquent. If even an ordinary school can be a breeding-ground for delinquent values, an approved school is even worse. The danger is obvious, and has been pointed out for a century or more. It is therefore odd that so little is done to prevent juvenile first offenders from

10. See ss. 1 and 2 of the Children Act, 1948: the parent can appeal to a court.

being sent to such institutions. Adult first offenders are to some extent protected by law from imprisonment, chiefly to avoid this very danger (see pages 76 and 152); but the Act of 1958 did not apply to juveniles, nor does the latest legislation contain anything on these lines. The reason may lie in the assumption that, because the regimes of juvenile institutions are planned with much more attention to reformation than those of prison, the danger of 'contamination' is negligible; but this is a very doubtful inference.

It may also have been assumed that courts would very seldom send a first offender to an approved school or borstal. In fact, substantial percentages of approved school boys have no previous records of offences[11]; and though the borstal percentage[11] is lower it is by no means negligible. It is conceivable that all these 'first offenders' were known by the courts to be boys with a history of unprosecuted delinquency[12], although this alone does not seem to justify an institutional measure before less drastic ones have been tried. It is more likely, however, that in some cases the main consideration in the courts' mind was the gravity of the offence or the parents' obvious inability to control their son.

A general prohibition, however, on the removal of juveniles from home as a result of their first appearance in court could easily be qualified by exceptions, of which the following seem the most important:

(i) cases in which the juvenile seems to be beyond parental control;

(ii) cases in which removal seems necessary for the safety or welfare of others;

(iii) cases in which the behaviour seems to be the result of mental disorder of a nature or degree which justifies in-patient treatment or care.

I am not, of course, implying that if the case falls within one of these exceptions the juvenile should automatically be removed from home: merely that if so the court should not be debarred from taking this step.

11. For approved school boys the 1967 percentage was 10·7 per cent.
For borstal lads the 1966 percentage was 3·5 per cent.
For senior detention centres the 1966 percentage was 12·5 per cent.
For junior detention centres it was 11·1 per cent.

12. Which could be known to the court either because the police had records of earlier warnings or because the boy asked for other offences to be taken into account.

It is not easy to think of a cogent objection to a proposal on these lines. Occasionally, it is true, someone who works in an institution for delinquent juveniles is heard to argue that if they were sent to his establishment at an earlier stage in their careers it would have a better chance of success with them. Such evidence as there is seems at first to support this; the fewer the boy's previous appearances in court the more likely he is to keep out of trouble. But this would be so even if he had been put on probation. In effect, therefore, the argument is that boys who might, for all we know, respond to a measure which does not involve removal from home should nevertheless be sent to an approved school or detention centre, as the case may be. If, of course, there were evidence that 'first offenders' had markedly higher success rates when, say, they are sent to approved schools than when they are put on probation, this would put the argument on a sounder footing: but at present such statistics as we have are in favour of probation.[13]

THE COMPOSITION OF JUVENILE COURTS

Finally, what sort of people should take these decisions? This cannot be answered simply by harking back to Chapter 11, with its discussion of the possible functions of a sentencing authority. For the position of a juvenile court differs in important ways from that of a criminal court for adults. The latter's most difficult problems arise over the proof of an individual's guilt; in a juvenile court this is seldom disputed, and, even when it is, the offences involved raise less difficult issues of fact or law. In contrast, the disposal of a convicted adult is in the nature of things a much simpler problem than the disposal of a juvenile. The main reason for this is that in the case of adults the choices are fewer, more clearly defined, and more closely controlled by law. Whether this should be so or not is another question; but it is not accidental. The greater variety of measures for juveniles reflects our feeling that in their case the best choice has a much greater chance of effecting a real change of outlook, while a mistaken choice is even more likely to lead to an anti-social career.

This being so, what can be done to ensure that the choices are made by people with an adequate understanding of the situations with which they are trying to deal and of the measures which are at their disposal? There are two main courses. One

13. See Hammond's Table 5 in *The Sentence of the Court.*

lies in the careful selection and training of those who preside over the juvenile course. Belgium, for example, has the *juge des enfants*, a lawyer who is committed to a career in the judiciary and who has had special training and experience in juvenile problems. A full-time professional, however, is not essential to this solution: Sweden has experimented with Child Welfare Boards composed of teachers, medical officers, clergymen and 'persons known for their interest in and devotion to the welfare of children and youth'. The unpopular English White Paper of 1965[14] proposed 'family councils' consisting of 'social workers of the children's service and other persons selected for their understanding and experience of children . . .'.

The other solution is to be content with a low degree of expertise in the people who preside, but to simplify and control their decisions, and above all to ensure that the trained agents who have to carry out these decisions are given enough latitude to apply them as their training and experience dictate. This seems to be the solution aimed at by the White Paper of 1968, which offers the court only three choices[15] where a child under fourteen is concerned: binding over the parents, placing the child under supervision, or committing him to the care of a local authority. It is evident that the effect of any of these measures in practice depends very much on the agency which is responsible for keeping an eye on the child and family, or for looking after the child after his removal.

Although these two solutions are not completely incompatible they are obviously independent alternatives. Which is the better? In theory it should be possible to compare the experience of countries which have tried them. In practice this is less valuable than it sounds because of the wide variation in the types of case with which the courts in different countries are trying to deal. In north American cities, for example, the cases which reach the juvenile courts seem to be much more serious than those which reach their English counterparts: most of the young offenders who appear before our magistrates would have been dealt with out of court in the U.S.A., either by the police or by the probation department.

There are a few general considerations, however, which point in one direction or the other. If the objective is flexibility of

14. See note 3, page 179.
15. Plus a fourth – a hospital or guardianship order – in cases of mental disorder.

treatment, so that it can be modified by the agent in the light of the juvenile's progress, then there is little point in training a professional sentencer to make a complex choice at the outset between a wide variety of measures.

If on the other hand the court's function is seen as more than that of a decision-maker, a case can be made out for the professionally trained sentencer. In the first place, it can be argued that one of his responsibilities is to protect the child and his family against unjustifiable or excessive measures: and that in order to perform this task properly he must learn what is involved in, say, a care order.[16]

Secondly, one may believe that the very process of dealing with the child or his family in court can be beneficial. Some magistrates obviously hope that what they say to the offender or his parents will have a corrective effect. The White Paper of 1965 was based on a slightly more sophisticated assumption: that its family councils, who were supposed to have unhurried discussions with parents and if possible reach agreement with them on the right way to deal with their child, would thus increase the success rate of their measures. Certainly this is less naïve than the belief that homilies in court have a lasting effect. The logical conclusion of both assumptions, however, is that the people who are to deliver these homilies or hold discussions with parents must be selected and trained with this in view: it is not enough to have benches filled by people who are successful parents and shop-keepers, or even successful parents and skilled manual workers, if their task is to deal with people who are often unsuccessful both with their families and in their work.

The strength of these arguments for a specially trained corps of sentencers varies with the situation in the society in question. If its social agencies are deficient in the quality of their staffs or their material resources, the courts' protective function is important. If the society is one in which authority (or an élite) has such prestige that an appearance before a magistrate can bring about permanent changes of outlook, there is a case for using magistrates in this way. If, at the other extreme, the society

16. Incidentally, let no magistrate imagine that he can do this by a one-day visit to a 'community home'. Only a stay in one, eating and sleeping in the boys' quarters (not in the headmaster's house!), will begin to give him some idea of what it is really like. The same is true of all institutions. Yet I know very few people – even among research workers – who have actually done this or tried to do it.

is very egalitarian, with values which lay great stress on the rightness of group decisions, the 'family council' might well be effective.

Undoubtedly there are societies which fit these descriptions. Equally certainly, modern England does not, although it probably did fit the first two at earlier stages in its history. In our case, too, there are additional arguments in favour of the other solution. The training of our social workers – especially in the field of child care and probation – has already reached a high standard, and is based on the assumption that they will be given considerable discretion. For better or worse, we are also committed to cheap justice, in the shape of spare-time magistrates, and the alternative would cost a great deal without guaranteeing spectacularly better results. The fact that we are to some extent committed to this line of development does not prove that it is rational; but the other arguments suggest that it is in fact the more far-sighted choice for a modern society.

Chapter 14

Some Residual Problems

Let me recapitulate and then deal with some final issues.

My first contention, on which the whole book hinges, was that the main aim of any penal system must be the reduction of prohibited conduct, but that this must be tempered by both economic considerations and humanity if the system is to be practicable and tolerable. The aims which raise serious difficulties are ordinary retribution and denunciation. Retribution as a limiting principle raises more difficulties than humanity as a limiting principle, and there is little point in adopting both. Retribution as a distributive principle has a strong appeal, but cannot be universally applied unless we give up several very desirable forms of preventive interference, or indulge in double-think by regarding them as outside the penal system.

A penal system designed by an economic reductivist, observing limits dictated not by retributive justice but by humanity, would differ in some important respects from our present one. It would be less ambiguous and illogical. It would distinguish less sharply between actual and likely harm, and between intention and inadvertence. It would lay far less emphasis on consistency in sentencing. On the other hand, it would not be either intolerably severe or unrealistically lenient.

As for the sorts of behaviour which are prohibited by the criminal law, these are so diverse that it is very difficult to formulate a general principle which will help in deciding whether a given sort should be penalized or not. The principles offered by Beccaria, Bentham and their successors have been *limiting* principles rather than positive justifications. Lord Devlin's attempt to offer 'the smooth functioning of society and the preservation of order' has suffered unfairly because he associated it with his opposition to the Wolfenden Report's recommendations on the subject of homosexual acts. Not only does it underlie much of our penal thinking, but it seems to be as nearly value-free as can be expected of any positive justification. It must be combined, however, with a careful comparison of the costs, benefits and side-effects of law enforcement and other means of reducing whatever conduct seems contrary to the principle.

For the criminal law is only one of many reductive techniques, preventive or corrective. The most useful distinction between preventive techniques is based on the extent to which they are 'focused' on likely law-breakers. As regards unfocused measures, we seem to have no evidence at all about the effectiveness of moral education in schools, and some not very reassuring evidence about the negative effects of mass media. The evidence as regards slum-clearance is discouraging, although measures such as these are justified on other grounds. As regards more focused measures most, but not all, of the evidence is also depressing. Prevention by reducing opportunities for law-breaking seems a more promising area for exploration, but is outside the scope of this book.

An unfocused measure which must receive special attention, however, because of its close connexion with law enforcement, is general deterrence. Most attempts to assess its efficacy fail because an essential condition of measurement is overlooked. Taxpayers in Illinois seem to respond to the threat of sanctions, as well as to appeals to conscience. On the other hand, murderers in New Zealand seem to be unaffected by the difference between the death penalty and long imprisonment; and the same is possibly true of most committers of personal violence. As for more common offences, the results of the Government Social Survey's interviews with young males are interesting. Most of them greatly over-estimated their chances of being detected, so that an enormous increase in police efficiency would be required to raise their estimates further. As for the consequences of detection, most ranked the probable penalty below their family's opinion of them, the loss of their job, and the general stigma of a court appearance. This is less surprising when it is noted that only a minority thought a custodial sentence was likely for most of the offences mentioned. Only *mamdatory* custodial sentences, which are unthinkable for most types of offender, are at all likely to be more effective as deterrents; and *exemplary* sentences are not a real solution to the dilemma. In other words, although commonsense suggests – and no one has disproved – the belief that penalties deter some potential offenders from some types of offence, the prospect of *increasing* the effectiveness of penalties as deterrents is very limited.

Focused measures consist largely of sentences which are intended as corrective (precautionary sentences are discussed later). Those of general applicability are custodial, supervisory, financial and nominal, although there are other measures which are of use for special categories. Psychological treatment does not seem to be generally applicable, nor could any society afford it if it were.

Measuring the efficacy of corrective measures presents several serious difficulties, and the most we can hope to do is assess *comparative efficacy*. A few hard variables – sex, age, previous convictions, previous time spent in institutions, and type of offence – are definitely associated with the probability of reconviction. When these are allowed for, financial measures seem most successful, followed by nominal, supervisory and custodial sentences in that order. Two possibilities, however, have to be borne in mind. One is that courts select the better prospects for fines and discharges; but this can hardly explain away entirely the discouraging results of probation. The other is that the results would be much better if the offenders who are likely to respond negatively to each measure could be identified and treated otherwise.

Penologists therefore set considerable store by pre-sentence diagnosis. So far as mentally disordered offenders are concerned, this is useful and practicable; it is even possible to suggest broad groups for which psychiatric examination should be the rule. The prestige and idealization of psychiatric diagnosis, however, has led penologists to hope for too much from pre-sentence reports about mentally normal offenders, and especially 'first offenders'. In the case of offenders who will either offend again or refrain from doing so irrespective of the sentence, it does not matter what measure the court chooses. As for 'selectively responsive' offenders, it is unlikely that they are responsive to only one choice, and in any case very difficult to identify the wrong choice or choices. Consequently, sentencers can probably maximize the number of correct choices by a 'strategic' sentencing sequence. With obvious exceptions – especially in the case of dangerous offenders – a financial or nominal penalty should be tried first, followed by probation, a suspended custodial sentence and finally actual custody.

The underlying assumptions of the sentencing system need

close examination in the light of modern developments. Some seem inevitable: that the sentencer can deal only with a convicted offender, and that the sentence must take one of the forms allowed by law. Other assumptions – that the penalty should be irrevocable and that it should be chosen by the persons who preside over the trial of guilt – are already being modified or questioned. The assumption that the choice of sentence should not vary from one area to another is a serious obstacle to experimentation. As for the 'individualization' of sentences, while this is an improvement on the rigidity of nineteenth-century sentencers, it makes more sense as a principle for *penal agents*. In particular, there is no point in the variety of the lengths of prison sentences which courts – and especially higher courts – can impose. No prison sentence should be of less than six months; and an offender's first prison sentence should have an upper limit of, say, two years in actual custody. A second or subsequent sentence should have a higher upper limit, but five years seems enough for this. (Very short sentences apart, there is no evidence that a longer sentence is a more effective corrective, and a little evidence – though very scanty – that it is not.) These limits could in practice be lowered by automatic remission for good conduct; and within these lower limits the actual date of release should be determined by the prison service.

Measures designed to incapacitate the offender can take several forms, some applicable only to certain types of offence. Only capital punishment and secure custody are of universal effectiveness, and since the former is obsolescent it is the latter which requires most consideration. It should be restricted to a very small minority of offenders: those with a substantial probability of repeating a type of offence likely to result in irremediable harm. (Other apparently incorrigible recidivists should be accommodated in carefully supervised hostels, provided with work, and made to pay part at least of the cost of their upkeep: the victims of their crimes should be compensated.) Precautionary detention should be sharply distinguished from corrective detention and should be served in different prisons. Only in exceptional circumstances, in which it is highly likely that the offender's propensity for his offences will soon be removed by some definite event or technique, should a corrective custodial sentence also be regarded as a precautionary one; and a long precautionary sentence should never be imposed as a corrective. Consequently there should be no attempt to make the conditions of corrective and precautionary detention comparable, and the latter should be made as tolerable as possible, even at considerable expense. A minimum duration for precautionary detention, longer than the maximum for a corrective sentence, should be fixed by legislation, statutory or subordinate. It would be unnecessary to let sentencers determine the minimum in individual cases, and most undesirable to let them determine so far in advance the actual date of release, which should be a matter for the executive. If there are grounds for distrusting the executive, a procedure for automatic review by an independent authority should be established. If all this is done we should be prepared to impose precautionary detention if there is evidence, from experts or statistics, that the offender is even slightly likelier than not to repeat his offences.

Some degree of control over sentencers is a feature of all civilized penal systems. Mandatory sentences are unpopular and rare; but semi-mandatory ones are open to less objection, and in certain circumstances precautionary imprisonment should be semi-mandatory. In contrast, attempts to prohibit some types of sentence in certain circumstances are quite common: imprisonment for 'first offenders' is an example. Precautionary imprisonment should be prohibited for all but the minority of offenders defined on page 139. Psychiatrists can in practice prevent a hospital order or psychiatric probation order; and by the same token probation officers should have power to veto an ordinary probation order. Another form of control, the appeal against sentence, would be improved if the prosecution as well as the accused had a right of appeal, and if sentencers were obliged to justify their sentences either by indicating that they regarded them as normal or by giving reasons for departing from the norm.

To transfer the sentencing function completely from magistrates, recorders and judges to a sentencing authority would not yield enough benefit in the way of better decisions to justify the delay and cost; but there would be advantages in entrusting a specially constituted authority with certain sentencing tasks, such as

(i) the disposal of petty, inadequate but relatively harmless recidivists;

(ii) experimentation with new types of measure before they are made generally available to courts;

(iii) the imposition of precautionary sentences.

All civilized penal systems recognize grounds for mitigating penalties or exempting offenders from them altogether. Most of these grounds are either superstitious or based on retributive reasoning; but some can be justified by humane and economic reductivism. The most important groups which earn exemption or mitigation are the immature and the mentally disordered. Some are dealt with by non-penal services without being (officially at least) identified as offenders; some are officially identified as such, but handed over to non-penal services; some are officially identified and dealt with under the criminal law. There is a point in this tripartite system, for each part of it is appropriate for some situations: but complete exemption from it – at least in the case of the mentally disordered – is becoming increasingly rare, and it is arguable that it should be abolished.

As for juvenile offenders, the evolution of non-penal measures and non-criminal procedures has been accompanied by a tendency to raise the minimum age for prosecution, until the so-called 'age of criminal responsibility' has become an obsolete distinction. It is more realistic to talk of the 'age of criminal independence', meaning by this the age until which any courts should be obliged to take into account the possibility that the juvenile is amenable to the influence of his parents, but after which it may – but is not of course obliged to – proceed on the assumption that the offender is morally independent of them. The exact age which should be fixed for this purpose should be determined by considering the ages adopted for other distinctions, such as consenting to marriage or sexual intercourse, voting and contracting (but not, on the whole, by regard to the compulsory school age). In non-criminal proceedings the standard of proof need not be as high as in criminal proceedings, but should not be relaxed to the same extent if the court is considering the removal of the child from his home. The normal sequence of measures for a juvenile offender should be a nominal measure (giving the parents their chance to influence their child), followed by supervision (giving the supervisor a chance to influence the parents), then the threat of removal, and finally actual removal; but this sequence must of course be subject to exceptions. There should be a general prohibition, however, with few exceptions, on the removal of juvenile offenders from home on their first appearance in court. On the whole, though flexibility of treatment is desirable, it should be achieved not by diversifying the courses open to the *court* but by confining it to the simple choice between leaving the child to his parents, placing him (and perhaps the family) under supervision, and handing him over to an agency; and by giving *agencies* as much freedom as possible in carrying out the supervision or treatment, especially in the light of the juvenile's progress.

DISCUSSION

One or two general points can be made about these proposals. As the Preface pointed out, they are designed for a society that is reasonably peaceful, affluent and ignorant. They are also designed for a society that is prepared to trust its prisons, probation departments and other social agencies (such as those responsible for children) with considerable power over the lives of offenders. It is probably true to say that in England, as well as other countries, the modern tendency is to trust agencies rather more, and sentencers rather less, than formerly. Our loss of confidence in our sentencers may not be wholly justifiable, for we have probably expected too much of them; but as far as agencies are concerned our increasing trustfulness can be justified on several grounds. The standard of education and training of their staffs has improved, and is continuing to do so. This is partly the result of the agencies' own growing awareness of their deficiencies, but partly also the result of outside pressures on them. For their work is subject to an increasingly critical scrutiny from government departments, legislators and news media. Thirdly, the sheer volume of individuals for whom agencies are obliged to take responsibility is itself a safeguard of sorts. Overcrowded custodial establishments are not anxious to keep inmates longer than prudence suggests. Overworked probation officers do not have the time to exercise oppressive supervision.

It is true that, while all these factors combine to ensure that *on the whole* social agencies do not carry their control over offenders to excessive lengths, they cannot prevent the occasional case in which this happens. Penal agencies have their share – sometimes more than their share – of stupid, moralistic, sadistic or possessive employees; and their power over unpopular individuals intensifies the dangers of these shortcomings. In custodial establishments – including those for juveniles – there is the added risk of persecution by powerful inmates. A penal system which does not contain some sort of safeguard against these possibilities cannot be regarded as satisfactory. In British juvenile establishments the safeguard is the inmate's right to a private

interview with an inspector or visiting magistrate.[1] Adult
prisoners, too, have the right to speak to visiting magistrates,
and also to write to the Home Secretary and to their members of
Parliament: but their letters may be read, though not censored,
by the prison staff, and they can be punished for 'making a false
and malicious allegation against an officer' (Rule 47). The Home
Office receive very large numbers of complaints, either direct
from prisoners or through M.P.s, and the sheer volume of them
is a problem with which any form of safeguard would have to
cope. If the complaint is of improper treatment, the staff of the
establishment concerned have to be asked for their version of
what the prisoner is alleging, which is usually less startling than
his. Normally the official report is accepted, but occasionally
the persistence of similar allegations by different prisoners, or the
intervention of a determined M.P. or one of the news media,
obliges the Home Secretary to order a more formal investigation.
Sometimes this is carried out by a committee drawn from the
visiting magistrates of the prison; sometimes an independent
person – usually a senior member of the legal profession – is
appointed. In either case the result is a published report. Finally,
a member of the House of Commons who is not satisfied with the
official answer to his inquiries about an individual's case can
refer it to the Parliamentary Commissioner for Administration
(the British equivalent of the Scandinavian Ombudsman), who
in the short time since he was appointed has already investigated
a small number of complaints from prisoners.

The main tasks of any system for the protection of the offender
are to ensure that he can bring his complaint to the attention of
someone who is both impartial and competent to take it up with
authority; and to discriminate between justifiable complaints and
those inspired by malice or paranoia. At one extreme it must
guard against the possibility of false accusations by inmates
whose objectives may be revenge, the relaxation of security or
simply the demoralization of those in charge of them. At the
other, it must be able to penetrate the consistent evidence of a
group of staff who feel morally justified in their treatment of an
exceptionally troublesome offender.

This being so, one or two features of the English system are
open to question. Is it advisable to use 'visiting magistrates'
both for disciplinary tribunals and for hearing private complaints

1. Depending on whether the establishment is an approved school,
remand home, detention centre or borstal.

from prisoners? Or to ask them to hold formal inquiries into allegations against the prison for which they are, to a certain extent, responsible? On the other hand, is it any better to entrust inquiries of this kind to busy Queen's Counsel, whose experience of prison and prisoners is confined to criminal trials? How easy is it for administrators, who are trained to avoid both embarrassment for their Ministers and friction with penal agents, to achieve the suspicious impartiality which a thorough investigation demands? The answer to these awkward questions may prove to be the Parliamentary Commissioner: it is too soon to say. Since his function, however, is the investigation of 'maladministration', and he is debarred from criticizing policy or decisions which are a proper use of discretionary powers, there are many aspects of the treatment of offenders on which he cannot be asked to report.[2]

It may be that the eventual remedy will be a specialist Ombudsman with power to investigate the conduct of penal agencies (including hostels and probation departments). I do not imply that there are many abuses for him to detect: on the contrary, I believe that they are rare, though not unheard of. Yet even if very few of his investigations disclosed improprieties, the remainder would perform the valuable function of reassuring that section of public opinion which distrusts penal agencies. If progress means allowing more and more discretion to penal agencies – as it probably does – it is necessary both to protect the offender against the occasional act of inhumanity and to give the public confidence in the integrity of its agents.

Finally, let me try to forestall two general criticisms of my proposals as a whole. Any sort of reform – whether of penal systems or other social institutions – is at risk of encountering the objection that it would be unacceptable to public opinion. Although I have dealt with the humanitarian and economic aspects of my suggestions, I have usually chosen to ignore the political issue. In fact, since none of my ideas is inhumane or uneconomic it would be difficult to show why any of them are likely to be so unpopular that they could not be publicly put forward. This is beside the point, however. There ought to be room for the sort of discussion in which political practicability – as distinct from other sorts – is out of order as a basis for argu-

2. The two examples of cases involving prisoners which are given in his Fourth Report are not reassuring. One involved a prisoner who wanted to bring legal proceedings against his ex-wife; the other a prisoner who wanted more frequent payments to enable his wife to visit him.

ment, and in which it is possible to work out rational ways of achieving objectives without having to consider at each step what the man in the street can be persuaded to swallow. One is more likely to get somewhere if one works out where one wants to go before seeing what routes are open – unless, of course, one is satisfied with mere movement, irrespective of its direction.

It is true that many improvements in penal systems have been achieved by opportunism or even by accident, when some *cause célèbre* has created a temporary climate of opinion which is favourable to some measure, or even demands it. We would not have had a Court of Criminal Appeal until several years later than we did if it had not been for the unfortunate Adolf Beck (see page 156). This very example, however, illustrates the dangers of opportunism without more fundamental thinking: for, as we have seen, the result of the legislation of 1907 was a one-sided system of appeal which, half a century later, was defended by the Donovan Committee as too 'traditional' to rationalize.

A criticism of a different sort is that there are problems which this book does not really face. For example, ever since 'the train-robbers' took more than two and a half million pounds (of which only a third of a million was recovered) from a mail train in 1963, the problem of how to sentence them has been raised at almost every discussion of sentencing principles at which I have been present. Their actual sentences ranged from thirty years (for seven men with previous records of crime) to three years (for a solicitor with a clean record who was found guilty of conspiring to obstruct the course of justice). One of the express aims of the long sentences was retributive – to prevent the robbers from enjoying the benefits of the unrecovered loot – but no doubt its corollary was the aim of warning other professionals that the judges would do their best to ensure that their crimes would not pay either.

Having argued not only against retributive sentencing but also against the occasional exemplary sentence, I cannot of course support this reasoning, although I have supported a deterrent tariff. So far as corrective prison sentences are concerned I have proposed an upper limit of five years for men with previous experience of imprisonment (as most of the train-robbers had), but I have also proposed a longer, indeterminate, precautionary sentence for men who are more likely than not to repeat crimes which carry a substantial risk of irremediable harm. Could it be argued that the train-robbers fell into this category? Certainly there was little doubt about the likelihood that several of them would resort to further planned robberies if released within a few years. But were their crimes likely to cause irremediable harm? From the financial point of view it is difficult to argue that this was so; it seems to require the loss of more than two and a half million pounds to accelerate this country's inflationary career. The justification for a precautionary sentence in their case would have been that they were armed[3], and demonstrated their readiness to use their weapons by injuring the train-driver and striking one of the Post Office staff.

It is questionable, however, whether it is legitimate to test a sentencing system by facing it with highly exceptional cases. If, as I propose, the system proper is supplemented by a sentencing authority with the function of dealing with specially problematic classes of offenders in ways not necessarily open to ordinary courts, the system itself need not be tinkered with so as to fit the exceptional case, but should simply provide for the case to be remitted to the sentencing authority.

A more frequent problem, however, which I have not attempted to solve is the petty but incorrigible offender, who does not respond to financial, supervisory or custodial measures, but whose offences are not harmful enough to justify precautionary detention. To this group belong the chronic drunk, the drug-addict, the sexual exhibitionist or importuner, and a large number of petty thieves and confidence-men.

This too is quite true: but again there is a very good reason for it. There are many penal problems which cannot be solved simply by changes in the law of sentencing or in the administration of the system, but must await new developments in the techniques of psychiatry, psychology, medicine, social engineering or case-work.

The more realistic the technicians in these fields, the more willing they are to admit that at present there are some types of behaviour for which, once they become chronic, there is at present no very effective treatment, and which at best we can only hope to prevent, or perhaps detect at such an early stage that treatment has some chance of success. This is especially true of behaviour which psychiatrists and psychologists tend to regard as a symptom of 'personality disorders' or addiction. From the

3. At least with iron bars and coshes, and perhaps with guns: see the account by ex-Detective-Superintendent M. Fewtrell (1964, pp. 13–15).

penological point of view, one of the most unfortunate features of such disorders is that those who suffer from them gravitate sooner or later into the orbit of the penal system, which is then criticized for its inability to cure them. Sometimes the behaviour itself is prohibited by the criminal law; but, even if it is not, the disapproval with which more normal people react to it may drive the individual into associations and ways of life which bring him into conflict with the law or its agents. In either case, the penal system is in the position of a sump, unable to do more than receive and retain the human material with which the machinery of the other social services cannot deal. It is the only service which is not allowed to close its doors to the unco-operative client.

Although our techniques for dealing with such deviants will no doubt gradually improve, there are some aberrations which are more likely to be reduced by prevention than by cure, and prevention is a net which always lets a few fish through. It is difficult to believe in a future society which will not have to cope with the problem of incorrigibility. Indeed, if all the types of behaviour which present this problem today were eliminated tomorrow, societies would soon – after an uneasy period of self-searching – find new targets for disapproval and official inter-ference. Some of the targets exist already, and simply escape attention because of more obvious ones. If drug addiction and alcoholism became things of the past, nicotine addiction would probably take their place as a focus for social concern. Some targets, on the other hand, would be created by raising standards, as we have done in the last hundred years where parents' treat-ment of their children is concerned. Moreover, it is highly probable that the higher we raise standards in this or other directions the harder it becomes to prevent or rectify sub-standard behaviour, simply because the standard is approaching closer to what is normal.

It would hardly be fair to censure a system for failing to apply remedies which have not yet been invented. Nevertheless, on the assumption that the technicians will from time to time succeed in improving their corrective techniques, it would be legitimate to criticize one which was so inflexible that improved techniques could not be effectively applied to the individuals who would benefit by them. It would also be legitimate to demand that any system should be sufficiently adaptable to allow experi-mentation with new ideas for treatment, within the limits of humanity. At least one of my proposals, namely a sentencing authority with a responsibility for experiments, is designed to increase the rather low adaptability of all the penal systems known to me.

Appendix A

A Sentencing Model

(by Nigel Walker, Michael Willmer[1] and Roy Carr-Hill[2])

The aim of this paper is to suggest an approach to the study of reconviction statistics which, though unorthodox, may eventually prove profitable.

In order to illustrate our points we have used data from Dr W. H. Hammond's follow-up of male offenders who were convicted during March and April 1957 in the Metropolitan Police District. Being the only study so far reported which compares the results of all four of the main types of sentence (nominal, financial, supervisory and custodial) when imposed on an English sample of adults, it seems the best for our purpose. We have confined our illustration to the most numerous age-group into which Dr Hammond sub-divided his adults, the twenty-one to twenty-nine-year-olds. His data are shown in Table 5. Some of the figures were published in *The Sentence of the Court* (1964); some were supplied to us by Dr Hammond for the purpose of this paper. We are greatly indebted to him, not only for the trouble which he took to do this, but also for some extremely helpful comments on our argument. We should make it clear, of course, that neither he nor the Home Office is responsible for the use which we have made of the data.

The key to our approach is the concept of a 'model': that is, a visual or intellectual device which assists explanatory or predictive thinking. Examples of models are the genes and chromosomes of genetics, the isobars of meteorologists or the contour lines of geographers. It is important to realize that in order to be useful and workable a model does not have to be a picture of reality. Genes were invented before they were actually observed; and nobody expects ever to be able to observe isobars or contour lines.[3]

1. Research Fellow, Nuffield College, Oxford.
2. Research Student, Nuffield College, Oxford.
3. For a fuller discussion of scientific models, see, for example, R. B. Braithwaite, *Scientific Explanation* (1953), or the less mathematical *Philosophy of Science* by S. Toulmin (1953).

Every sentencer who chooses his sentences with the aim of correcting offenders – and there can be very few nowadays who do not have this in view most of the time[4] – must, whether

TABLE 5

THE DISTRIBUTION OF SENTENCES AND RECONVICTIONS
AMONG MALES AGED TWENTY-ONE TO TWENTY-NINE
IN DR W. H. HAMMOND'S METROPOLITAN SAMPLE

		numbers reconvicted
1. *Men receiving their first sentence*		
Discharged	68	22
Fined	170	33
Put on probation	61	30
Imprisoned	49	21
	348	
2. *Men receiving their second sentence*		
Discharged	34	20
Fined	50	23
Put on probation	39	28
Imprisoned	75	53
	198*	
3. *Men receiving their third sentence*		
Discharged	8	3
Fined	26	19
Put on probation	20	14
Imprisoned	56	31
	110*	
4. *Men receiving their fourth sentence*		
Discharged	3	1
Fined	14	10
Put on probation	14	10
Imprisoned	43	33
	74*	

* Excluding three offenders dealt with by other means.

he is aware of it or not, be basing his decisions on some sort of model – that is, on some set of assumptions about offenders which helps – or appears to help – him to tell whether this

4. We are not ignoring other aims, such as retribution, deterrence, denunciation or the protection of the public; but this article is about corrective sentencing. 'Correction' is used to include both the reformation and the deterrence of the individual offender, since it is seldom possible to tell which of these processes is taking place.

offender should be fined, imprisoned or dealt with by one of the other measures at his disposal. If the sentencer is psychologically sophisticated it will be a fairly complex model; if not, it will be simpler. One of the purposes of this article is to consider how complex it really has to be. For the essential point of a model is that – if it is properly constructed – its complexity is no greater than is necessary for the efficient performance of its task. Contour lines on maps are an exceedingly simple device, but sufficient to enable one to make several useful sorts of prediction – for example, whether one will be able to see Village X from Hill Y, or whether Ridge Z will obstruct the line of sight.

The analogy of a map is a good one, because it helps to make clear the difference between a sentencer and a psychologist, psychiatrist or social worker whose task it is to report on and sometimes to treat an offender. The latter are like geographers, who need complex maps to describe the districts in which they are interested: maps which show vegetation, land use, population distribution, surface geology, annual rainfall and so on. The sentencer, on the other hand, whose task is to choose between a limited number of possible measures, is rather like the motorist who simply wants to drive through the same district by the best roads. All he needs is a road-map, uncomplicated by the detail of the geographer's atlas.

This article therefore approaches sentencers' models from the opposite direction to most – if not all – textbooks of penology. Instead of emphasizing the enormous complexity of human nature and inferring from this that sentencers cannot operate efficiently without an accurate and sophisticated diagnosis of each offender it asks 'How simple could a sentencer's model be without failing in its tasks?' It therefore begins with the simplest possible model, and proceeds to consider what refinements are needed in order to meet *sentencers'* requirements, as distinct from the requirements of, say, psychologists or social case-workers.

The first step is to consider how a sentencer's model should represent an offender. What should the symbols on the map stand for? Not necessarily, as we have seen, for the concepts of psychology, psychiatry or social case-work. But if not these, then what? The answer is to be found in the nature of the sentencer's objective. If – as we are assuming in this discussion – his aim is the choice of a measure that will correct the offender, then his model should represent offenders as likely to respond, or not to respond, to the correctives at his disposal. The symbols on his map will stand for 'responsiveness' or 'non-responsiveness'. Thus for a sentencer who has to choose between nominal, financial, supervisory and custodial measures when sentencing a mentally normal adult offender the most helpful representation of an offender would be one which indicated his probable response to each of these types of corrective.

At this point an important objection must be raised. Is it realistic to think in terms of Smith's responsiveness to probation and non-responsiveness to fines as if this were a more or less fixed characteristic, analogous to his immunity or non-immunity to smallpox? Is it not more realistic to assume that his responsiveness is *conditional*, and that whether he goes straight or not during whatever period is chosen for the follow-up will depend as much on environmental factors – such as the reaction of his family or his employers to his conviction – as on the fine or the way in which he is managed by his probation officer? It is true that there may be offenders whose responsiveness (or lack of it) can be regarded for practical purposes as unconditional; but for the moment we do not need to assume that they exist in more than negligible numbers.

As a first step, therefore, let us construct a simple model, based on three assumptions:

(i) that the four permissible types of sentence – nominal, financial, supervisory and custodial – are imposed with the frequencies shown in our table;

(ii) that Hammond's first offenders are drawn from a population of individuals whose responsiveness to sentences is conditional and indistinguishable. This assumption will, of course, appear highly artificial to those who are accustomed to emphasize the need for individualization in corrective sentencing; and at a later stage we shall show that there are advantages in assuming that the population with which we are concerned is of at least two kinds. For the moment, however, our aim is maximum simplicity;

(iii) that each of the four types of sentence involves a certain probability that an offender subjected to it will be reconvicted, *and that this probability remains the same whether he is being sentenced for the first, second, third or fourth time.* This too will appear a highly artificial assumption. It is a way, however, of taking account of the differing reconviction rates associated with different types of sentence without begging any questions as to the responsiveness of offenders or the relative importance of the sentence itself and the offender's subsequent vicissitudes; and the assumption that the probability remains constant is of course in accordance with the aim of maximum simplicity. This model needs a little explanation. Essentially it is one in which it is not possible for the sentencer at the time of sentence to say 'This man is more likely to be reconvicted than that man' or even 'This man is more likely to be reconvicted than that man if both are subjected to such-and-such a measure'. The differing probabilities of reconviction belong, as it were, to the measure and not to the man, and are constant; but it is assumed that it is impossible for anyone to tell in advance which of the individual offenders subjected to a given measure will be among the percentage that will be reconvicted. Although *prima facie* plausibility is not an important consideration in an argument such as ours, this model is not as implausible as it looks at first sight. It merely requires us to suppose that every man who is convicted for the first time of an indictable offence is indistinguishably likely to be reconvicted (we do not need to know how likely), but that this likelihood is unequally affected by different penal measures.

Readers who are more at home with models that can be visualized may find it helpful to think of this model as one in which each offender is a particle of identical size and shape, while the sentences are sieves through which the particles pass. Each of the sieves, however, is rather crudely constructed, and the sizes of its apertures vary, some being large enough to let offenders through, some small enough to retain them, with the result that each time the offenders pass through it roughly the same percentage is retained. The percentage of holes which are too small is different in each of the four sieves.

The model is illustrated in Figure 3. Let T be the total number of first offenders. Let α_1 be the proportion of these offenders who are sentenced to be discharged; β_1 the proportion of these offenders who are fined; γ_1 the proportion of the offenders who are given a sentence of probation; and δ_1 be the proportion of offenders who are sent to prison. Similarly α_i is the proportion of offenders sentenced for their ith crime who are given a discharge and so on. Let q_α be the probability (at the first, second, third or fourth court appearance) that an offender who is given a discharge will be reconvicted; q_β=the probability that an offender who is fined will be reconvicted; q_γ=the probability that an offender who is given a term of probation will be reconvicted; and q_δ=the probability that an offender who is given a term of imprisonment will be reconvicted.

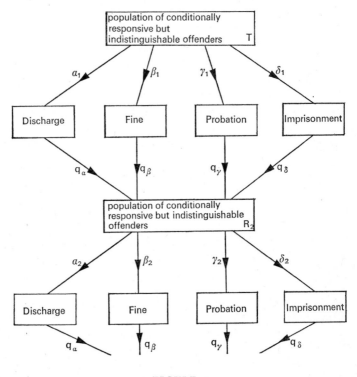

FIGURE 3

THE SIEVE MODEL

If so, the number of persons reconvicted out of those who receive a discharge on their first sentence is given by $R_{2a}=q_a T\alpha_1$: and similarly for the other types of sentence. It follows, therefore, that the total number of offenders who are convicted a second time, R_2, is given by the equation

$$R_2 = R_{2a} + R_{2\beta} + R_{2\gamma} + R_{2\delta}$$

The number of these offenders who are reconvicted after receiving a discharge on the second occasion, R_{3a}, is given by the equation

$$R_{3a} = q_a R_2 \alpha_2.$$

Other quantities can be calculated in a similar way.

The extent to which estimates of reconvictions based on this model can be made to correspond with Hammond's data[5] is shown in Figure 4 (the estimates being based on the values $q_a=0.378$ $q_\beta=0.283$ $q_\gamma=0.580$ $q_\delta=0.588$, and the data being factored as if the original cohort consisted of 1,000 individuals). The agreement between the estimates and the actual observations was good enough to encourage us to pursue our reasoning a little further.

We then refined our simplest model in two ways. First, we abandoned the assumption that the population is completely indistinguishable so far as responsiveness is concerned, and introduced the notion of a group of offenders ($N=z$) who are unconditionally unresponsive to any sentence, at least on the first, second, third or fourth court appearance. The remainder of the population, however, was assumed to be conditionally and indistinguishably responsive as before. (Readers who found the simile of the sieve helpful should think of these universally unresponsive offenders as particles which are small enough to pass through any of the apertures in any of the sieves.) We still assumed, however, that sentencers, when choosing between measures, were unable to distinguish universally unresponsive offenders from the rest (an assumption which can hardly be called artificial). On these assumptions, the number of first offenders who receive a discharge on their first appearance in court, R_{2a}, is given by the equation

$$R_{2a}=\alpha_1(T-z)q_a+\alpha_1 z$$

Similar equations hold for the other quantities at all four court appearances. The values used in drawing the theoretical curves were:

$$z=75 \quad q_a=0.281 \quad q_\beta=0.168 \quad q_\gamma=0.481 \quad q_\delta=0.422$$

As an alternative refinement, we introduced a group of 'universally responsive' offenders ($N=u$) who were certain not to be reconvicted whatever form of sentence was imposed on them (that is, in terms of the sieve simile, too large to pass

5. When comparing estimates based on our model with Dr Hammond's numbers of actual reconvictions, we deliberately proceeded on the simple, if artificial, assumption that his 348, 198, 110 and 74 convicted men were samples from stages in the career of a single cohort of 'first offenders'. There were of course alternatives (also artificial) which were open to us, but this seemed preferable.

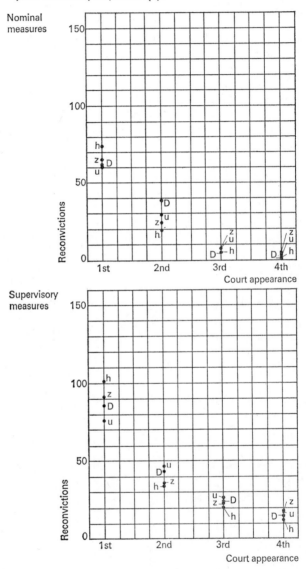

KEY
D = reconvictions based on Dr Hammond's data for 21—29 age-group
h = ⎤ estimates from models which assume offender populations
z = ⎥ that are homogeneous (h), or homogeneous with a universally
n = ⎥ unresponsive minority (z), or roughly half homogeneous and
     ⎦ half universally responsive (u).

Nominal measures

Reconvictions

1st   2nd   3rd   4th
Court appearance

Supervisory measures

Reconvictions

1st   2nd   3rd   4th
Court appearance

FIGURE 4

RECONVICTIONS PREDICTED BY THE SIEVE MODEL

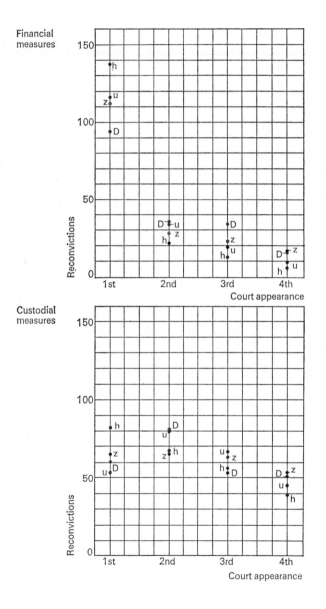

through any aperture in any sieve). As before, we assumed that sentencers were either unaware of the existence of this group or unable to distinguish its members from the remainder of the population. The resulting equations were of the form

$$R_{2a} = (T-u)\alpha_1 q_a$$

and we used the following values in drawing the theoretical curves:

$$u = 450 \quad q_a = 0\cdot565 \quad q_\beta = 0\cdot433 \quad q_\gamma = 0\cdot794 \quad q_\delta = 0\cdot692$$

The results of both refinements can be seen in Figure 4. On the whole Hammond's data agree slightly less with the model which includes a small minority of universally unresponsive offenders than with the model which includes a larger number of universally responsive offenders. It would of course have been possible to achieve better agreement still with a model which included both sub-groups as well as a conditionally and indistinguishably responsive residue. Moreover, it proved possible to construct models in which 'q' had only two values instead of four[6] – one for nominal and financial measures and one for supervisory and custodial measures – and which agreed only slightly less with Hammond's data.

There would have been little point, however, in straining after a very high level of agreement with data drawn from a single sample and a fairly narrow age-group. Our aim has been merely to show the possibilities of extremely simple models which beg no questions and make no unnecessary assumptions about the responsiveness of individual offenders to the main sorts of sentence. One of the next steps must be to find data which will increase (or decrease) our confidence in models of this kind. Meanwhile, however, one or two further points can be made.

The difference between a model which includes a small sub-group of universally unresponsive offenders and one which includes a large number of universally responsive ones is of considerable importance. For only if the sub-group accounts for a sizeable percentage of the total population of offenders is it worth while to seek criteria by which the members

6. If z and u=0, $q_{a\beta} = 0\cdot311$ and $q_{\gamma\delta} = 0\cdot585$

If z=75 and u=0, $q_{a\beta} = 0\cdot201$ and $q_{\gamma\delta} = 0\cdot448$

If z=0 and u=450, $q_{a\beta} = 0\cdot473$ and $q_{\gamma\delta} = 0\cdot730$

of the sub-group might be identified at the sentencing stage. It is perfectly possible to conceive of a model which fitted all the data closely by the inclusion of one or more sub-groups, each of which was so small in relative numbers that there was little hope of defining criteria which would correctly identify its members without incorrectly identifying too many non-members. At what point the size of a sub-group becomes 'negligible' in this precise sense depends of course on the discriminatory power of the criteria. If it were discovered that all offenders with easily remarked characteristics such as tattoo-marks never responded, while those without tattoo-marks sometimes responded, it would be worth while to tell sentencers to proceed on this assumption. In real life, however, where criteria seem to be more subjective and less powerful in discrimination, the notion of negligible sub-groups must be accepted.

Consequently, it is of great importance to decide whether we should be thinking in terms of a model with a negligible sub-group of incorrigibles or a very large sub-group of universally and unconditionally responsive offenders. Without more data than have been made available to us we cannot point to the correct choice. What we can point out is that in a situation in which diagnostic research could be directed either towards criteria for identifying incorrigibles or towards criteria for identifying universally and unconditionally responsive offenders, the inference that the latter (if our model is at all appropriate) are in all probability far more numerous suggests that research concerned with them is more likely to pay off.[7]

Our relatively simple model, however, may be too simple. We may eventually be forced to think in terms of sub-groups of offenders who

(i) are unconditionally and selectively responsive to one or more but not all measures at the time of sentence;

and/or

(ii) change the nature of their responsiveness from one conviction to the next.

Only a sample of penal careers (based if possible on a cohort and complete enough to stretch from first to, say, eighth

---

7. There are other interesting but subsidiary questions. For example, over how wide an age-group can 'q' be regarded as a constant? (For the response of offenders to the different measures may well vary with age.) Or again, does 'q' have similar or (more probably) different values when applied to a non-metropolitan sample?

conviction) could help to decide this. Again, however, we must emphasize that such sub-groups, though improving the performance of the model, may turn out to be negligible from the point of view of diagnostic research.

Glossary of Unfamiliar Terms

age of criminal independence:
a proposed term for the age at which courts are no longer required (although still allowed) to involve an offender's parents or guardians when considering how to deal with him, not to be confused with the age of criminal responsibility (*q.v.*).

age of criminal responsibility:
the age at which a person becomes liable to criminal prosecution for an act or omission prohibited by the criminal law.

approved schools:
institutions to which juveniles could be committed by summary or superior courts as a result either of criminal proceedings or of care, protection or control proceedings, for a period of not less than six months (with exceptions) or more than three years (again with exceptions). Some of the schools were provided by local authorities, some by religious and philanthropic societies. There were separate schools for different age-groups, and for girls. As a result of the Children and Young Persons Act, 1969, the schools will be absorbed in the wider category of 'community homes' (*q.v.*), although most of them seem likely to remain in existence.

assize court:
a court presided over by a judge, sitting in turn at each of the towns in his 'circuit', with a jury to decide questions of guilt.

attendance centres:
centres which young male offenders in the ten-to-seventeen age-group may be ordered to attend for one or two hours on Saturdays. Physical training, cleanliness and handicrafts are important features of their regimes. Most of the centres are run by police. There are experimental centres for the seventeen-to-twenty-one age-group provided and run by the Prison Department. For

economic reasons attendance centres are not provided for rural districts.

borstals:

custodial institutions to which offenders between their seventeenth and twenty-first birthdays may be sent by superior courts for 'training' for a period of not less than six months (with exceptions) or more than twenty-four months. They range from secure to 'open' borstals, and include borstals for girls. They are provided and staffed by the Prison Departmnet of the Home Office.

care order:

an order of a juvenile court committing a person under the age of sixteen to the care of a local authority, and conferring on the authority the powers and duties of a parent (the equivalent of a pre-1969 'fit-person' order).

case-work:

a technique or group of techniques for dealing with disapproved conduct or situations by personal influence on individuals, as distinct from coercion or material assistance. See also *social case-work*.

clear-up percentage:

the percentage of offences reported to the police which are traced to the offenders, whether or not they are prosecuted.

client:

a technical term in social case-work (*q.v.*) for the individual who is the focus for the case-worker's attention.

cohort:

a group selected for follow-up so that it includes all the persons born (or sentenced, or released from prison, as the case may be) between certain dates: less precisely, a sample taken from such a group.

community homes:

'an integrated system of residential establishments' which supersede children's homes and hostels, approved schools (*q.v.*), remand homes, probation homes and hostels, detention centres (*q.v.*) and borstals so far as juveniles under seventeen are concerned, as a result of the Children and Young Persons Act, 1969.

corrective (measure):
a measure intended to prevent an offender from offending again, either by individual deterrence (*q.v.*) or by reformation (*q.v.*).

crown court:
a court which, like an assize court (*q.v.*), is presided over by a judge, with a jury to determine questions of guilt, but which sits only in a fixed place (e.g. the Manchester Crown Court).

day-fine (system):
a fine calculated by estimating what part of a day's earnings the offender can be expected to pay: a system of fining in terms of numbers of day-fines.

detention centre:
a secure custodial establishment to which young males found guilty of imprisonable offences may be sent for short periods, usually three months. Physical training, hard work and restricted leisure are the important features of their regimes.

deterrence, general:
the discouragement of potential offenders by the prospect of objectionable measures.

deterrence, individual:
the discouragement of an offender from offending again by the recollection of objectionable treatment.

deterrible:
a useful neologism meaning 'in a state of mind in which one is capable of being deterred'.

exemplary sentence:
one of abnormal severity, intended to discourage potential imitators.

extended sentence:
a form of precautionary (*q.v.*) prison sentence for recidivists (*q.v.*) which was substituted for preventive detention (*q.v.*) by the Criminal Justice Act, 1967. Its length is fixed by the court, but must not exceed ten years (five years in the case of offences carrying maximum prison terms of less than five years). It does not, however, exclude the possibility of parole (*q.v.*) or the right to remission (*q.v.*). For the conditions which make an offender eligible for an extended sentence, see page 133.

first offender:
the usual term for an offender who has been found guilty of an offence for the first time. In the First Offenders Act, 1958, however, it means in effect a person who is convicted for the first time *since his seventeenth birthday* of an *indictable* offence.

'fit person' order:
see *care order*.

follow-up:
an attempt to trace the subsequent career of a sample of individuals, usually for a limited period and usually with a view to assessing the efficacy of some form of treatment.

higher (criminal) courts:
i.e. an assize court (*q.v.*), crown court (*q.v.*), or quarter sessions (*q.v.*): such courts sit with juries and are presided over by judges or (in the case of quarter sessions) experienced lawyers.

hospital order:
an order by a criminal court under s. 60 of the Mental Health Act, 1959, committing the offender compulsorily to a mental hospital. See also *restriction order*.

imprisonable offence:
an ugly but convenient term for an offence for which an adult may (but not necessarily must) receive a prison sentence.

indeterminate sentence:
a custodial sentence for which the maximum duration is not specified by the law or by the sentencer.

indictable offence:
one for which an adult could in certain circumstances be tried in a higher court (*q.v.*): offences involving serious violence, sexual molestation, dishonesty or danger to the state are indictable. See also *non-indictable offence*.

juveniles:
persons for whom court procedures are modified because of their youth. See also *young adults*.

legal naturalism:
the assumption that legal sub-divisions of criminal (or other) forms of conduct correspond to natural sub-divisions.

life sentence:
a sentence of imprisonment which leaves the date of release to be decided by the executive (in England, the Home Office). Release is on licence, which in Britain lasts, in theory at least, for the rest of the offender's life.

lower (criminal) courts:
courts presided over by stipendiary or lay magistrates, who try issues of guilt without the help of a jury and either sentence the offender within their limited powers or remand him to quarter sessions (*q.v.*) for sentence.

mandatory sentence:
one which the court must impose on an adult who has been convicted (e.g. life imprisonment for murder). See also *semi-mandatory sentence*.

model:
a visual or intellectual device (such as algebra) which helps in explanatory or predictive thinking about observable phenomena: see page 203.

Montero's aim:
the use of the penal system to protect identified offenders against unofficial retaliation.

nominal measure:
one which imposes no financial penalty, supervision, custody or other disability or restraint: e.g. a discharge.

non-indictable offence:
one which can be tried only by a lower (summary) court, with its limited sentencing powers. Most motoring offences are non-indictable.

Ombudsman:
a Scandinavian official whose function is to investigate complaints by members of the public of maladministration from which they have suffered.

Parliamentary Commissioner for Administration:
the newly created British equivalent of the Ombudsman (*q.v.*). His functions are defined by the Parliamentary Commissioner Act, 1967.

parole:
the release of a prisoner before the due date, subject to the possibility of recall for failure to comply with specified conditions, which normally include supervision: to be distinguished from 'remission' (*q.v.*).

penal agent, agency:
a person with the function of carrying out an order of the court, e.g. a probation officer or prison officer: an organization with this function.

penal humanitarian:
one who believes that the penal system should be such as to cause the minimum of suffering by its attempts to achieve its aims.

precautionary (measure):
a measure intended to prevent an individual from committing an offence by making it physically difficult for him to do so, e.g., especially, by imprisonment.

preventive detention:
a form of precautionary (*q.v.*) prison sentence for recidivists which was replaced in 1968 by the 'extended sentence' (*q.v.*).

probation order:
an order by a criminal court under s. 3 of the Criminal Justice Act, 1948, placing the offender under the supervision of a probation officer.

psychiatric probation order:
a probation order which includes a requirement that the offender shall undergo psychiatric treatment as an out-patient or in-patient: see s. 4 of the Criminal Justice Act, 1948.

quarter sessions:
a local court, with a jury to decide questions of guilt, presided over by a recorder who is an experienced barrister or (in the case of county sessions) by a group of magistrates with a chairman who is almost always an experienced lawyer.

quasi-indictable offence:
a non-indictable offence which is sufficiently similar to an indictable offence to be thought worth recording in the Criminal Record Office files (e.g. a non-indictable assault).

recidivist:
strictly speaking, any offender who breaks the law again after penal treatment. The term is usually reserved, however, for 'multiple recidivists' who fail to respond to several sentences; those who have so far relapsed only once are called 'primary recidivists'.

reconviction:
a conviction of an already convicted offender on a subsequent occasion; in English reconviction statistics the term usually refers only to a reconviction for an indictable or quasi-indictable offence (*q.v.*).

reductivism, reductivist:
the view that the over-riding aim of a penal system should be the reduction of the frequency of conduct prohibited by the criminal law; a person who holds this view.

reformation:
a lasting improvement in the extent to which a person obeys the law or social norms.

remission:
an automatic reduction of a prison sentence, which can be forfeited in whole or part for indiscipline: to be distinguished from 'parole' (*q.v.*).

repentance:
a feeling of regret and culpable responsibility for an act or omission.

restriction order:
an order by a higher court directing that an offender on whom it has just imposed a hospital order (*q.v.*) shall not be discharged from hospital without the authority of the Home Secretary.

retaliation:
the infliction of suffering on a person to satisfy the victims of his acts or omissions, or those who sympathize with the victims.

retribution:
the infliction of suffering on a person solely because of a past act, and in accordance with a divinely or socially approved code: not to be confused with retaliation (*q.v.*) or repentance (*q.v.*).

semi-determinate sentence:
a custodial sentence of which the maximum (and sometimes the minimum) duration is fixed either by law or by the sentencer, leaving the executive free to choose the exact date for release.

semi-mandatory sentence:
a mandatory sentence (*q.v.*) which the court may (but not must) avoid imposing in exceptional circumstances (which are usually defined).

sentencer:
a person presiding over a criminal court who has the power to impose a penal measure.

sentencing authority:
a proposed body other than a criminal court which would have the task of choosing penal measures for offenders, or for some categories of offender.

social case-work:
the application of case-work (*q.v.*) to types of social pathology (as distinct from, e.g., industrial problems).

social inquiry:
an investigation of an individual's career, circumstances and family in order to assist in decisions for his disposal or in his treatment.

star (prisoner):
one who is serving his first prison sentence (or, exceptionally, one who is treated as if he were).

stipendiary magistrate:
a full-time, salaried magistrate, with legal training. Such magistrates are appointed only in a few large cities.

young adults:
persons for whom special penal measures, such as borstal, but not necessarily special court procedures, are reserved.

Appendix C

A Decision by the
Norwegian Supreme Court
on an Appeal by the Prosecution
against Sentence[1]

The defendant, a young man of nineteen from an ordinary good home, had committed between thirty and forty larcenies and grand larcenies to provide money for amusement and restaurant life. The Oslo City Court gave him a suspended sentence of ten months' imprisonment, refused the prosecution request that he be placed in a 'work school', and made an order for compensation. The prosecution appealed.

EXTRACT FROM JUDGEMENT RENDERED BY
THE NORWEGIAN SUPREME COURT DATED
28 APRIL 1962[2]
[In the Supreme Court]
Mr Justice Hiorthøy said:
'. . . The Public Prosecutor has appealed from the judgement to the Supreme Court on grounds of insufficient punishment. The declaration of appeal urges that in view of the need for general observance of the law it cannot be correct to apply a suspended sentence in the case of such extensive and persevering criminal activity. . . . In the first place, it is pleaded that the petition for placing the accused in a work school ought to have been allowed, but if this is not allowed a non-suspended prison sentence ought to be imposed even if the accused has not previously been punished.

'The facts of the case and the personal conduct of the prisoner will appear from the judgement of the City Court.

'I have come to the conclusion that the appeal ought to be allowed, and that the accused should be sentenced to be placed in a work school.

1. Referred to in Chapter 10.
2. From *Norsk Retstidende* 1962, pages 365 ff. I am indebted to Professor Johannes Andenaes of Oslo University for providing me with a translation from the transcript.

'In the Act of 1 June 1928, relating to the reformative treatment of juvenile delinquents, it is stipulated as a condition for such placement that the convicted person is in need of reformative influence in a work school in order to abstain from committing further offences, and that such placement would be expedient. The experts agree that the latter condition has been fulfilled in this case. I refer in this respect to the statement of 16 October 1961 by Dr Christensen, the Police Medical Officer which is quoted in the extract of the decision of the City Court, and to the statement given by the expert, Mr Bergsvein Hov, Director, which is also quoted there. It will also appear from the decision of the City Court that Mr Bødal, Director of the work school for juvenile delinquents, has recommended such placement.

'While the City Court also agreed that such placement would be expedient, it felt – although with some doubt – that placement would not be necessary in order to keep the accused from committing further offences. It is understood that, in taking this attitude, the City Court was largely influenced by a statement made by the Police Medical Officer during the main trial, to the effect that the situation had changed somewhat since she made her statement in writing, the accused "having now shown some initiative". She still felt that placement in a work school would be expedient, but she was in doubt as to the need for such placement. Mr Hov, the Director, also expressed doubt as to whether placement in a work school would be necessary in order to keep the accused from committing further offences.

'The above-mentioned initiative relates to the information given to the City Court that on 31 October 1961 the accused took up employment with N.E.B.B. as a winder of electric motors, that he is now in regular employment there, and that it was his intention to continue in this position and to take the necessary courses in order to become a skilled worker. However, the hopes that the accused would show greater steadiness in his work and greater willingness to perform it later proved somewhat unjustified. It has been stated before the Supreme Court that as early as 5 March last he terminated his work with N.E.B.B., and as a reason for so doing he says that he was transferred, owing to insufficient work, to a new position involving the performance of occasional jobs, for which he received far less pay, Kr. 3.– per hour. He has now applied for a new position, but there is no indication that he has resumed regular work.

'It will appear from the personal data that the accused has not shown much steadiness in his employment after having completed his school education. In the course of somewhat more than two years he has been employed in as many as seven different enterprises, and the information given regarding his conduct at N.E.B.B. shows that he has not changed in this respect. In view of the other information given about him, I would therefore assume that there is a considerable risk that, now that he has no work, he will again try to obtain money to pay for restaurant visits and other amusements by means of criminal offences. In weighing this risk I cannot refrain from attaching considerable importance to the very large number of burglaries and thefts which he has committed. It is true that most of these offences have been concentrated in a relatively short period of time, four or five months during 1961. However, he had already in 1959 begun to commit offences of exactly the same kind. In these circumstances I feel that there are compelling reasons for placing him in a work school.

'I vote for the following

judgement:

1. Bjørn Berg, born 1 September 1943, is ordered to be placed in a work school for young offenders in accordance with § 1 of the Act of 1 June 1928.
2. The punishment imposed by the City Court is annulled.
3. Costs are not awarded.'

Mr Justice Endresen: 'In the main and in the conclusion I agree with the Justice giving the leading vote.'

Mr Justice Bendiksby, Mr Justice Eckhoff and Mr Justice Thrap: 'Likewise.'

References

Advisory Council on the Treatment of Offenders (1957): Report: *Alternatives to Short Terms of Imprisonment* (H.M.S.O.).

Assembly Office of Research of the California Legislature (1968): 'Crime and Penalties in California' (cyclostyled, not on sale).

Bagley, C. (1965): 'Juvenile Delinquency in Exeter', *Journal of Urban Studies*, II, 1, pp. 33 ff.

Beccaria, C. (1764): *Of Crimes and Punishments (Dei Delitti e delle pene)* (anonymous English translation 1767, J. Almond, London).

Bentham, J. (1789): *An Introduction to the Principles of Morals and Legislation* (T. Payne, London).

Bentham, J. (1830): *The Rationale of Punishment* (Robert Heward, London).

Beutel, F. K. (1957): *Some Potentialities of Experimental Jurisprudence as a New Branch of Social Science* (University of Nebraska Press).

Braithwaite, R. B. (1953): *Scientific Explanation* (Cambridge University Press).

Cadogan Committee (1938, Cmd 5684): *Corporal Punishment* (H.M.S.O.).

Cases at law:

    Ashman's case (1858) 1 Foster & Finlason 88

    Beck's case: see Watson, E. R. (ed.)

    R. v. *Crehan* [1962] 1 All E.R. 608

    R. v. *Hilliard* (1899) in Public Records Office file HO/144/278A/61209

    R. v. *Hodgson* [1968] *Criminal Law Review*, 46

    R. v. *Reeves* [1963] report in *The Times*, 20 November

    R. v. *Simcox* [1964] *Observer*, 15 March

    R. v. *Smith* [1961] A.C. 290

R. v. *Turner* (1966) 51 Criminal Appeal Reports, 72
Vassal v. *Harris* (1964) *Criminal Law Review*, 322.

Denning, Lord (1950): Minutes of Evidence taken before the Royal Commission on Capital Punishment, Ninth Day (H.M.S.O.)

Devlin, J. Daniel (1961): *Police Charges* (Police Review Publishing Co., London).

Devlin, P. (1959, 1965 revised and expanded): *The Enforcement of Morals* (Oxford University Press).

Donovan Committee (1965, Cmnd 2755): *Report on the Court of Criminal Appeal* (H.M.S.O.).

Durkheim, Émile (1895): *The Rules of Sociological Method* (*Les Règles de la méthode sociologique*) (translation by S. A. Solovan and J. H. Moeller, ed. G. E. G. Catlin, University of Chicago Press).

Eichman, C. J. (1966): *The Impact of the Gideon Decision upon Crime and Sentencing in Florida: A Study of Recidivism and Sociocultural Change* (Monograph No. 2 of the Florida Division of Corrections, Research and Statistics Section).

Eysenck, H. J. (1960): *Handbook of Abnormal Psychology* (Pitman, London).

Eysenck, H. J. (1964): *Crime and Personality* (Routledge, London).

Ferguson, T. (1952): *The Young Delinquent in his Social Setting* (Oxford University Press).

Fewtrell, M. (1964): *The Train Robbers* (Barker, London).

Folkard, S., *et al.* (1966): *Probation Research: A Preliminary Report* (Home Office Studies in the Causes of Delinquency and the Treatment of Offenders No. 7, H.M.S.O.).

Glaser, D. (1964): *The Effectiveness of a Prison and Parole System* (Bobbs-Merrill, Indianapolis).

Gowers Commission (1953, Cmnd 8932): *Capital Punishment* (H.M.S.O.).

Grant, J. and M. (1959): 'A Group Dynamics Approach to the Treatment of Non-conformists in the Navy', *Annals of the American Academy of Political and Social Science* (March).

Halloran, J. D. (1964): *The Effects of Mass Communication with Special Reference to Television: A Survey* (Television Research

Committee Working Paper No. 1, Leicester University Press).

Halloran, J. D. (1967): *Attitude Formation and Change* (Television Research Committee Working Paper No. 2, Leicester University Press).

Hammond, W. H. (1960): Appendix D of *The Use of Short Sentences of Imprisonment by the Courts* (Report by the Scottish Advisory Council on the Treatment of Offenders, H.M.S.O.).

Hammond, W. H. (1964, 1966 revised): Part VI of *The Sentence of the Court* (Home Office, H.M.S.O.).

Hammond, W. H., and Chayen, E. (1963): *Persistent Criminals* (H.M.S.O.).

Hart, H. L. A. (1959, 1962, 1968): 'Prolegomenon to the Principles of Punishment' (Presidential Address to the Aristotelian Society, 1959), *Proceedings of the Aristotelian Society*, 1959–60, or in *Punishment and Responsibility* (Oxford University Press).

Home Office (1965, Cmnd 2742): *The Child, the Family and the Young Offender* (H.M.S.O.).

Home Office (1968, Cmnd 3601): *Children in Trouble* (H.M.S.O.).

Hood, R. G., and Taylor, I. (1968): 'Second Report on the Effectiveness of Pre-sentence Investigations in Reducing Recidivism', *British Journal of Criminology*, VIII, 4, pp. 431 ff.

Jarvis, F. V. (1965): 'Inquiry before Sentence', in *Criminology in Transition* (ed. T. Grygier *et al.*, Tavistock Publications, London).

Latey Committee (1967, Cmnd 3342): *The Age of Majority* (H.M.S.O.).

Lloyd George, Gwilym (1956): speech in debate on capital punishment, *Hansard's Parliamentary Debates*, 16 February, Vol. 548, cols. 2543–4.

Longford, Earl of (1961): *The Idea of Punishment* (Chapman, London).

McCord, W. and J., and Zola, I. K. (1959): *Origins of Crime: A New Evaluation of the Cambridge-Somerville Youth Study* (Columbia University Press).

Mannheim, H., and Wilkins, L. T. (1955): *Prediction Methods in Relation to Borstal Training* (H.M.S.O.).

Mathieson, T. (1965): *The Defences of the Weak* (Tavistock Publications, London).

Mill, J. S. (1859): *On Liberty* (Parker, London).

Miller, W. B. (1962): 'The Impact of a "Total Community" Delinquency Control Project', *Social Problems*, X, 2, pp. 168 ff.

Montero, P. D. (1916): *El Derecho Protector de los Criminales* (Madrid).

Montesquieu, Charles de Secondat, Baron de (1748): *The Spirit of the Laws* (*De l'Esprit des lois*) (translation 1750, Nourse & Vaillant, London).

Morton, G. D. (1962): *The Function of Criminal Law in 1962* (Canadian Broadcasting Company Publications, Toronto).

Parliamentary Commissioner for Administration (1968): *Fourth Report: Session 1967–8* (H.M.S.O.).

Power, M. J. (1967): 'Delinquent Schools', *New Society* (19 October).

Powers, E., and Witmer, H. (1951): *An Experiment in the Prevention of Delinquency* (Columbia University Press).

Prison Rules, 1964 (Statutory Instrument No. 388, H.M.S.O.).

Radzinowicz, L. (ed.) (1957): *Sexual Offenders* (Cambridge Department of Criminal Science Survey, Macmillan, London).

Rollin, H. R. (1969): *The Mentally Abnormal Offender and the Law* (Pergamon, Oxford).

Royal Commission on Capital Punishment: see Gowers Commission.

Schur, E. M. (1963): *Narcotic Addiction in Britain and America* (Tavistock Publications, London).

Schwartz, R. D., and Orleans, S. (1967): 'On Legal Sanctions', *University of Chicago Law Review*, XXXIV, pp. 274 ff.

Seebohm Committee (1968, Cmnd 3703): *Local Authority and Allied Personal Social Services* (H.M.S.O.).

Sellin, T., and Wolfgang, M. (1964): *The Measurement of Delinquency* (John Wiley, New York).

Statutes, England and Wales:

    1688 An Act declaring the Rights and Liberties of the Subject. . . . 1 Wm. & Mar. II, c. 2

    1907 Criminal Appeal Act. 7 Edw. 7, c. 23

    1933 Children and Young Persons Act. 23 Geo. 5, c. 2

    1948 Children Act. 11 & 12 Geo. 6, c. 43

    1948 Criminal Justice Act. 11 & 12 Geo. 6, c. 58

    1952 Hypnotism Act. 15 & 16 Geo. 6 and 1 Eliz. 2, c. 46

1958 First Offenders Act. 6 & 7 Eliz. 2, c. 31

1967 Parliamentary Commissioner Act. 15 & 16 Eliz. 2, c. 13

1967 Criminal Justice Act. 15 & 16 Eliz. 2, c. 80.

1969 Children and Young Persons Act. 17 & 18 Eliz. 2.

Stephen, J. F. (1874): *Liberty, Equality, Fraternity* (Smith, Elder, London).

Stephen, J. F. (1883): *A History of the Criminal Law of England* (3 vols., Macmillan, London).

Thomas, D. A. (1963): 'Sentencing – The Case for Reasoned Decisions', *Criminal Law Review*, pp. 243 ff.

Tornudd, P. (1968): 'The Preventive Effect of Fines for Drunkenness', in *Scandinavian Studies in Criminology*, Vol. II (ed. N. Christie, Tavistock Publications, London).

Toulmin, S. (1953): *The Philosophy of Science* (Hutchinson, London).

Trolle, J. (1945): *Syv Maaneder Uden Politi* (Copenhagen), cited by J. Andenaes (1966), 'The General Preventive Effects of Punishment', *University of Pennsylvania Law Review*, CXIV, 7, pp. 949 ff.

Walker, N. D. (1957): *A Short History of Psychotherapy* (Routledge, London).

Walker, N. D. (1968): *Crime and Insanity in England*, Vol. I (Edinburgh University Press).

Walker, N. D., Hammond, W. H., and Steer, D. J. (1967): 'Repeated Violence', *Criminal Law Review*.

Watson, E. R. (ed.) (1925): *The Trial of Adolf Beck* (Hodge, Edinburgh).

West, D. J. (1963): *The Habitual Prisoner* (Macmillan, London).

Willcock, H. D., and Stokes, J. (1968): *Deterrents to Crime Among Youths aged 15 to 21* (Government Social Survey Report No. SS 356, Part II, obtainable from the Librarian of the Government Social Survey, London).

Wilson, J., Williams, N., and Sugarman, B. (1967): *Introduction to Moral Education* (Penguin, London).

Wolfenden Committee (1957, Cmnd 247): *Homosexual Offences and Prostitution* (H.M.S.O.).

The New Yugoslav Criminal Code (1951), in *New Yugoslav Law*, II–III (Federation of Jurists' Association of Yugoslavia Belgrade).

Further Reading

The following list is intended for the reader who wishes to pursue a topic dealt with in this book.

Chapter 1
H. L. A. Hart (1968): *Punishment and Responsibility* (Oxford University Press), especially Chapter 1.
B. Wootton (1963): *Crime and the Criminal Law* (Stevens, London).
W. Moberly (1968): *The Ethics of Punishment* (Faber, London).

Chapter 2
P. Devlin (1965 edition): *The Enforcement of Morals* (Oxford University Press).
H. L. A. Hart (1963): *Law, Liberty and Morality* (Oxford University Press).

Chapter 3
J. R. Wilson, N. Williams and B. Sugarman (1967): *Introduction to Moral Education* (Penguin, London).

Chapter 4
J. Andenaes (1966): 'The General Preventive Effects of Punishment', *University of Pennsylvania Law Review*, CXIV, 7, pp. 949 ff.
R. M. Jackson (1967): *Enforcing the Law* (Macmillan, London).

Chapter 5
N. D. Walker (1968 edition): *Crime and Punishment in Britain* (Edinburgh University Press), Part 3.

Chapters 6–8
Home Office (1964): *The Sentence of the Court* (H.M.S.O.), especially Part VI.

R. G. Hood (1967): 'Research on the Effectiveness of Punishments and Treatment', in *Collected Studies in Criminological Research*, Vol. I (Council of Europe).

The Report of the Streatfeild Committee on the Business of the Criminal Courts (1961, Cmnd 1289, H.M.S.O.), Part B.

Chapter 9

R. M. Jackson (1967): *Enforcing the Law* (Macmillan, London).

Chapter 10

N. D. Walker (1968 edition): *Crime and Punishment in Britain* (Edinburgh University Press), Chapter 15.

Report of the Dove-Wilson Committee on Persistent Offenders (1932, Cmd 4090, H.M.S.O.).

W. H. Hammond and E. Chayen (1963): *Persistent Criminals* (H.M.S.O.).

D. J. West (1963): *The Habitual Prisoner* (Macmillan, London).

Chapter 11

R. M. Jackson (1967): *Enforcing the Law* (Macmillan, London), Chapter 6.

D. A. Thomas (1963): 'Sentencing – The Case for Reasoned Decisions', *Criminal Law Review*, pp. 243 ff.

Chapter 12

B. Wootton (1963): *Crime and the Criminal Law* (Stevens, London), Chapter 3.

Chapter 13

The Kilbrandon Report on Children and Young Persons, Scotland (1964, Cmnd 2306, H.M.S.O.).

O. Nyquist (1960): *Juvenile Justice* (Macmillan, London).

Index